CHATGPT DALL.E 3

COMPLETE GUIDE

THIRD EDITION

BY

DR. HESHAM MOHAMED ELSHERIF

Who Should Read This Book?

If you've picked up this book, you might be curious about the intended audience. To put it succinctly, this book is a guide for anyone and everyone interested in leveraging the transformative potential of ChatGPT, including its underlying formulas, modules, and applications. Let's delve a little deeper into the sectors and professions that would benefit most from the insights contained within these pages.

1. **E-commerce Professionals**: The modern e-commerce landscape demands intuitive, responsive, and customer-centric approaches. If you're in the realm of online retail and want to improve customer service, automate queries, or even use ChatGPT for product recommendations, this book will provide you with the practical knowledge to integrate the technology seamlessly.

2. **Educators and Teachers**: The power of AI isn't limited to commerce. Educators can tap into ChatGPT to create interactive lesson plans, provide instant feedback, and engage in personalized student interactions. Dive into the chapters that discuss constructing effective educational prompts and watch as your teaching transforms.

3. **Corporate and Professional Email Managers**: Writing professional emails, especially in large quantities, can be a daunting task. With ChatGPT, not only can you draft emails efficiently, but you can also tailor them to be more effective and targeted. This book offers guidance on creating prompts that yield polished and professional email content, ensuring your communication is both efficient and effective.

4. **Marketers**: In a rapidly changing digital world, marketers need to be at the forefront of technological advancements. ChatGPT offers tools for customer engagement, market research, content creation, and more. Understand how to craft intricate prompts for specific marketing objectives, from gathering consumer insights to generating creative campaign ideas.

5. **AI Enthusiasts and Hobbyists**: Even if you're not affiliated with a specific sector mentioned above, but have a burning curiosity about ChatGPT, its architecture, and potential, you will find a wealth of information here. Learn about the underlying formulas,

delve deep into its modules, and experiment with it based on the comprehensive guidance provided.

Moreover, a special section of this book is dedicated to constructing advanced and complex prompts. Whether you're a beginner trying to navigate the intricacies of AI or a seasoned expert aiming to push the boundaries of what ChatGPT can achieve, the methodologies outlined here will empower you to communicate with this AI in a way that fetches optimal responses.

In essence, this book serves as both a primer and a deep dive into the world of ChatGPT. Regardless of your prior knowledge or intended application, the insights and hands-on strategies within these pages will enhance your understanding and application of one of the most groundbreaking AIs of our time. Happy reading!

Dr. Hesham Mohamed Elsherif

Table of Contents

Chapter1: Introduction

ChatGPT, part of OpenAI's GPT (Generative Pre-trained Transformer) series, represents a transformative step in the domain of artificial intelligence and natural language processing. Stemming from the broader GPT architecture, ChatGPT is specifically designed to handle conversational tasks, simulating human-like interactions in a wide range of topics and applications.

Background and Origins:

The GPT series was born out of the need to develop more adaptive and context-aware models for natural language tasks. Building on the Transformer architecture introduced by Vaswani et al. in 2017, GPT models utilize a deep learning technique that significantly improves the handling of sequences, which is paramount in language-based tasks.

1. The Era Before Transformers: Before the rise of transformer architectures, recurrent neural networks (RNNs) and convolutional neural networks (CNNs) were the dominant architectures for processing sequential data like text. While effective to a degree, they had their limitations in handling long-range dependencies in sequences and scaling efficiently with increasing data and parameters.

2. Birth of the Transformer: In 2017, a paper titled "Attention is All You Need" was introduced by Vaswani et al. This paper proposed the Transformer architecture, which eliminated recurrence and instead relied wholly on attention mechanisms to draw global dependencies between input and output. The architecture allowed for parallel processing of sequences and was found to be more efficient and scalable than its predecessors.

3. Rise of the GPT Architecture: Building upon the transformer foundation, OpenAI introduced the Generative Pre-trained Transformer (GPT). The underlying principle was simple yet powerful: first, train a large model on a vast corpus of text in an unsupervised manner, allowing it to learn grammar, facts, reasoning abilities, and even some biases present in the data. Then, fine-tune this model on specific tasks to achieve state-of-the-art performance.

4. ChatGPT's Emergence: While the earlier versions of GPT showcased strong capabilities in various NLP tasks, there was an increasing demand for models specifically tailored for conversational AI. This led to the evolution of ChatGPT, a variant of GPT, optimized for human-like interactions across a plethora of topics. It inherited the knowledge base of GPT but was further refined to handle conversational nuances better.

5. The Significance of Large Scale: One of the hallmarks of the GPT series, including ChatGPT, is the scale. Each subsequent version has had billions, if not trillions, of parameters. This massive scale, combined with diverse training data, enables the model to store vast amounts of information and generate incredibly diverse and coherent outputs. However, it's worth noting that the size also brings challenges in terms of computational requirements and potential amplification of biases.

6. The Ecosystem Around GPT: With the success of the GPT architecture, there's been a surge in research and applications based on it. From fine-tuned versions for specific industries to platforms offering GPT-powered services, the architecture has, in many ways, set a new standard in the field of natural language processing.

Training and Mechanism:

Like its siblings in the GPT family, ChatGPT is trained on massive datasets to capture the nuances of language. It starts with unsupervised learning, where it predicts the next word in a sequence from large amounts of text. Once this foundation is established, fine-tuning on narrower datasets with specific tasks can be performed.

The sheer size of the model, combined with its training on diverse data, enables ChatGPT to generate coherent, contextually relevant, and often human-like responses. It uses the accumulated knowledge from its training data to generate answers, tell stories, simulate characters, assist with tasks, and much more.

1. Two-Step Training Process:

a. Unsupervised Pre-training:
Before being fine-tuned for specific tasks, ChatGPT is subjected to unsupervised training on vast amounts of text data. This phase, often referred to as pre-training, allows the model to learn grammar, facts, some reasoning abilities, and even biases present in the data. The model is trained to predict the next word in a sequence, a task known as language modeling.

b. Task-Specific Fine-tuning:
After the pre-training phase, ChatGPT is further refined on narrower datasets designed for specific tasks or domains. This phase helps in

tailoring the model's generalized knowledge to be more effective in particular applications, including conversation.

2. The Power of Attention Mechanisms:

a. Self-Attention:
At the heart of the GPT series, including ChatGPT, is the self-attention mechanism. This allows each word (or token) in an input sequence to focus on different parts of itself, thus determining which parts of the sequence are relevant to a particular word.

b. Multi-Head Attention:
To capture information at multiple scales and from different subspaces, the transformer architecture uses multiple attention heads. Each head can potentially learn different types of relationships or dependencies in the data.

3. Positional Encoding:
Transformers and, by extension, ChatGPT don't inherently understand the order of sequences, unlike RNNs. To handle this, positional encodings are added to the embeddings, allowing the model to consider the position of words within a sequence.

4. Depth and Width: Large-Scale Architectures:
ChatGPT, especially the later versions, boasts deep architectures with numerous layers and a vast number of parameters. This scale allows the model to store and process extensive amounts of information, contributing to its ability to generate nuanced and coherent outputs. The depth aids in complex patterns recognition, while the width allows for a richer representation.

5. Decoding Strategies:

a. Greedy Decoding:
In this method, at each step, the model picks the word with the highest probability as its next word. It's deterministic but can sometimes lead to repetitive or suboptimal outputs.

b. Beam Search:
Here, the model keeps track of multiple sequences (beams) at once, expanding all of them simultaneously and keeping the ones with the highest probabilities. It's more computationally intensive than greedy decoding but often produces better results.

c. Sampling:
Instead of always picking the most probable next word, the model

samples from its distribution. This method can introduce randomness and creativity into the outputs.

6. Regularization Techniques:
Techniques like dropout and layer normalization are used within the model's architecture to prevent overfitting and ensure smoother training.

3. Applications:

ChatGPT's versatility allows it to be applied in numerous scenarios:

Applications of ChatGPT:

1. Customer Support:

- Automated Help Desks: Businesses utilize ChatGPT to power chatbots that answer frequent inquiries, significantly reducing response times.

- Guided Troubleshooting: For issues with products or software, ChatGPT can guide users through diagnostic steps, offering solutions based on the user's input.

- Feedback Collection: Chatbots can gather feedback about products, services, or user experience, providing valuable insights for businesses.

2. Content Creation:

- Blogging Assistance: ChatGPT can help bloggers by suggesting content outlines, generating article introductions, or even proposing titles.

- Scriptwriting: Film and theater professionals can use ChatGPT for brainstorming dialogues or plot elements.

- Advertising and Marketing: Brands can leverage ChatGPT to draft ad copies, generate slogans, or craft marketing messages.

3. Education:

- Homework Assistance: Students can consult ChatGPT for explanations on academic topics, seek clarifications, or even get help with problem-solving.

- Language Learning: ChatGPT can act as a conversational partner, helping language learners practice real-time conversations.

- Research Assistance: Scholars and researchers can use ChatGPT for brainstorming, paper outlining, or even generating abstracts.

4. Entertainment:

- Interactive Storytelling: ChatGPT can power interactive fiction platforms where users direct the story's path through their choices and interactions.

- Video Game Characters: Game developers can use ChatGPT to simulate non-playable characters (NPCs) with deep and interactive dialogues, enhancing the gaming experience.

- Virtual Companions: For lonely or elderly individuals, ChatGPT-powered companions can offer conversation, narrate stories, or engage in general chatter.

5. Technical Applications:

- Code Writing Assistants: Developers can seek suggestions for code snippets, get debugging help, or understand specific programming concepts.

- Data Analysis: Data scientists can use natural language queries to ask ChatGPT to perform specific data analyses or even generate reports.

6. Health and Well-being:

- Mental Health Chatbots: While not a replacement for professional care, ChatGPT can provide immediate responses in mental health apps, offering comfort or directing users to helplines.

- Health Information: Users can seek general health and wellness information, though it's essential to consult professionals for personalized advice.

7. Business and Productivity:

- Meeting Summarization: ChatGPT can assist in summarizing long meetings or converting spoken content into written notes.

- Idea Brainstorming: Teams can use ChatGPT as a brainstorming tool, proposing ideas or refining existing concepts.

8. E-commerce:

- Product Descriptions: E-commerce platforms can use ChatGPT to generate or refine product descriptions, enhancing the shopping experience.

- Shopping Assistants: ChatGPT can guide shoppers, offering product recommendations based on their preferences.

4. Strengths and Limitations:

Strengths of ChatGPT:

1. Vast Knowledge Base:

- **General Knowledge:** Due to its training on vast and diverse datasets, ChatGPT has a broad knowledge of a myriad of topics, from history and science to pop culture.

- **Language Mastery:** The model possesses strong grammatical understanding and can fluently communicate in multiple languages.

2. Adaptability:

Diverse Interactions: ChatGPT can handle a wide range of tasks and interactions, from simple Q&A to storytelling and more complex dialogues.

- **Customization:** Through fine-tuning, ChatGPT can be tailored to specific industries or applications, making it versatile across sectors.

3. Scalability:

- **Handling High Volume:** For businesses, ChatGPT can simultaneously manage a large number of users, especially useful in applications like customer support.

- **Continuous Learning:** With each version and iteration, the GPT models, including ChatGPT, have shown improvement, indicating the potential for continued refinement and growth.

4. Cost Efficiency:

- **Reducing Operational Costs:** Automating tasks like customer queries can lead to cost savings for businesses.

- **Accessibility:** For individuals or small businesses, using models like ChatGPT can be more accessible than hiring specialists for specific tasks.

Limitations of ChatGPT:

1. Lack of Deep Understanding:

- **Surface-Level Responses:** While ChatGPT can produce human-like text, it doesn't genuinely understand content. It generates responses based on patterns in its training data without actual comprehension.

- **Absence of Context:** ChatGPT lacks a persistent memory of past interactions, which means each query is treated in isolation without the context of previous conversations.

2. Sensitivity to Input Phrasing:

- **Inconsistent Answers:** Slight changes in the phrasing of a question can yield different answers, revealing the model's sensitivity to input.

3. Risk of Generating Misinformation:

- **Erroneous Outputs:** ChatGPT can, at times, produce information that is incorrect or misleading.

- **Amplifying Biases:** Since it's trained on vast internet data, ChatGPT can inherit and even amplify biases present in those datasets.

4. Ethical Concerns:

- **Potential Misuse:** In the wrong hands, ChatGPT could be used to generate misleading information, fake news, or harmful content.

- **Job Displacement:** As with many automation tools, there's a concern about ChatGPT replacing jobs, especially in areas like customer support.

5. Verbosity:

- **Redundancy:** The model sometimes provides answers that are longer than necessary, reiterating points or over-explaining.

6. Dependence on Prompts:

- **Requirement for Clear Instructions:** The quality of the output is often highly dependent on how the input prompt is crafted. It might necessitate iterative prompting to obtain the desired response.

5. Ethical and Societal Implications:

The development and widespread use of models like ChatGPT raise important ethical questions, particularly concerning the potential for misuse in spreading misinformation, the implications on employment in sectors like customer service, and the broader societal impact of humans increasingly interacting with AI entities.

1. Misinformation and Fake News:

- **Generating False Information:** With its ability to craft coherent and plausible text, ChatGPT could be exploited to create misleading articles, bogus news stories, or counterfeit narratives.

- **Amplifying Biases:** As ChatGPT is trained on vast internet datasets, it can inadvertently reproduce or even amplify existing biases, leading to outputs that might be racially, politically, or culturally prejudiced.

2. Dependence on Machines:

- **Reduced Human Interaction:** As more sectors adopt AI-driven communication, there's a potential reduction in human-to-human interactions, which could impact societal dynamics.

- **Over-reliance on AI:** There's a risk that people might become overly reliant on AI for information, potentially hindering critical thinking or personal research efforts.

3. Job Displacement:

- **Automation of Roles:** With ChatGPT's potential in customer service, content creation, and more, certain jobs might become redundant. While AI can handle high volumes efficiently, the human touch could be lost.

- **Economic Repercussions:** If widespread job displacement occurs without adequate upskilling or reskilling opportunities, it could lead to economic challenges, including increased unemployment.

4. Privacy Concerns:

- **Data Handling:** While ChatGPT doesn't remember individual interactions, there's always concern about how user data is handled, especially if the platform it's integrated into doesn't prioritize user privacy.

- **Impersonation Risks:** ChatGPT's proficiency in generating human-like text could be misused to impersonate individuals, leading to potential scams or fraud.

5. Mental Health Implications:

- **Overattachment:** Especially in applications like virtual companionship, users might develop an unhealthy attachment to AI entities, potentially hampering real human relationships.

- **Misguidance:** In applications related to mental health or well-being, there's a risk of ChatGPT providing inadequate or inappropriate advice, which could be harmful to individuals seeking genuine help.

6. Accessibility and Digital Divide:

- **Unequal Access:** Advanced technologies, while promising, might not be equally accessible to all socio-economic classes, potentially widening the digital divide.

- **Cultural Biases:** Since models like ChatGPT are often trained on predominantly English, Western-centric datasets, they might inadvertently marginalize or misinterpret non-Western cultures and languages.

7. Intellectual Property and Originality:

- **Content Creation:** If ChatGPT is used extensively in fields like writing, art, or music, questions arise about the originality of such content and who holds the intellectual property rights.

- **Devaluation of Human Creativity:** There's a potential risk of undermining the value of human creativity and effort if AI-generated content becomes indistinguishable from human-produced work.

8. Regulation and Accountability:

- **Lack of Oversight:** The rapid advancement of AI technologies often outpaces regulatory frameworks, leading to a lack of oversight or standards.

- **Determining Responsibility:** In cases where ChatGPT or similar models produce harmful outputs or make decisions with adverse consequences, it becomes challenging to ascertain responsibility, given the absence of human intentionality.

Chapter 2: ChatGPT Prompts

Chatbot models like ChatGPT, which are based on OpenAI's GPT (Generative Pre-trained Transformer) architectures, rely heavily on prompts to generate responses. Understanding prompts and how they function is critical to harnessing the full power of these models. Here's a comprehensive overview:

What is a Prompt?

In the context of models like ChatGPT, a prompt is a piece of text input that the user gives to the model. The model takes this input and generates an output based on its training data and the patterns it has learned. The prompt serves as a way to instruct or guide the model in generating its response.

How Prompts Work in ChatGPT:

1. **User Input**: The user sends a text query, or prompt, to the model.

   Explanation: This is the initial step where a user sends a piece of text to the model. The nature of this text determines the direction in which the conversation will move.

   Example: A user might send a simple question like, "Who wrote 'Pride and Prejudice'?" This is the user's input prompt.

2. **Model Processing:** The model processes the prompt using the neural weights it has learned during training.

   Explanation: Once the model receives the input, it processes it using billions of parameters that have been trained on a diverse range of internet text. These parameters allow the model to understand context, recognize patterns, and generate relevant responses.

   Example: When presented with the above question, ChatGPT checks patterns in its training to identify relevant information associated with the book 'Pride and Prejudice'.

3. **Response Generation**: The model returns a text response that, ideally, addresses the prompt appropriately.

Explanation: Based on the processed input and the patterns recognized, the model produces a text output that ideally aligns with the user's query.

Example: In response to the earlier prompt, the model might reply, "Jane Austen wrote 'Pride and Prejudice'."

Factors Influencing Prompt Responses:

1. **Explicitness**: The clearer and more explicit your prompt, the more precise the model's response will likely be.

2. **Length**: While GPT models can handle long prompts, there's a maximum token limit (e.g., 2048 tokens for GPT-3). If a conversation exceeds this, you'd need to truncate, omit, or otherwise shrink your text.

3. **Training Data**: ChatGPT's responses are based on patterns in its training data. If a topic was not present or was underrepresented in its training data up to the last update, the model might not have comprehensive or up-to-date knowledge on it.

4. **Temperature Setting**: This is a parameter you can adjust when querying the model. A higher temperature (e.g., 0.8) makes output more random, while a lower value (e.g., 0.2) makes it more deterministic.

5. **Max Tokens Setting**: This restricts the length of the response. For instance, setting max tokens to 50 might truncate longer responses.

Additional Factors in Prompt Processing:

Prompt Context:

Explanation: The model can consider previous messages in a conversation to provide contextually relevant answers. This allows for back-and-forth interactions that make sense as a cohesive conversation.

Example:

User: "Tell me about 'Pride and Prejudice'."

ChatGPT: "It's a novel written by Jane Austen, first published in 1813. It's a romantic fiction about the manners and matrimonial machinations among the British gentry of the early 19th century."

User: "What's the main theme of the book?"

ChatGPT: "The main theme of 'Pride and Prejudice' is the importance of love and understanding in marriage. It also delves into issues of class, reputation, and the pitfalls of first impressions."

Inferred Intent*:*

Explanation: Sometimes, the model tries to infer the user's intent based on the phrasing or the nature of the question.

Example:

User: "I need a poem about winter."

ChatGPT: (Inferring that the user wants a creative piece) "Winter's embrace, so cold and deep, / Blankets the earth in a frozen sleep. / Snowflakes dance, light and free, / Painting a world of white for all to see."

Prompt Ambiguity*:*

Explanation: If a prompt is ambiguous, the model might either ask for clarification or generate a response based on patterns it deems most likely relevant.

Example:

User: "Tell me about apple."

ChatGPT might interpret this in multiple ways: as the fruit, the tech company, etc. A possible response could be, "Are you referring to the fruit or the technology company, Apple Inc.?"

Tips for Effective Prompting:

1. **Be Clear and Direct:** If you want information on a specific topic, it's often better to be explicit about it.

2. **Specify the Format**: If you want the answer in a specific format (e.g., a list, a short summary), mention it in the prompt.

3. **Iterative Prompting**: If the initial response isn't satisfactory, you can refine the prompt and ask again, or ask follow-up questions.

4. **Systematic Experimentation**: Trying different phrasings or approaches to a question can give you insights into how the model understands and responds.

Use Cases:

1. **Information Retrieval**: Using prompts to extract specific knowledge from the model.

2. **Creative Writing**: Providing a story start or scenario and asking the model to continue.

3. **Tutoring**: Asking the model to explain concepts or solve problems step-by-step.

4. **Translation**: Providing text in one language and prompting for a translation in another.

5. **And many more!** The potential applications of ChatGPT with effective prompting are vast.

Limitations:

- **Bias and Neutrality**: Since ChatGPT is trained on vast amounts of internet text, it might sometimes exhibit biases present in its training data. This makes the phrasing and nature of prompts even more critical, as they can inadvertently lead to biased outputs.

- **Over-Reliance on Prompts**: While effective prompting can achieve desired outputs, over-relying on the model without critical evaluation can lead to misinformation or undesired outcomes.

Developing Complicated and Compound ChatGPT Prompts:

Creating complicated compound prompts can sometimes be a strategy to extract more nuanced or specific information from models like ChatGPT. These prompts are typically layered, multi-faceted, and may combine different types of queries. Here are some examples along with explanations:

Combining Historical with Hypothetical:

Prompt: "Assuming Shakespeare had access to a modern computer, how might he have reacted to word processing software, given what we know about his writing habits and the tools available in his time?"

Explanation: This prompt combines historical knowledge (Shakespeare's writing habits and the tools of his era) with a hypothetical scenario (his reaction to modern word processing software).

Merging Scientific Explanation with Creative Extension:

Prompt: "Explain the process of photosynthesis in plants and then craft a short story where plants have evolved to harness solar energy for more advanced purposes beyond just making food."

Explanation: The first part seeks a scientific explanation, while the second part demands a creative extrapolation based on the given science.

Blending Personal Opinion with Factual Information:

Prompt: "Describe the economic impacts of the COVID-19 pandemic during 2020-2021, and then share what you, as a model, perceive as the most significant long-term change for global economies based on this event."

Explanation: The first segment is about factual historical economic data, while the second seeks the model's "opinion" (or its inferred analysis based on training data).

Juxtaposing Literature Review with Modern Context:

Prompt: "Summarize the themes explored in George Orwell's '1984' and discuss how they might resonate with or differ from the concerns of a digital society in 2023 concerning surveillance and privacy."

Explanation: The prompt first requests a literary review and then requires a comparative analysis with contemporary issues.

Integrating Technical Explanation with Ethical Consideration:

Prompt: "Outline the basic principles of how deep learning neural networks operate and subsequently discuss the ethical implications of using such technologies for facial recognition in public spaces."

Explanation: The prompt begins with a technical inquiry and segues into an ethical discussion related to the application of the technology.

Fusing Instructional Request with Evaluation:

Prompt: "Provide a step-by-step recipe for making a traditional Italian lasagna, and then evaluate how adopting plant-based alternatives for meat and cheese might alter its taste and cultural authenticity."

Explanation: Initially, the prompt asks for a set of instructions (a recipe), followed by an evaluative discussion on changes and their implications.

When crafting complicated compound prompts, it's essential to ensure clarity in each segment of the prompt to get relevant and coherent responses.

Chapter 3: ChatGPT Formula

What is the ChatGPT Formula?

At its core, the term "ChatGPT formula" refers to the structured approach or methodology users employ to craft prompts and interact with ChatGPT effectively. Given the model's sensitivity to input phrasing, the way questions or prompts are structured can significantly influence the nature and accuracy of the response. Therefore, understanding and optimizing this formula is crucial for anyone looking to harness the full potential of ChatGPT.

Best Practices for Crafting the ChatGPT Formula:

Explicitness: One of the key components of the ChatGPT formula is being clear and explicit. Vague or ambiguous questions can lead to similarly vague answers.

Example: Instead of asking, "What's the weather like?", specify the location and date: "What's the weather like in Paris on September 5th, 2023?"

Iterative Prompting: If the initial response isn't satisfactory, users can iterate and refine their prompts, seeking clarity or nudging the model towards a more desirable answer.

Example: If the query "Tell me about black holes" results in a very basic response, you can follow up with, "Can you explain the physics behind black holes in more detail?"

Guided Responses: Asking ChatGPT to think step-by-step or debate the pros and cons before arriving at an answer can yield more thoughtful and comprehensive outputs.

Example: Instead of "What are the benefits of solar energy?", ask "Can you list and elaborate on the benefits and drawbacks of solar energy?"

Setting the Context: Sometimes, setting a context or providing a brief backstory can guide the model to generate more tailored responses.

Example: "Imagine you're explaining to a 10-year-old. What is photosynthesis?"

Temperature and Token Settings: For advanced users, tweaking parameters like "temperature" (which influences randomness) and "max tokens" (which limits response length) can further optimize outputs.

Example: For creative tasks, a higher temperature might be desired for varied outputs, while for factual queries, a lower temperature can yield more consistent answers.

Real-world Examples of Effective ChatGPT Formula Use:
Educational Setting: A teacher could guide the model to craft age-appropriate explanations: "Explain the concept of gravity as you would to a third-grade student."

Business Applications: A market analyst might seek specific data: "List the advantages and disadvantages of investing in the tech sector in 2022."

Content Creation: An author could seek inspiration for a story set in a specific era: "Provide a brief overview of daily life in 18th century France for a nobleman."

Technical Assistance: A programmer could ask for a specific coding solution: "Provide a Python code snippet for a function that calculates the factorial of a number."

ChatGPT Advanced Formulas:

1. System and User Tokens: To create a more structured dialogue or to simulate a multi-turn conversation, users can use system and user tokens to alternate between instructions and queries.

- *Example:*
  [System] You are a historian specializing in Ancient Rome. [User] Tell me about Julius Caesar's contributions to Rome. This method sets a context and ensures that responses align with the predefined expertise.

2. Prompt Chaining: Chain prompts to guide the model through a series of related or sequential thoughts. This can be useful for complex problem-solving or multi-step tasks.

- *Example:*
  Explain the process of photosynthesis. Now, based on that, how do plants thrive in limited sunlight?

3. Temperature and Token Tweaking: While often used in standard interactions, mastering the balance of "temperature" (determining randomness) and "max tokens" (limiting output length) is an art in itself, especially for specialized tasks.

- *Example:*
  For brainstorming creative story ideas, you might set a higher temperature (e.g., 0.8) for varied outputs. For concise factual answers, a lower temperature (e.g., 0.2) with a reduced token count can give precise results.

4. Role Play and Scenario Simulation: Instruct the model to play a specific character or role. This can be valuable for creative tasks, debate simulations, or specialized knowledge retrieval.

- *Example:*
  You are Sherlock Holmes. Explain the process of deductive reasoning you'd use to solve a mystery.

5. Conditional and Hypothetical Queries: Frame your prompts in a conditional or hypothetical manner to explore potential outcomes, predictions, or solutions.

- *Example:*
  If quantum computing becomes mainstream in the next decade, how might it impact current encryption methods?

6. Socratic Questioning: Engage the model in a Socratic dialogue where answers are followed by deeper probing questions. This iterative method can lead to more profound insights.

- *Example:*
  Why is the sky blue? Followed by, What causes that specific scattering of shorter wavelengths? And so on.

7. Meta-Prompts: Ask the model about its own functioning, training data, or the best ways to interact with it. This introspective approach can yield valuable insights into optimizing subsequent interactions.

- *Example:*
  How are you trained to handle controversial topics? or What's the best way to ask you about historical events for accurate answers?

8. Feedback Loops: Have the model refine or critique its own outputs. This can be a method to refine answers or improve upon initial outputs.

- ***Example:***
  After getting a response, you might ask, Can you simplify the previous answer? or Provide a counterargument to your last statement.

Chapter 4: ChatGPT for eCommerce

Incorporating ChatGPT into an e-commerce business can enhance the user experience, improve customer support, and even drive sales. Here's a step-by-step strategy to integrate ChatGPT into your e-commerce venture:

1. Business Model & Niche Selection:

- **Example**: Let's assume you want to sell handmade crafts.

2. Platform & Website Development:

- **Example**: Use platforms like Shopify, WooCommerce, or Magento.

- Integrate ChatGPT as an on-site chatbot to assist visitors.

3. Product Listing & Inventory Management:

- **Example**: List handmade crafts such as jewelry, pottery, and embroidered items.

- ChatGPT can help answer questions like "How many items are in stock?" or "Can I see more photos of this product?"

4. Customer Service Enhancement with ChatGPT:

- Train ChatGPT to answer frequently asked questions (FAQs) about your products, shipping policies, returns, etc.

- **Example**: A customer might ask, "What's the return policy for jewelry?" and ChatGPT could instantly provide the information.

5. Personalized Shopping Experience:

- Use ChatGPT to provide product recommendations based on user queries.

- **Example**: A visitor might ask, "Do you have pottery with a floral design?" ChatGPT can then showcase relevant products.

6. Shopping Cart & Checkout Assistance:

- Use ChatGPT to guide customers through the checkout process, answering questions about payment methods, shipping, or applying discounts.

- **Example**: If a customer asks, "How do I use my discount code?", ChatGPT can guide them step-by-step.

7. Feedback & Reviews Collection:

- After purchase, ChatGPT can ask customers for feedback or to leave a product review.

- **Example**: "Did you like your floral pottery? Would you mind leaving a review?"

8. Retargeting & Marketing:

- Integrate ChatGPT into email marketing campaigns or messenger apps. When users respond, ChatGPT can assist with queries.

- **Example**: Send an email about a new pottery collection, and if customers reply with questions, ChatGPT can provide answers.

9. Data Collection & Analysis:

- Collect data on the most common queries ChatGPT handles. This will provide insights into what customers are looking for or any challenges they face on the site.

- **Example**: If many customers ask about shipping duration, consider making that information more prominent on the site.

10. Continuous Training & Improvement:

- Continuously feed ChatGPT with updated information about products, policies, and promotions.

- Review chat logs regularly to identify areas where the model might be faltering and retrain it as needed.

- **Example**: If ChatGPT struggles with questions about a new product category, such as wooden crafts, provide more training data around that category.

11. Expansion & Scalability:

- As your e-commerce business grows, consider introducing multi-language support with ChatGPT or integrating it with other systems like inventory management or CRM.

- **Example**: If expanding to a non-English speaking market, train ChatGPT in the local language to serve those customers.

12. Stay Updated & Innovate:

- As AI and chatbot technology evolve, be ready to update and upgrade your ChatGPT instance to leverage new features or better performance.

- **Example**: If a new version of ChatGPT becomes available with better product recommendation abilities, consider implementing it.

ChatGPT Prompts and Modules needed for eCommerce:

In the following section, I will expand the ChatGPT prompts and modules needed for each strategy point to establish a successful ecommerce business.

Business Model & Niche Selection:

1. **Market Analysis & Trends:**

- **Prompt**: "Provide an analysis of the current market trends in the e-commerce sector."

- **Module**: Integrate web scraping and analytics tools to constantly update ChatGPT on prevailing market trends.

Example: ChatGPT might return, "Based on recent data, sustainable products and eco-friendly goods have seen a 20% increase in demand in the e-commerce sector."

2. **Niche Opportunities:**

- **Prompt**: "Identify untapped niches within the sustainable products sector."

- **Module**: Analyze keyword search data, social media mentions, and emerging industries to highlight potential niches.

Example: "Bamboo-based household items and reusable silicone food storage products are emerging niches within the sustainable products sector."

3. **Competitive Landscape:**

- **Prompt**: "Detail the competitive landscape for bamboo-based household items in the e-commerce space."

- **Module**: Integrate with e-commerce platforms and business databases to provide data on current players, their market share, and customer reviews.

Example: "There are currently 15 major players in the bamboo-based household items sector, with 'BambooLiving' leading with a 30% market share. Reviews suggest customers are looking for more innovative designs."

4. **Customer Pain Points:**

- **Prompt**: "What are the common pain points for customers buying bamboo-based products online?"

- **Module**: Analyze customer reviews, feedback, and comments from various platforms to extract common complaints or wishes.

Example: "Customers often mention a lack of product durability and express a desire for a wider variety in design."

5. **Business Model Suggestions:**

- **Prompt**: "Suggest business models for launching an e-commerce platform for bamboo-based items, addressing identified pain points."

- **Module**: Combine knowledge from successful e-commerce models with customer feedback data to generate tailored business model suggestions.

Example: "Considering the demand for design variety, consider a crowd-sourced design model. Allow designers to submit designs for bamboo products, and let the community vote. Top designs go into production, offering variety and addressing durability concerns."

6. **Monetization Strategies:**

- **Prompt**: "Propose monetization strategies for the suggested crowd-sourced design model."

- **Module**: Use data on popular monetization methods, their success rates, and fitment with the business model to suggest strategies.

Example: "1. Take a percentage from each sale of designer-submitted products. 2. Offer a premium subscription where subscribers get early access to new designs. 3. Allow designers to pay a fee for promoting their designs on the platform's homepage."

7. **Risk Assessment:**

- **Prompt**: "What potential risks are associated with the crowd-sourced design model?"

- **Module**: Analyze historical data of similar models, current market conditions, and potential challenges to highlight risks.

Example: "Risks include potential copyright infringements from submitted designs, variability in product quality, and the challenge of keeping the community engaged."

Platform & Website Development:
1. **Platform Selection:**

- **Prompt**: "Recommend the most suitable e-commerce platforms for selling handmade crafts with a primary audience in the U.S."

- **Module**: Analyze popular e-commerce platforms based on their features, scalability, pricing, and reviews, specific to the desired niche and target market.

Example Response: "Shopify, WooCommerce (on WordPress), and BigCommerce are top choices for selling handmade crafts to a U.S audience. Shopify offers ease of use, WooCommerce provides customization, and BigCommerce is scalable for growing businesses."

2. **Design Theme Suggestions:**

- **Prompt**: "Suggest design themes that resonate with the handmade crafts niche."

- **Module**: Scour the web for popular design aesthetics for handmade crafts sites, emphasizing visual appeal and user experience.

Example Response: "Consider rustic, minimalist, or artisanal themes. Websites like 'ThemeForest' or Shopify's theme store have specific themes like 'Crafty', 'Handmade Artisans', and 'Natural Goods'."

3. **Feature Integration:**

- **Prompt**: "List essential features to integrate for an e-commerce site selling handmade crafts."

- **Module**: Refer to best practices and trends for e-commerce sites, especially those related to handmade crafts.

Example Response: "Key features include a product gallery, zoom-in functionality, customer reviews section, a blog for craft stories, integration with social media for sharing, and a detailed 'About the Artisan' page."

4. **Checkout Optimization:**

- **Prompt**: "Propose strategies to streamline the checkout process for higher conversion."

- **Module**: Analyze data from successful e-commerce sites, identifying common barriers to purchase and their solutions.

Example Response: "1. Implement a one-page checkout. 2. Offer multiple payment gateways. 3. Provide guest checkout options. 4. Showcase security badges for trust. 5. Use progress indicators."

5. **Mobile Optimization:**

- **Prompt**: "What are the key considerations for optimizing the website for mobile users?"

- **Module**: Refer to mobile e-commerce UX best practices and potential pitfalls.

Example Response: "Ensure responsive design, utilize large, touch-friendly buttons, simplify navigation with a hamburger menu, optimize images for faster loading, and implement mobile-friendly checkout like Apple Pay or Google Wallet."

6. **SEO & Visibility:**

- **Prompt**: "Provide SEO best practices for a handmade crafts e-commerce site."

- **Module**: Pull from up-to-date SEO guidelines, focusing on e-commerce specific strategies.

Example Response: "1. Optimize product descriptions with relevant keywords. 2. Use high-quality images with alt tags. 3. Implement schema markup. 4. Create a blog for craft-related content to attract organic traffic. 5. Optimize meta tags and URLs."

7. **Security Measures:**

- **Prompt**: "List essential security measures for an e-commerce platform."

- **Module**: Analyze common e-commerce security threats and best practices for mitigation.

Example Response: "1. Use SSL certificates for encrypted data transmission. 2. Implement a firewall and regular malware scans. 3. Stay updated with platform patches. 4. Use secure payment gateways. 5. Educate customers on safe online shopping practices."

8. **User Testing & Feedback:**

- **Prompt**: "How should we approach user testing for our e-commerce platform?"

- **Module**: Provide strategies based on successful user testing methodologies.

Example Response: "Start with alpha testing among the internal team. Progress to beta testing with select customers. Implement tools like Hotjar to understand user behavior. Gather feedback, iterate, and refine the user experience."

Product Listing & Inventory Management:

1. **Product Categorization:**

- **Prompt**: "Recommend an optimal product categorization structure for a diverse range of handmade crafts."

- **Module**: Analyze current market trends and competitive benchmarks to provide a comprehensive categorization strategy.

Example Response: "Categories can include: Jewelry (sub-categories: necklaces, rings, bracelets), Pottery (sub-categories: vases, plates, mugs), Textiles (sub-categories: scarves, blankets, clothing)."

2. **Product Description & SEO:**

- **Prompt**: "Provide guidelines for crafting SEO-optimized product descriptions for handmade pottery."

- **Module**: Draw from SEO best practices and keyword research specific to the handmade pottery niche.

Example Response: "1. Use relevant keywords such as 'handcrafted ceramic vases' or 'artisanal pottery bowls'. 2. Limit descriptions to 150-250 words, making them concise yet informative. 3. Highlight unique features, origin, and the artisan's inspiration."

3. **Inventory Tracking:**

- **Prompt**: "Suggest tools or methods for real-time inventory tracking for a small e-commerce business."

- **Module**: Integrate information from popular inventory management software solutions, highlighting those that cater to small businesses.

Example Response: "Tools like TradeGecko, Stitch Labs, or Zoho Inventory provide real-time inventory tracking suitable for small e-commerce operations. They offer integrations with popular e-commerce platforms and automate restocking alerts."

4. **Pricing Strategy:**

- **Prompt**: "Propose a pricing strategy for premium handmade crafts, factoring in costs, competition, and perceived value."

- **Module**: Combine cost analysis, competitor pricing data, and premium product positioning to generate a comprehensive pricing strategy.

Example Response: "1. Calculate the total cost of production. 2. Mark up by 50% for direct costs. 3. Consider a 20% premium for unique craftsmanship. 4. Regularly benchmark against competitors and adjust. 5. Offer bundle deals or discounts for returning customers."

5. **Stock Alerts:**

- **Prompt**: "Design an alert system for low-stock items to ensure timely replenishment."

- **Module**: Use data from inventory levels and sales velocity to project when products will run out, triggering automatic alerts.

Example Response: "Implement a threshold system. For products that sell 10 units a day and take 5 days for restocking, set the alert threshold at 60 units. Once inventory drops below this, trigger an automatic restocking alert."

6. **Product Photography Guidelines:**

- **Prompt**: "Provide best practices for photographing handmade crafts for online listings."

- **Module**: Refer to successful e-commerce platforms and photography guidelines for optimal product presentation.

Example Response: "1. Use natural lighting or a softbox. 2. Opt for neutral backgrounds. 3. Capture multiple angles. 4. Showcase size context (e.g., a ring next to a coin). 5. Edit for clarity but keep colors true to life."

7. **Return & Storage Management:**

- **Prompt**: "Outline a process for managing returns and reintegrating items into the inventory for handmade crafts."

- **Module**: Incorporate best practices from inventory management and customer service perspectives.

Example Response: "1. Designate a 'Returns' section in your storage. 2. Inspect returned items for damage. 3. If intact, update inventory count and place the item back in general stock. 4. If damaged, decide on repairs, discounts, or discards. 5. Update inventory system accordingly.

8. **Scaling Inventory with Growth:**

- **Prompt**: "Propose strategies to scale inventory management as sales volume increases."

- **Module**: Forecast based on current growth trends and integrate solutions tailored for larger operations.

Example Response: "1. Migrate to a more robust inventory management system. 2. Consider warehouse or third-party logistics partnerships for storage. 3. Automate reorder processes based on predictive analytics. 4. Introduce barcoding for faster item tracking."

Customer Service Enhancement with ChatGPT:
1. **Tailored Responses Based on Purchase History:**

- **Prompt**: "Offer support based on a user's recent purchase of a 'Blue Crystal Pendant'."

- **Module**: Integrate with the user's purchase history to provide context-aware responses.

Example User Query: "I have an issue with my recent purchase."
Example ChatGPT Response: "I see you recently bought a 'Blue Crystal Pendant'. What seems to be the issue with it?"

2. **Interactive Troubleshooting:**

- **Prompt**: "Guide a customer through troubleshooting a faulty product."

- **Module**: Use decision-tree logic to navigate the user through step-by-step solutions based on their responses.

Example User Query: "My electronic gadget isn't turning on." **Example ChatGPT Sequence**:

- "Let's troubleshoot. Have you ensured it's charged?"

- "Try a different charging cable and see if that works."

- "If the problem persists, it might be an internal issue. Would you like to process a return or exchange?"

3. **Personalized Recommendations:**

- **Prompt**: "Recommend complementary products based on a user's past purchases and browsing history."

- **Module**: Analyze user behavior and purchase data to offer personalized product suggestions.

Example Response: "Given your interest in vintage watches, you might appreciate our new collection of antique pocket watches."

4. **Real-time Order Status:**

- **Prompt**: "Update a user on the current status of their order."

- **Module**: Integrate with the order tracking system to fetch real-time updates.

Example User Query: "Where's my order #45678?" **Example ChatGPT Response**: "Your order #45678 is currently in transit and is expected to be delivered tomorrow."

5. **Feedback and Reviews:**

- **Prompt**: "Request feedback from a user after a resolved customer service interaction."

- **Module**: Integrate feedback collection forms or surveys at the end of a support interaction.

Example Response: "I'm glad we could assist you! Would you mind providing feedback on your support experience? It'll help us improve."

6. **Handling Complex Queries:**

- **Prompt**: "Identify when a user's query is too complex and suggest human assistance."

- **Module**: Use sentiment analysis and query complexity metrics to determine when to hand off to a human agent.

Example User Query: "I've had multiple issues with my orders, and I'm frustrated!" **Example ChatGPT Response**: "I'm truly sorry for the inconvenience. Let me connect you with a member of our support team for immediate assistance."

7. **Promotions and Offers:**

- **Prompt**: "Inform users about ongoing promotions or special deals related to their interests."

- **Module**: Access current promotional data and match it with user behavior and preferences.

Example User Query: "Are there any deals on sneakers?" **Example ChatGPT Response**: "Yes, we currently have a 'Buy One Get One 50% Off' promotion on select sneaker brands. Would you like to check them out?"

8. **Proactive Assistance:**

- **Prompt**: "Offer help when a user spends too much time on the checkout page."

- **Module**: Monitor user activity on specific pages and trigger proactive assistance prompts.

Example ChatGPT Initiative: "It seems you've been on the checkout page for a while. Can I assist you with the process?"

9. **Cultural and Linguistic Adaptations:**

- **Prompt**: "Adapt responses based on the user's cultural and linguistic preferences."

- **Module**: Identify user's geographical location or language preference and adapt responses accordingly.

Example User Query (in French): "Combien coûte la livraison?"
Example ChatGPT Response: "La livraison standard coûte 5€. Si vous dépensez plus de 50€, la livraison est gratuite!"

Personalized Shopping Experience*:*

1. **Product Recommendations Based on History:**

- **Prompt**: "Recommend products based on a user's past purchase of 'vintage leather boots'."

- **Module**: Integrate with the user's purchase history and the product recommendation engine to suggest similar or complementary items.

Example Response: "Given your past purchase of vintage leather boots, you might like our collection of leather jackets and leather care kits."

2. **Dynamic Interaction Based on Browsing Behavior:**

- **Prompt**: "Engage a user who's spent considerable time browsing 'summer dresses' without making a purchase."

- **Module**: Track user behavior to identify potential purchase hesitations and intervene with helpful suggestions.

Example ChatGPT Initiative: "Noticed you're checking out our summer dresses! Do you have any questions or would you like some style recommendations?"

3. **Tailored Discounts and Offers:**

- **Prompt**: "Propose a special offer to a user who often buys 'organic skincare products'."

- **Module**: Analyze user purchase frequency and preferences to provide tailored promotions.

Example Response: "We appreciate your love for our organic skincare range! Here's an exclusive 20% discount for your next purchase in this category."

4. **Outfit or Set Recommendations:**

- **Prompt**: "Create an outfit ensemble based on a user's interest in 'denim jackets'."

- **Module**: Link up with a fashion recommendation system, considering current fashion trends and available inventory.

Example Response: "Pairing that denim jacket with a white tee, black skinny jeans, and ankle boots would give a chic street style look. Want to explore these matching items?"

5. **Feedback-based Recommendations:**

- **Prompt**: "Adjust product suggestions based on a user's feedback about preferring 'minimalist jewelry'."

- **Module**: Adapt recommendations dynamically based on real-time feedback given during the conversation.

Example Response: "Thank you for sharing your preference. Check out our minimalist jewelry collection, featuring delicate chains and subtle designs."

6. **Interactive Quizzes for Tailored Suggestions:**

- **Prompt**: "Guide a user through a 'Find Your Style' quiz."

- **Module**: Design a series of interactive questions to determine user preferences, culminating in tailored product suggestions.

Example ChatGPT Sequence:

- "Do you prefer gold or silver jewelry?"

- "Do you like statement pieces or subtle designs?"

- "Based on your choices, here are some handpicked items for you!"

7. **Updates on Favorites or Wishlist Items:**

- **Prompt**: "Notify a user about a restock of an item in their wishlist."

- **Module**: Integrate with the user's wishlist or favorites and the inventory management system for real-time stock updates.

Example Response: "Good news! The 'Ruby Heart Pendant' from your wishlist is now back in stock."

8. **Localized Product Recommendations:**

- **Prompt**: "Suggest products based on the user's location."

- **Module**: Use geolocation data to recommend products popular in or tailored to that region.

Example User Query: "I'm shopping from Canada. What do you recommend?" **Example ChatGPT Response**: "Considering the Canadian winters, you might love our range of cozy knit sweaters and thermal leggings."

Shopping Cart & Checkout Assistance:

1. **Cart Review and Feedback:**

- **Prompt**: "Provide an overview of items currently in the user's shopping cart."

- **Module**: Integration with the e-commerce platform's cart system to fetch real-time cart contents.

Example User Query: "What's in my cart right now?" **Example ChatGPT Response**: "You have 3 Items in your cart: 'Handmade Blue Scarf', 'Leather-bound Journal', and 'Scented Candle Set'."

2. **Promotions and Discounts Application:**

- **Prompt**: "Guide the user on applying a discount code during checkout."

- **Module**: Step-by-step guidance based on the platform's checkout UI.

Example User Query: "How do I use my discount code?" **Example ChatGPT Response**: "At the checkout page, you'll see a field labeled 'Discount Code'. Enter your code there and click 'Apply'. The discount will be automatically deducted from your total."

3. **Shipping and Delivery Options:**

- **Prompt**: "Detail the available shipping options and their costs."

- **Module**: Extract shipping policies and costs from the platform's database.

Example User Query: "How much is shipping?" **Example ChatGPT Response**: "We offer Standard Shipping at $5 (3-5 business days) and Express Shipping at $10 (1-2 business days). Orders above $50 qualify for free Standard Shipping."

4. **Address and Payment Queries:**

- **Prompt**: "Help a user with entering billing and shipping addresses."

- **Module**: Visual guidance based on UI, with possible validation of address formats.

Example User Query: "I'm confused about entering my address." **Example ChatGPT Response**: "No worries! Start by entering your street number and name. Follow with the city, state, and postal code. Ensure the country selected at the top is correct. If your billing and shipping addresses are the same, you can check the 'Same as Shipping Address' box."

5. **Upselling at Checkout:**

- **Prompt**: "Recommend add-on products based on items in the user's cart."

- **Module**: Sync with recommendation algorithms and inventory to suggest complementary products.

Example Response: "Since you're buying a journal, would you be interested in our premium pen set? It's a favorite among our journal enthusiasts."

6. **Troubleshooting Payment Issues:**

- **Prompt**: "Assist a user facing payment errors."

- **Module**: Provide common solutions based on known payment gateway error messages.

Example User Query: "My credit card isn't going through." **Example ChatGPT Response**: "I'm sorry for the inconvenience. Please ensure:

1. The card details entered are correct.

2. You have sufficient balance.

3. The card hasn't expired. If the issue persists, consider using an alternate payment method."

7. **Security Reassurances:**

- **Prompt**: "Reassure the user about payment security."

- **Module**: Highlight the e-commerce platform's security protocols and certifications.

Example User Query: "Is my payment information safe?" **Example ChatGPT Response**: "Absolutely. We use end-to-end encryption and comply with PCI DSS standards. Plus, we never store your credit card information."

8. **Order Confirmation and Next Steps:**

- **Prompt**: "Explain to the user what happens post-checkout."

- **Module**: Outline the post-purchase process, from order confirmation to delivery.

Example Response: "Once you've completed your purchase, you'll receive an order confirmation email. You can track your order's progress from your account dashboard. We'll also send you email updates when your order ships and is out for delivery."

Feedback & Reviews Collection:

1. Initiating Feedback After Purchase:

- **Prompt**: "Request feedback from a user who has just received their 'Vintage Leather Handbag'."

- **Module**: Integration with order and delivery systems to initiate feedback requests post-delivery.

Example ChatGPT Initiative: "We noticed you've recently received your 'Vintage Leather Handbag'. We'd love to hear your thoughts! Could you rate it from 1-5?"

2. Detailed Product Review:

- **Prompt**: "Guide a user through submitting a detailed review for their recent purchase."

- **Module**: Implement a structured review template for users to fill out, capturing aspects like quality, usability, and value for money.

Example Response: "We're thrilled you're willing to share your thoughts. Let's start with:

1. How would you rate the product quality on a scale of 1-5?

2. Describe your favorite feature of the product.

3. Do you think it offers value for its price?"

3. Capture Feedback on Customer Service:

- **Prompt**: "Inquire about a user's recent interaction with the customer service team."

- **Module**: Reference the user's recent customer service interactions and present a satisfaction survey.

Example ChatGPT Initiative: "You recently contacted our support team. How was your experience? Please rate our response time, helpfulness, and resolution on a scale of 1-5."

4. Incentivized Review Requests:

- **Prompt**: "Offer an incentive for providing a product review."

- **Module**: Integrate promotional codes or loyalty points systems to reward users for their reviews.

Example Response: "Thank you for purchasing our 'Summer Floral Dress'. Share a review and get a 10% discount on your next purchase!"

5. **Feedback on Website Experience:**

- **Prompt**: "Ask the user about their browsing and shopping experience on the website."

- **Module**: Use a combination of open-ended and structured questions to capture detailed feedback.

Example ChatGPT Initiative: "We're always working to improve. How was your shopping experience today? Were you able to find products easily? Was the checkout process smooth?"

6. **Capture Negative Feedback Constructively:**

- **Prompt**: "Engage a user who seems dissatisfied with a product or service."

- **Module**: Use sentiment analysis to detect negative feedback and then engage the user constructively to understand the issues.

Example User Query: "I'm not happy with the quality of the shoes I ordered." **Example ChatGPT Response**: "I'm truly sorry to hear that. Can you tell me specifically what you didn't like? Your feedback will help us make necessary improvements."

7. **Real-time Feedback During Browsing:**

- **Prompt**: "Engage users who have been browsing a specific section for an extended time without making a purchase."

- **Module**: Monitor user behavior to identify potential confusion or decision paralysis and then prompt for feedback.

Example ChatGPT Initiative: "You've been exploring our 'Tech Gadgets' section for a while. Is there something specific you're looking for or any feedback you'd like to share about our selection?"

8. **Post-Return Feedback Collection:**

- **Prompt**: "Inquire about the reasons behind a product return to understand potential product or service gaps."

- **Module**: Link feedback prompts to return and refund processes to capture insights.

Example ChatGPT Initiative: "We noticed you returned the 'Bluetooth Headset'. Could you share why it didn't meet your expectations? Your feedback will help us enhance our offerings."

Retargeting & Marketing:

1. **Cart Abandonment Reminders:**

- **Prompt**: "Engage a user who added items to their cart but didn't complete the purchase."

- **Module**: Integration with the cart system to detect abandoned carts and initiate timely reminders.

Example ChatGPT Initiative: "Hey! We noticed you left a 'Vintage Wall Clock' in your cart. Still interested? Here's a 10% off code to sweeten the deal: CART10."

2. **Product Recommendations Based on Browsing History:**

- **Prompt**: "Recommend products to a user based on their recent browsing of 'sports equipment'."

- **Module**: Access browsing history to suggest relevant products.

Example Response: "We saw you were checking out sports equipment. Our newly arrived 'Aero-Dynamic Badminton Racket' has been getting rave reviews. Want to take a look?"

3. **Feedback-based Marketing:**

- **Prompt**: "Market new product arrivals based on a user's feedback about loving 'vintage accessories'."

- **Module**: Match user feedback with relevant marketing campaigns.

Example ChatGPT Initiative: "Since you love vintage accessories, you might be thrilled with our just-arrived collection of 'Retro Sunglasses'. Check them out!"

4. **Engaging Dormant Users:**

- **Prompt**: "Engage a user who hasn't shopped or interacted with the platform in the last six months."

- **Module**: Identify dormant users and target them with re-engagement campaigns.

Example ChatGPT Initiative: "Long time no see! We've missed you. Here's a 20% off code on your next purchase to welcome you back: WELCOME20."

5. **Upselling and Cross-Selling:**

- **Prompt**: "Suggest complementary products based on a user's purchase of 'wireless earbuds'."

- **Module**: Sync with recommendation algorithms to suggest related items.

Example Response: "Enjoying your new wireless earbuds? Our 'Protective Earbud Case' might be the perfect accessory to keep them safe!"

6. **Newsletter Sign-ups:**

- **Prompt**: "Encourage users to sign up for newsletters for the latest updates and offers."

- **Module**: Integrate with email marketing platforms to facilitate sign-ups.

Example ChatGPT Initiative: "Stay in the loop with our latest collections and exclusive deals! Want to sign up for our newsletter?"

7. **Promoting Limited-Time Offers:**

- **Prompt**: "Inform users about ongoing sales or limited-time promotions."

- **Module**: Access current promotional data to notify users.

Example Response: "Heads up! Our summer sale is on. Enjoy up to 50% off on select items until this weekend."

8. **Feedback Loop for Marketing Campaigns:**

- **Prompt**: "Ask users for feedback on recent marketing campaigns to understand their effectiveness."

- **Module**: Initiate feedback forms or quick surveys post-campaign.

Example ChatGPT Initiative: "Did you enjoy our 'Winter Wonderland' campaign? Your feedback helps us create better experiences for you."

9. **Geo-targeted Promotions:**

- **Prompt**: "Promote products or offers specific to a user's location."

- **Module**: Use geolocation data to push relevant promotions.

Example User Query: "Any deals for customers in California?" **Example ChatGPT Response**: "Absolutely! Customers in California get free shipping for the entire month. Happy shopping!"

Data Collection & Analysis:

1. **User Preferences Survey:**

- **Prompt**: "Conduct a quick survey to gauge user preferences about 'summer fashion'."

- **Module**: Initiate an interactive survey, capturing responses and storing them for analysis.

Example ChatGPT Initiative:

- "Which summer fashion trend are you most excited about: Bohemian, Nautical, or Vintage?"

- "On a scale of 1-5, how important is sustainable fashion to you?"

2. **Behavioral Data Collection:**

- **Prompt**: "Track and analyze a user's browsing pattern on the website."

- **Module**: Integration with site analytics to monitor user behavior, such as pages visited, time spent, and click-through rates.

Example Analysis: "Users spending over 10 minutes in the 'shoe' section are 60% more likely to make a purchase."

3. **Feedback on New Features or Products:**

- **Prompt**: "Gather feedback on a new website feature or product rollout."

- **Module**: Engage users with structured questions, capturing their initial reactions and detailed feedback.

Example ChatGPT Initiative: "We've introduced a new 'Virtual Try-On' feature for our eyewear collection. Have you tried it? Please share your thoughts!"

4. Customer Satisfaction Metrics (CSAT, NPS):

- **Prompt**: "Measure user satisfaction after a purchase or support interaction."

- **Module**: Deploy standard satisfaction metrics, analyzing scores and open feedback.

Example ChatGPT Sequence:

- "On a scale of 1-10, how likely are you to recommend our platform to a friend?"

- "What's one thing we could improve?"

5. Demographic Data Collection:

- **Prompt**: "Collect demographic information for targeted marketing campaigns."

- **Module**: Integrate non-intrusive questions into regular interactions, ensuring user privacy.

Example ChatGPT Initiative: "For personalized product recommendations, could you share your age range? (Optional)"

6. Identify and Analyze User Pain Points:

- **Prompt**: "Engage users to understand common problems or issues they face on the platform."

- **Module**: Use sentiment analysis to detect negative feedback and engage the user to gather more specifics.

Example User Query: "The checkout process is quite confusing."
Example ChatGPT Response: "Sorry to hear that. Could you specify what you found confusing? Your feedback helps us improve."

7. Market Research and Trend Analysis:

- **Prompt**: "Gather insights on upcoming market trends or user preferences for future products."

- **Module**: Implement interactive questionnaires, collecting and analyzing data for market insights.

Example ChatGPT Initiative: "Which upcoming tech gadget are you most excited about: Foldable Phones, AR Glasses, or Smart Watches?"

8. **Product Usage and Experience:**

- **Prompt**: "Understand how users interact with or use a product post-purchase."

- **Module**: Periodic check-ins post-purchase to gather data on product usability, durability, and satisfaction.

Example ChatGPT Initiative: "It's been a month since you bought our 'Eco-friendly Yoga Mat'. How's your experience been? Any feedback?"

9. **User Testimonials and Stories:**
- **Prompt**: "Collect positive experiences or stories from satisfied users for marketing purposes."

- **Module**: Engage with users post-purchase or post-interaction, requesting them to share their experiences.

Example ChatGPT Initiative: "We're thrilled you loved the 'Handcrafted Wooden Desk'. Would you mind sharing your experience for our testimonial section?"

Continuous Training & Improvement:

1. **User Feedback Analysis:**

- **Prompt**: "Request feedback after a user has engaged with ChatGPT for assistance."

- **Module**: Post-interaction survey or quick feedback mechanism to rate and review the chatbot experience.

Example ChatGPT Initiative: "Thanks for chatting! On a scale of 1-5, how would you rate your interaction today? Any suggestions for improvement?"

2. **Misunderstanding Detection:**

   - **Prompt**: "Identify and log instances where ChatGPT failed to understand or respond accurately to user queries."

   - **Module**: Use sentiment analysis or explicit user feedback markers (e.g., "That's not what I asked") to detect and record misunderstandings.

Example User Query: "How do I return a product?" **Incorrect ChatGPT Response**: "Our products are made of high-quality materials." **User Feedback**: "That's not helpful."

3. **Integration with External Data Sources:**

   - **Prompt**: "Stay updated with the latest in e-commerce trends and user behavior."

   - **Module**: Regularly ingest and learn from external data sources, market reports, and user behavior analytics to refine interactions.

Example Input: Feed data from a report showing a rise in demand for "sustainable fashion". **Post-Training ChatGPT Initiative**: "Interested in fashion? Check out our trending sustainable fashion collection!"

4. **Routine Test Interactions:**

   - **Prompt**: "Regularly test ChatGPT with a set of benchmark queries."

   - **Module**: Scheduled test interactions to evaluate the chatbot's accuracy, speed, and relevance. Compare outcomes with expected responses.

Example Test Query: "What's your return policy?" **Expected Response**: "Our return policy allows returns within 30 days of purchase. The product should be unused and in its original packaging."

5. **Iterative Feedback Loop:**

   - **Prompt**: "Analyze user feedback and iteratively refine the chatbot's training."

   - **Module**: Compile and analyze both quantitative (e.g., satisfaction scores) and qualitative (e.g., user comments) feedback. Use this analysis to continuously train and improve ChatGPT's database.

6. Scenario-Based Training:

- **Prompt**: "Train ChatGPT for specific e-commerce scenarios or upcoming promotions/events."

- **Module**: Create scenario-based training modules, especially for sales events, product launches, or identified user pain points.

Example Scenario: "Black Friday Sales" **Training Data**: Feed ChatGPT with information about Black Friday deals, common queries, and expected high-traffic products.

7. Engaging with Other Bots:

- **Prompt**: "Allow ChatGPT to engage with other chatbots or AI models."

- **Module**: Organize periodic interactions between ChatGPT and other AI solutions to exchange information and train on diverse data points.

Example Interaction: ChatGPT conversing with a chatbot from a tech store to understand queries related to electronics.

8. Enhance Multimodal Capabilities:

- **Prompt**: "Train ChatGPT to handle multimodal inputs, like images or voice."

- **Module**: If the e-commerce platform supports image search or voice queries, enhance ChatGPT's capability to interpret and respond to such inputs.

Example User Input: An image of a red dress. **Expected ChatGPT Response**: "Looking for a red dress? Here are some options we have!"

9. Domain-Specific Updates:

- **Prompt**: "Update ChatGPT's knowledge about specific e-commerce domains regularly."

- **Module**: Periodic training sessions focused on specific domains or categories within the e-commerce platform, especially rapidly evolving ones.

Example Domain: "Smart home gadgets" **Training Data**: Latest releases, top brands, common user queries, and concerns related to smart home gadgets.

Expansion & Scalability:

1. **Multilingual Support:**

   - **Prompt**: "Translate and respond to user queries in various languages to support global markets."

   - **Module**: Integration with real-time translation services to allow ChatGPT to engage users in their native language.

Example User Query (in Spanish): "¿Cómo puedo devolver un producto?" **Expected ChatGPT Response (in Spanish)**: "Puede devolver un producto dentro de los 30 días posteriores a la compra. Asegúrese de que el producto esté sin usar y en su embalaje original."

2. **Regional Product Recommendations:**

   - **Prompt**: "Suggest products based on regional popularity or relevance."

   - **Module**: Analyze user's location data and browsing history to recommend regionally trending or relevant products.

Example ChatGPT Initiative for a user in Australia: "Looking for something to beat the summer heat? Our collection of sun hats is quite popular in Australia right now."

3. **Dynamic Integration with Growing Inventory:**

   - **Prompt**: "Stay updated with the ever-expanding product range."

   - **Module**: Real-time syncing with the inventory management system to learn and recommend from the latest additions.

Example User Query: "Show me the latest arrivals in women's footwear." **Expected ChatGPT Response**: "Certainly! Here are the newest additions to our women's footwear collection..."

4. **Handling Increased User Load:**

   - **Prompt**: "Ensure consistent performance during peak user interactions."

- **Module**: Cloud-based scalability solutions to handle increased user loads, especially during sales or promotions.

Example Scenario: Black Friday Sale. **Implementation**: Automatic scaling of ChatGPT's cloud resources during expected high-traffic times.

5. Expansion to New Platforms and Channels:

- **Prompt**: "Integrate ChatGPT into emerging platforms such as mobile apps, social media channels, or third-party marketplaces."

- **Module**: APIs or SDKs to integrate ChatGPT into multiple platforms, ensuring a consistent user experience everywhere.

Example Implementation: Integration of ChatGPT into the brand's Instagram store for immediate query resolution.

6. Customization for Different Market Segments:

- **Prompt**: "Adapt ChatGPT's responses based on the demographic or market segment."

- **Module**: Profile analysis to tailor interactions based on user age, preferences, past interactions, etc.

Example User Profile: Male, aged 18-24, interested in tech. **Expected ChatGPT Initiative**: "Did you check out our latest gaming laptops? They're a hit among tech enthusiasts!"

7. Integration with Expanding External Tools:

- **Prompt**: "Synchronize with new CRM, ERP, or other systems as the business scales."

- **Module**: Modular architecture and APIs that allow seamless integration with emerging tools or software the business adopts.

Example Scenario: Integration with a new CRM system. **Implementation**: Ensure ChatGPT can fetch user interaction histories and preferences from the new CRM.

8. Enhanced Security for Growing User Data:

- **Prompt**: "As the user base grows, ensure data security and compliance."

- **Module**: Regular updates, patches, and security audits. Ensure compliance with data protection regulations of different regions.

Example Implementation: GDPR compliance for users from the European Union, ensuring data privacy and right to erasure.

9. Feedback Mechanism for Continuous Refinement:

- **Prompt**: "As the business grows, gather feedback on ChatGPT's performance from a wider audience."

- **Module**: Scalable and segmented feedback collection systems to understand the diverse needs and experiences of a growing user base.

Example ChatGPT Initiative: "Help us serve you better! Share your feedback about this chat experience and get a 5% discount on your next purchase."

Stay Updated & Innovate:

1. Market Trend Analysis:

- **Prompt**: "Keep abreast of emerging e-commerce and industry trends."

- **Module**: Integrate with data analytics tools that track market trends and feed this data to ChatGPT for better user interactions.

Example Input: Trending data shows an increasing interest in "sustainable fashion". **Expected ChatGPT Initiative**: "Looking for eco-friendly choices? Explore our curated range of sustainable fashion."

2. Adapting to Evolving Tech Landscape:

- **Prompt**: "Stay updated with advancements in tech and integrate them into the platform."

- **Module**: Regularly update ChatGPT's capabilities, such as integrating AR for product trials or voice search functionality.

Example User Voice Command: "Show me blue summer dresses in size M." **Expected ChatGPT Response**: "Sure! Here are blue summer dresses in size M for you."

3. **Feedback-based System Evolution:**

- **Prompt**: "Adapt and evolve based on user feedback and requirements."

- **Module**: Periodically collect, analyze, and implement changes based on feedback regarding ChatGPT's performance and user needs.

Example Feedback: "It would be great if the chatbot could help with size recommendations." **Implementation**: Integration of a size recommendation engine into ChatGPT.

4. **Continuous Learning from Diverse User Interactions:**

- **Prompt**: "Learn from each user interaction to refine responses and recommendations."

- **Module**: Implement machine learning techniques to allow ChatGPT to adapt and improve its interactions over time based on user behaviors and preferences.

Example Learning Scenario: If a user frequently inquires about "vegan products", prioritize vegan options in future product recommendations.

5. **Integration with Emerging Platforms:**

- **Prompt**: "Stay updated by integrating with emerging social media platforms or e-commerce channels."

- **Module**: Expand the reach of ChatGPT by integrating it with emerging platforms like new social media shopping features or virtual reality marketplaces.

Example Integration: Embedding ChatGPT into shopping features on platforms like TikTok or Snapchat for real-time product queries.

6. **Exploring New Engagement Mechanisms:**

- **Prompt**: "Innovate in how ChatGPT engages with users."

- **Module**: Introduce gamified interactions, storytelling, or themed engagements to make user interactions more engaging and enjoyable.

Example ChatGPT Initiative: "Join our 'Treasure Hunt' game! Answer riddles to find hidden discounts across our website."

7. Proactive Updates & Notifications:

- **Prompt**: "Provide users with proactive updates on products, offers, or industry news."

- **Module**: Integrate with the e-commerce platform's notification system to push relevant and timely updates to users.

Example ChatGPT Initiative: "Breaking News! The newest smartphone model you've been waiting for is now available on our platform."

8. Integration with External Knowledge Bases:

- **Prompt**: "Access and deliver information from external sources."

- **Module**: Link ChatGPT with external databases or knowledge repositories to provide users with updated industry news, product reviews, or related content.

Example User Query: "How does Product X compare with its competitors?" **Expected ChatGPT Response**: "Based on recent reviews and comparisons, Product X offers better battery life but lacks the camera features of its main competitor. Would you like a detailed comparison?"

9. Exploring Novel AI Capabilities:

- **Prompt**: "Experiment with new AI functionalities and capabilities."

- **Module**: Regularly update ChatGPT with the latest AI research and tools – from better sentiment analysis to predictive behaviors.

Example Implementation: Predicting when a user might abandon a cart and proactively offering assistance or discounts to ensure conversion.

Chapter 5: ChatGPT for Teachers

Creating an effective educational experience with ChatGPT requires strategic planning to ensure learning objectives are met while keeping students engaged. Here's a step-by-step strategy:

1. Define the Learning Objectives:

- Determine what you want students to learn or achieve.

- Example: If teaching history, an objective might be, "Students will understand the causes and impacts of the American Civil War."

2. Know Your Audience:

- Understand the proficiency level and background of your learners.

- Example: If your learners are high school students, the depth and complexity of questions they pose to ChatGPT might differ from those of college students.

3. Choose a Suitable Interface:

- Decide whether you want to use a raw interface like the OpenAI Playground, or if you want to integrate ChatGPT into a Learning Management System (LMS) using the API.

- Example: For younger students, you might want an interface with additional safety and filtering features.

4. Develop Guided Activities:

- Design structured activities or questions that students can pose to ChatGPT.

- Example: "Ask ChatGPT to explain the differences between the North and South leading up to the American Civil War."

5. Encourage Open Exploration:

- Allow time for students to ask ChatGPT their own questions related to the topic.

- Example: After a session on the Civil War, students might be curious about specific battles, leaders, or the daily life of soldiers.

6. Incorporate Group Activities:

- Students can work in groups to draft questions, research, or challenge ChatGPT for more comprehensive answers.

- Example: A group project could involve creating a timeline of major events, with each student using ChatGPT to research specific events.

7. Facilitate Critical Thinking:

- Teach students to critically analyze the answers they receive, cross-reference with other sources, and challenge any inconsistencies.

- Example: "Compare ChatGPT's response about the causes of the Civil War with our textbook. Discuss any discrepancies in your groups."

8. Provide Feedback Loops:

- Allow students to share their interactions and findings with the class and discuss their experiences.

- Example: "Share an interesting fact or insight you learned from ChatGPT today."

9. Promote Ethical Use:

- Ensure students understand the importance of ethical interactions, even with AI, and the dangers of disinformation.

- Example: "While ChatGPT is a tool, it's essential to treat it respectfully and understand that it doesn't have emotions or consciousness. Always cross-reference information."

10. Continuous Assessment:

- Periodically assess students' understanding and adjust the learning approach accordingly.

- Example: After a few sessions, provide a quiz or project to gauge how effectively students are integrating information from ChatGPT into their broader understanding.

11. Iterate & Improve:

- Based on feedback and results, make necessary changes to your strategy for using ChatGPT.

- Example: If students are finding the open exploration phase overwhelming, offer more structured guidance or examples to help them get started.

12. Stay Updated:

- As ChatGPT and similar technologies evolve, be prepared to update your strategies and approach.

- Example: Attend webinars or training sessions on AI in education to keep up-to-date.

ChatGPT Prompts and Modules for Teachers:

The following section I will expand the prompts and modules needed to establish each of the previous points in details using ChatGPT.

Defining Learning Objectives Using ChatGPT:

1. Understand the Basics:

Before you dive into complex prompts, introduce students or educators to the idea of well-defined objectives.

- **Prompt**: "ChatGPT, explain the importance of clear learning objectives in an educational setting."

- **Expected Outcome**: An overview of the purpose and benefits of having well-defined learning objectives.

2. Examples and Analysis:

Use ChatGPT to provide examples of objectives and then critically analyze them.

- **Prompt**: "Provide an example of a learning objective for a biology class on cellular structures."

- **Expected Outcome**: "By the end of this module, students will be able to identify and describe the functions of key cellular structures, including the nucleus, mitochondria, and endoplasmic reticulum."

- **Follow-up Prompt**: "Critique the provided learning objective. What are its strengths and weaknesses?"

- **Expected Outcome**: A discussion on how the objective is specific and linked to tangible outcomes, but might be broad for a single lesson.

3. **Objective Development Workshop**:

Encourage the creation of objectives through guided questions.

- **Prompt**: "Guide me step by step in creating a learning objective for a literature class studying Shakespeare's 'Romeo and Juliet'."

- **Expected Outcome**: A guided workshop-style response that takes the user through understanding the play's themes, identifying desired student outcomes, and then framing those in the form of an objective.

4. **Comparison with Curriculum Standards**:

Ensure that the developed objectives align with wider curriculum standards.

- **Prompt**: "Compare the objective 'Students will understand the significance of soliloquies in 'Romeo and Juliet'' with common high school literature standards."

- **Expected Outcome**: An analysis showing how the objective meets certain standards but may lack in other areas like critical analysis or comparison with other works.

5. **Real-world Application**:

Understanding how objectives tie into real-world skills or applications can deepen their significance.

- **Prompt**: "How can the learning objective 'Students will analyze the economic principles in 'The Wealth of Nations'' be relevant in today's global economy?"

- **Expected Outcome**: Insights into how understanding classic economic theories can provide context for current economic practices and systems.

6. **Feedback and Iteration**:

Use ChatGPT as a tool to refine objectives based on feedback.

- **Prompt**: "I've drafted the objective 'Students will know about the Civil War.' How can I make this more actionable and specific?"

- **Expected Outcome**: Suggestions to modify the objective to something like "Students will analyze the key causes of the Civil War and evaluate its long-term impact on American society."

7. **Bloom's Taxonomy Integration**:

Incorporate higher-order thinking skills by framing objectives around Bloom's taxonomy.

- **Prompt**: "Help me draft a learning objective for a physics class on Newton's Laws at the 'Application' level of Bloom's Taxonomy."

- **Expected Outcome**: "By the end of the lesson, students will be able to apply Newton's three laws to real-world scenarios, such as explaining the forces at play when a car comes to a sudden stop."

Through these complex modules and prompts, educators can interactively work with ChatGPT to draft, refine, and contextualize their learning objectives, ensuring they are clear, actionable, and tied to both curriculum standards and real-world relevance.

Knowing Your Audience Using ChatGPT:

1. **Basics of Audience Analysis**:

Before diving deep, get a primer on the concept of audience analysis.

- **Prompt**: "ChatGPT, why is audience analysis important in educational settings?"

- **Expected Outcome**: A thorough response on the significance of tailoring educational content according to the learners' needs, preferences, and backgrounds.

2. **Audience Profile Creation**:

Use ChatGPT to craft hypothetical audience profiles or understand real ones.

- **Prompt**: "Provide a detailed profile of a typical middle school student learning mathematics in an urban school setting."

- **Expected Outcome**: A profile detailing age range, possible prior knowledge, cultural factors, potential challenges, and more.

3. **Audience Adaptation Techniques**:

Ask ChatGPT for strategies to adapt material based on specific audience characteristics.

- **Prompt**: "How can I modify a lesson on the solar system for students who have visual impairments?"

- **Expected Outcome**: Suggestions on using tactile learning materials, audio descriptions, Braille resources, etc.

4. **Feedback Mechanism**:

Knowing your audience is an ongoing process. Understand how to gather and interpret feedback.

- **Prompt**: "What are effective strategies to collect feedback from high school students after a lesson on World War II?"

- **Expected Outcome**: Strategies such as anonymous surveys, open discussions, or reflection essays might be recommended.

5. **Cultural and Socio-Economic Sensitivities**:

Understanding cultural backgrounds and socio-economic differences is essential. ChatGPT can provide context.

- **Prompt**: "I'm teaching literature to a diverse class with students from multiple countries. How can I ensure cultural sensitivity when discussing Western classics?"

- **Expected Outcome**: Suggestions might include incorporating non-Western literature, creating safe discussion environments, and encouraging students to draw parallels with their own cultures.

6. **Learning Preferences and Styles**:

ChatGPT can offer insights into different learning styles and how to cater to them.

- **Prompt**: "Describe the characteristics of auditory learners and suggest techniques to engage them in an online class."

- **Expected Outcome**: A description of auditory learners followed by techniques like using podcasts, discussions, or mnemonic devices.

7. **Technology Familiarity**:

In a digital age, understanding the tech-savviness of your audience is key.

- **Prompt**: "I'm conducting an online coding workshop for senior citizens. What challenges might they face and how can I overcome them?"

- **Expected Outcome**: Insights into potential challenges like unfamiliarity with modern interfaces, slower typing speed, and strategies like hands-on assistance, patience, or simplified platforms.

8. **Assessment and Iteration**:

To truly know your audience, assess their grasp on material and iterate your approach.

- **Prompt**: "Suggest ways to assess the comprehension levels of a college audience after a lecture on quantum physics."

- **Expected Outcome**: Methods like quizzes, debates, or conceptual application projects might be recommended.

Through these modules and prompts, educators can engage with ChatGPT to deeply understand their audience. This comprehensive audience knowledge ensures the material is accessible, engaging, and effective for the learners.

Choosing a Suitable Interface Using ChatGPT:

1. **Introduction to Interface Options**:

Start with a foundational understanding of potential platforms and their significance.

- **Prompt**: "ChatGPT, outline the different interfaces one might use to integrate a chatbot into an educational setting."

- **Expected Outcome**: A broad overview of interfaces ranging from direct platforms like OpenAI Playground to Learning Management Systems (LMS) or custom web integrations.

2. **Platform Comparisons**:

Get a detailed comparison between popular platforms based on specific criteria.

- **Prompt**: "Compare the OpenAI Playground with integrating ChatGPT via API into Moodle in terms of flexibility and ease of use."

- **Expected Outcome**: A comparison highlighting the direct usage of Playground versus the customizability and potential complexities of using an API with Moodle.

3. **Interface Customization**:

Understand how different interfaces can be modified for specific educational needs.

- **Prompt**: "How can I customize a ChatGPT interface on a personal website to make it more engaging for primary school children?"

- **Expected Outcome**: Suggestions like adding colorful design elements, larger font sizes, or integrating multimedia elements for enhanced interaction.

4. **Safety and Security**:

Given that the audience might be younger or the content sensitive, understanding safety features is essential.

- **Prompt**: "What safety features should I consider when embedding ChatGPT in an e-learning platform for middle schoolers?"

- **Expected Outcome**: Recommendations such as profanity filters, content monitoring, restricted access, or parental controls.

5. **Accessibility Features**:

Ensure that all students, including those with disabilities, can access and use the interface.

- **Prompt**: "Provide guidelines to make a ChatGPT interface accessible for students with motor disabilities."

- **Expected Outcome**: Ideas like voice command integrations, compatibility with screen readers, or keyboard-only navigation.

6. **Optimizing Engagement**:

Ask for strategies to make the interface more engaging, ensuring sustained student interaction.

- **Prompt**: "Suggest ways to enhance student engagement when using ChatGPT in a virtual classroom setting."

- **Expected Outcome**: Proposals like gamifying interactions, integrating visual aids or multimedia, or using real-world problem-solving prompts.

7. **Integration with Other Tools**:

Understand how ChatGPT can be integrated with other educational tools and platforms.

- **Prompt**: "How can I seamlessly integrate ChatGPT into a platform like Blackboard or Google Classroom?"

- **Expected Outcome**: A step-by-step guide or suggestions on using the API, considering platform-specific features, or potentially leveraging third-party plugins.

8. **Feedback Collection**:

To continually improve the interface, gather feedback directly through it.

- **Prompt**: "Propose a method to collect user feedback on the ChatGPT interface within an LMS for college students."

- **Expected Outcome**: Strategies such as embedding feedback forms, encouraging forum discussions, or integrating real-time reaction features.

9. **Ongoing Iterations**:

As with any tool, ongoing improvements are key.

- **Prompt**: "After collecting feedback on a ChatGPT interface in a high school e-learning platform, what steps should be taken to implement changes?"

- **Expected Outcome**: Steps like analyzing common feedback trends, prioritizing changes based on educational impact, testing modifications, and rolling them out systematically.

By working through these detailed prompts and modules, educators and institutions can make informed decisions about the best interface to employ, ensuring ChatGPT serves as a beneficial tool in their specific educational context.

Developing Guided Activities Using ChatGPT:

1. **Introduction to Guided Activities**:

Begin with an understanding of the essence and importance of guided activities.

- **Prompt**: "ChatGPT, explain the significance of guided activities in the context of AI-driven learning."

- **Expected Outcome**: A response detailing how guided activities provide direction, structure, and clarity, helping to optimize learning experiences with AI tools.

2. **Activity Brainstorming**:

Use ChatGPT for brainstorming activity ideas based on specific subjects or themes.

- **Prompt**: "Provide five guided activity ideas for teaching the water cycle using ChatGPT to middle school students."

- **Expected Outcome**: A list of activities like interactive Q&A sessions, storytelling tasks where ChatGPT fills in details, or visual representation explanations.

3. **Refinement of Ideas**:

Refine and expand upon initial ideas with ChatGPT's input.

- **Prompt**: "I have an idea for a guided activity where students interview ChatGPT as if it were a historical figure. How can I enhance this activity for a lesson on Ancient Rome?"

- **Expected Outcome**: Suggestions like assigning specific roles (e.g., Julius Caesar, Cleopatra), providing students with context beforehand, or incorporating multimedia resources.

4. **Tailored Activities for Different Learning Styles**:

Ensure inclusivity by crafting activities suited to various learning preferences.

- **Prompt**: "Design a ChatGPT guided activity on the topic of photosynthesis for visual learners."

- **Expected Outcome**: Activities might involve asking ChatGPT to describe diagrams, creating mind maps, or visual storyboards based on ChatGPT's explanations.

5. **Integrating Real-world Contexts**:

Anchor abstract concepts in real-world scenarios for better understanding.

- **Prompt**: "Develop an activity using ChatGPT that explains the concept of compound interest in the context of saving money for college."

- **Expected Outcome**: An activity where students interact with ChatGPT to simulate different saving scenarios, analyzing how compound interest affects their savings over time.

6. **Collaborative Activities**:

Foster collaboration by designing group activities centered around ChatGPT.

- **Prompt**: "Propose a team-based activity where students use ChatGPT to explore the cultural implications of the Renaissance."

- **Expected Outcome**: A suggestion such as group projects where each team deep-dives into a particular aspect (e.g., art, science, philosophy) using ChatGPT, followed by a collaborative presentation.

7. **Feedback and Iteration**:

Iterate on activities based on student feedback and performance.

- **Prompt**: "After conducting a guided activity on the French Revolution using ChatGPT, many students felt overwhelmed. How can I simplify the activity for better comprehension?"

- **Expected Outcome**: Recommendations on breaking down the activity into smaller tasks, providing clearer guidelines, or focusing on fewer, more critical events.

8. **Interdisciplinary Activities**:

Craft activities that span multiple subjects, enhancing holistic learning.

- **Prompt**: "Design a guided activity using ChatGPT that intersects both geometry and art for high school students."

- **Expected Outcome**: An activity like exploring the geometrical principles in famous artworks or creating art based on specific geometric shapes and patterns with ChatGPT's guidance.

9. **Assessment Activities**:

Use ChatGPT not just for teaching, but also for assessment.

- **Prompt**: "How can I create a guided activity with ChatGPT to assess students' understanding of the human digestive system?"

- **Expected Outcome**: Ideas like a Q&A quiz, asking students to explain concepts back to ChatGPT and evaluating the accuracy, or simulating real-life scenarios involving digestion.

By systematically developing and refining guided activities with ChatGPT, educators can provide engaging, structured, and effective learning experiences. This ensures that learners benefit optimally from the integration of AI into their educational journey.

Encouraging Open Exploration Using ChatGPT:

1. **Introduction to Open Exploration**:

Begin by understanding the importance of open exploration in the educational context.

- **Prompt**: "ChatGPT, why is open exploration significant in a learning environment, especially when using AI-driven tools?"

- **Expected Outcome**: An explanation highlighting the value of autonomy, critical thinking, discovery-based learning, and the advantages of using AI to facilitate diverse inquiries.

2. **Scaffolded Exploration**:

Gradually lead students into open-ended tasks, providing some structure initially.

- **Prompt**: "Provide a semi-structured exploration activity on Renaissance art for high school students using ChatGPT."

- **Expected Outcome**: An activity such as "Begin by asking ChatGPT about three major artists of the Renaissance. Then, choose one artwork from each artist, inquire about its significance, and explore related themes or techniques."

3. **Brainstorming Sessions**:

Leverage ChatGPT to brainstorm questions or topics to explore.

- **Prompt**: "Help students brainstorm questions about space exploration they might want to explore further with ChatGPT."

- **Expected Outcome**: A list of intriguing questions like "How do black holes form?", "What are the challenges of Mars colonization?", or "Describe the lifecycle of a star."

4. **Diverse Exploration Avenues**:

Guide students to explore topics from various angles or disciplines.

- **Prompt**: "Suggest different interdisciplinary angles to explore the topic of 'Rainforests' using ChatGPT."

- **Expected Outcome**: Suggestions such as exploring rainforests through the lens of biology (flora and fauna), geography (distribution and features), anthropology (tribal cultures), or even economics (value and threats).

5. **Reflective Practices**:

After exploration, engage students in reflection to deepen their understanding.

- **Prompt**: "Propose a reflection activity for students after they explore the concept of 'Artificial Intelligence' with ChatGPT."

- **Expected Outcome**: Activities like journaling their newfound insights, discussing potential ethical concerns, or predicting future AI advancements.

6. **Challenge Assumptions**:

Encourage students to critically assess the information they receive.

- **Prompt**: "Design an activity where students critically evaluate ChatGPT's response on a controversial topic."

- **Expected Outcome**: An activity such as "Ask ChatGPT about the effects of global warming. Compare its response with peer-reviewed sources, noting any discrepancies or biases."

7. **Group-based Exploration**:

Encourage collective exploration where students collaborate.

- **Prompt**: "Sketch a group-based open exploration activity using ChatGPT centered around 'World Cultures'."

- **Expected Outcome**: A suggestion like dividing students into groups, each exploring a different culture, sharing interesting customs, practices, or histories, and then collaboratively creating a global culture mosaic.

8. **Documenting the Journey**:

Promote the documentation of their exploration, allowing for deeper reflection and sharing.

- **Prompt**: "How can students document their exploration journey of 'Ancient Civilizations' with ChatGPT?"

- **Expected Outcome**: Recommendations such as creating a digital portfolio, blogging their findings, or designing infographics based on their exploration.

9. **Feedback and Iteration**:

Seek feedback on the open exploration process to improve it continuously.

- **Prompt**: "After a session of open exploration with ChatGPT, how should educators gather feedback from college students to enhance the process?"

- **Expected Outcome**: Strategies like feedback forms, group discussions, or even having students suggest potential exploration topics for the future.

Promoting open exploration allows students to personalize their learning journey. By leveraging ChatGPT, educators can provide a vast, information-rich platform where students dive deep into topics of interest, honing their research, critical thinking, and independent learning skills.

Incorporating Group Activities Using ChatGPT:

1. **Understanding Group Dynamics**:

Begin by understanding the fundamentals of group work and its benefits.

- **Prompt**: "ChatGPT, explain the advantages of group activities in a learning environment and the dynamics that come into play."

- **Expected Outcome**: A detailed response highlighting the merits of collaboration, diverse viewpoints, shared responsibilities, and the dynamics of group roles, conflicts, and resolutions.

2. **Group Role Assignments**:

Use ChatGPT to suggest and describe roles within group activities.

- **Prompt**: "List potential roles students can take on in a group research project using ChatGPT."

- **Expected Outcome**: Roles such as Researcher, Recorder, Presenter, Time-keeper, and ChatGPT Navigator.

3. **Collaborative Exploration**:

Design activities where groups use ChatGPT to explore topics together.

- **Prompt**: "Create a collaborative exploration activity on the topic of 'sustainable energy sources' using ChatGPT for groups of five."

- **Expected Outcome**: A structured activity where each group member explores a specific energy source, shares findings, and collaborates to create a combined report or presentation.

4. **Group Challenges and Scenarios**:

Craft scenarios or problems for groups to solve using ChatGPT.

- **Prompt**: "Design a scenario-based activity where student groups use ChatGPT to address a community issue like water scarcity."

- **Expected Outcome**: An activity where groups brainstorm solutions, use ChatGPT for research and validation, and present actionable ideas.

5. **Debate and Discussion**:

Encourage groups to engage in debates using information sourced from ChatGPT.

- **Prompt**: "Propose a group debate activity about 'Genetically Modified Organisms (GMOs)' where ChatGPT is used for research."

- **Expected Outcome**: An activity structure where teams take pro and con positions, research their stance with ChatGPT, and engage in a structured debate.

6. **Peer Teaching**:

Leverage the "teach to learn" principle with group activities.

- **Prompt**: "Sketch an activity where student groups use ChatGPT to research and teach peers about various 'World Religions'."

- **Expected Outcome**: Guidelines for groups to research specific religions, develop lesson plans, and conduct mini-teaching sessions.

7. **Creative Collaborations**:

Promote creativity through group activities with ChatGPT.

- **Prompt**: "Design a group activity where students collaborate to write a short story set in the Medieval Ages using ChatGPT for historical accuracy."

- **Expected Outcome**: A structured activity guiding groups through brainstorming, using ChatGPT for historical details, and collaboratively crafting the story.

8. **Feedback and Reflection**.

Post-activity, have groups reflect on their collaboration and the role of ChatGPT.

- **Prompt**: "How can student groups reflect and provide feedback on their experience of using ChatGPT in a group project about 'Climate Change'?"

- **Expected Outcome**: Methods such as SWOT analysis, group discussions, feedback forms on ChatGPT's effectiveness, or reflective journals.

9. **Continual Improvement**:

Iterate on group activities based on experiences and outcomes.

- **Prompt**: "After conducting a group activity on 'Robotics Evolution' using ChatGPT, how should an educator refine the activity for future classes?"

- **Expected Outcome**: Steps like analyzing group outcomes, considering student feedback, addressing observed challenges, and tweaking activity guidelines.

By integrating group activities with ChatGPT, educators can combine the power of collaborative learning with AI-driven insights. This approach not only enhances knowledge acquisition but also fosters essential soft skills like teamwork, communication, and critical thinking.

Facilitating Critical Thinking Using ChatGPT:

1. **Introduction to Critical Thinking**:

Begin with a foundational understanding.

- **Prompt**: "ChatGPT, define critical thinking and explain its significance in today's educational landscape."

- **Expected Outcome**: A comprehensive explanation of critical thinking, its components, and its role in discerning information, especially in the age of information overflow.

2. **Questioning Information**:

Train students to question the information they receive.

- **Prompt**: "Provide an activity where students evaluate the credibility of a statement made by ChatGPT about the 'First Moon Landing'."

- **Expected Outcome**: A proposed activity involving students cross-referencing ChatGPT's information with multiple sources and assessing its accuracy.

3. **Scenario Analysis**:

Design hypothetical scenarios to challenge students' thinking.

- **Prompt**: "Craft a scenario related to 'Bioethics in Genetic Engineering' for students to dissect using critical thinking with ChatGPT's assistance."

- **Expected Outcome**: A scenario such as a hypothetical genetic modification and its societal implications, prompting students to explore ethical considerations, benefits, and potential drawbacks using ChatGPT.

4. **Debate and Contrasting Views**:

Present contrasting viewpoints to foster nuanced thinking.

- **Prompt**: "Design an activity where students debate the pros and cons of 'Artificial Intelligence in Healthcare' using information sourced from ChatGPT."

- **Expected Outcome**: Guidelines for researching arguments, preparing debate points, and critically evaluating each side's merits and concerns.

5. **Analyzing Assumptions and Biases**:

Encourage students to recognize underlying assumptions or biases in responses.

- **Prompt**: "Propose an activity where students identify potential biases in ChatGPT's explanation of 'The Industrial Revolution'."

- **Expected Outcome**: An activity structure prompting students to analyze ChatGPT's response, identify potential Western-centric or technology-focused biases, and compare with diverse sources.

6. **Solving Real-world Problems**:

Leverage ChatGPT for problem-solving exercises that require critical evaluation.

- **Prompt**: "Develop a group activity where students use ChatGPT to find solutions to 'Urban Overpopulation' and critically assess the feasibility of each solution."

- **Expected Outcome**: A multi-step activity where groups brainstorm solutions, research with ChatGPT, and critically evaluate each idea's viability, scalability, and potential impact.

7. **Reflective Practices**:

Promote self-reflection on critical thinking processes.

- **Prompt**: "How can students reflect on their critical thinking journey after exploring 'Modern Art Movements' with ChatGPT?"

- **Expected Outcome**: Methods such as reflective essays, group discussions, or self-assessment checklists on their analytical approach and insights.

8. **Limitations and Strengths**:

Understand ChatGPT's limitations to foster a more critical approach to its responses.

- **Prompt**: "List the potential limitations of ChatGPT when used as a primary research tool and how students can navigate them."

- **Expected Outcome**: Insights on limitations like lack of subjective analysis, potential for outdated information, or lack of nuance, coupled with recommendations for cross-referencing or seeking expert opinions.

9. **Continuous Feedback and Iteration**:

Encourage feedback to refine the critical thinking facilitation process.

- **Prompt**: "After conducting critical thinking exercises on 'Climate Change' using ChatGPT, how should feedback be collected and integrated for future lessons?"

- **Expected Outcome**: Suggestions like structured feedback forms focusing on ChatGPT's effectiveness, group retrospectives, or iterative changes based on observed challenges.

By systematically integrating ChatGPT into the critical thinking process, educators can provide students with a dynamic tool to challenge, validate, and deepen their analytical skills. This approach nurtures students who are better equipped to navigate the complex, information-rich world of the 21st century.

Providing Feedback Loops Using ChatGPT:

1. **Understanding Feedback Loops**:

Initiate with the fundamental importance and methodology behind feedback loops.

- **Prompt**: "ChatGPT, explain the concept and significance of feedback loops in the educational process."

- **Expected Outcome**: A detailed explanation of feedback loops, their iterative nature, and the role they play in improving learning outcomes and teaching methodologies.

2. **Direct Feedback Collection**:

Use ChatGPT to gather direct feedback from students post-lesson or activity.

- **Prompt**: "Design a set of questions that educators can pose to students after a lesson on 'Ecosystems' to gather feedback using ChatGPT."

- **Expected Outcome**: Questions like "What did you find most engaging about today's lesson?", "Which concepts remain unclear?", or "How do you feel about the pace of the lesson?"

3. **Feedback Analysis**:

Analyze the collected feedback to derive actionable insights.

- **Prompt**: "Given feedback from students that a lesson on 'Quantum Physics' was too fast-paced, how should the lesson be modified for future classes?"

- **Expected Outcome**: Recommendations such as breaking down complex topics further, incorporating more interactive elements, or setting prerequisite lessons to ensure foundational understanding.

4. **Feedback on ChatGPT Interactions**:

Understand students' experiences and feedback specific to ChatGPT interactions.

- **Prompt**: "Suggest a method to collect feedback from students about their interactions and learning experience with ChatGPT during a 'Renaissance Art' module."

- **Expected Outcome**: Methods such as anonymous online surveys, focus group discussions, or reflective journal entries focusing on the effectiveness, clarity, and engagement of ChatGPT.

5. **Iterative Feedback**:

Promote a continuous feedback mechanism throughout a course or module.

- **Prompt**: "Design a feedback loop mechanism for a semester-long course on 'Modern Literature' where ChatGPT is used for supplementary learning."

- **Expected Outcome**: A structured feedback system involving periodic check-ins, mid-semester feedback collection through ChatGPT, and end-of-semester reviews to iteratively improve the course.

6. **Feedback-driven Customization**:

Customize ChatGPT interactions based on regular feedback.

- **Prompt**: "If students feel that ChatGPT's explanations on 'Organic Chemistry' are too technical, how can educators guide them to interact with ChatGPT for simpler explanations?"

- **Expected Outcome**: Suggestions such as prompting students to ask ChatGPT for "layman's terms" explanations, breaking questions down, or seeking analogies and examples.

7. **Feedback on Group Activities**:

Gather feedback on collaborative and group-based activities involving ChatGPT.

- **Prompt**: "Propose a method to collect and analyze feedback after a group activity where students used ChatGPT to explore 'Ancient Civilizations'."

- **Expected Outcome**: Techniques like group feedback sessions, leader-facilitated reflections, or collaborative digital boards where students pin their feedback.

8. **Feedback for Future Integration**:

Collect suggestions for future integrations and applications of ChatGPT.

- **Prompt**: "How can educators gather student suggestions on potential topics or modules where ChatGPT integration might be beneficial?"

- **Expected Outcome**: Methods like open forums, suggestion boxes, or brainstorming sessions where students discuss and vote on potential ChatGPT applications.

9. **Review and Recap Sessions**:

Use feedback to create review sessions that address common areas of difficulty or interest.

- **Prompt**: "Based on feedback indicating confusion about 'Genetic Engineering', how can ChatGPT assist in a recap or review session?"

- **Expected Outcome**: Ideas like a Q&A session, breaking down the topic into subtopics, or interactive discussions facilitated by ChatGPT.

By integrating these feedback loop modules with ChatGPT, educators can ensure that the AI-enhanced learning experience is always evolving and improving. This iterative approach, driven by feedback, ensures that students' needs are consistently met, optimizing their learning experience.

Promoting Ethical Use with ChatGPT:

1. **Foundations of Ethical Use**:

Start by understanding the ethical implications and considerations of AI.

- **Prompt**: "ChatGPT, provide an overview of the ethical considerations when using AI tools in educational settings "

- **Expected Outcome**: A comprehensive explanation highlighting data privacy, potential biases, misuse of information, dependence on AI, and the importance of human discernment.

2. **Bias and Objectivity**:

Highlight the potential for AI to have biases based on training data.

- **Prompt**: "Provide an example of how AI, including tools like ChatGPT, might inadvertently display bias."

- **Expected Outcome**: An illustrative example, possibly highlighting how AI models can perpetuate stereotypes or misconceptions if trained on biased datasets.

3. **Ethical Exploration Activities**:

Use ChatGPT to simulate ethical dilemmas for students to dissect.

- **Prompt**: "Design a scenario-based activity exploring the ethical implications of AI in medical decisions."

- **Expected Outcome**: A hypothetical scenario, such as an AI recommending medical treatments, prompting students to consider ethical implications like trust, accountability, and potential biases.

4. **Privacy and Data Security**:

Emphasize the importance of protecting personal data and understanding AI's data usage.

- **Prompt**: "Outline best practices for students when sharing or seeking information using ChatGPT to ensure data privacy."

- **Expected Outcome**: Guidelines like avoiding sharing personal details, being cautious of potential phishing, and understanding the data handling practices of AI platforms.

5. **Healthy Dependence**:

Discuss the balance between leveraging AI for insights and not becoming overly reliant.

- **Prompt**: "Discuss the potential pitfalls of over-relying on AI tools like ChatGPT for academic research or learning."

- **Expected Outcome**: A discussion on issues such as lack of deep understanding, potential for misinformation, reduced critical thinking, or diminished interpersonal skills.

6. **Collaborative Ethical Discussions**:

Engage students in group discussions about ethical AI use.

- **Prompt**: "Craft a group discussion activity centered around the ethical implications of AI-driven surveillance in public spaces."

- **Expected Outcome**: An activity structure where students research, debate, and present on topics like privacy concerns, security benefits, societal implications, and trust in AI decision-making.

7. **Ethical Creation and Development**:

Introduce the ethics of AI creation, not just consumption.

- **Prompt**: "Describe the ethical considerations for developers when creating AI models for educational purposes."

- **Expected Outcome**: Insights on ensuring unbiased training data, transparency in AI decisions, respecting user privacy, and the potential impact on learning dynamics.

8. **Feedback on Ethical Experiences**:

Encourage feedback on any ethical concerns or observations students have while using

ChatGPT.

- **Prompt**: "Suggest a mechanism for students to report and discuss observed biases or ethical concerns when interacting with ChatGPT."

- **Expected Outcome**: Recommendations like an anonymous feedback system, regular ethical review sessions, or dedicated forums to discuss AI ethics.

9. **Ethical Guidelines and Best Practices**:

Establish and regularly update ethical usage guidelines for students.

- **Prompt**: "Help create a set of ethical guidelines for students using ChatGPT in a university research setting."

- **Expected Outcome**: Guidelines emphasizing data privacy, critical evaluation of AI generated information, citing AI tools appropriately in research, and promoting inclusive and unbiased interactions.

Promoting ethical use is not just about following rules but fostering an understanding of the broader implications of AI in society. By integrating these modules with ChatGPT, educators can ensure that students are not only savvy AI users but also ethically conscious digital citizens.

Continuous Assessment Using ChatGPT:

1. **Introduction to Continuous Assessment**:

Start by explaining the concept and importance of continuous assessment in the learning

process.

- **Prompt**: "ChatGPT, elaborate on the significance of continuous assessment in education and how it differs from traditional testing."

- **Expected Outcome**: A detailed explanation highlighting the benefits of ongoing evaluation, formative assessment, and personalized feedback.

2. **Assessment Criteria Definition**:

Use ChatGPT to define the criteria for specific assessments.

- **Prompt**: "Provide criteria for assessing a student's research paper on 'Climate Change' in a high school science class."

- **Expected Outcome**: A list of criteria such as research depth, citations, organization, and clarity.

3. **Constructive Feedback**:

Showcase how ChatGPT can provide constructive feedback on assignments.

- **Prompt**: "Give an example of how ChatGPT can provide constructive feedback on a student's essay about 'Shakespearean Sonnets.'"

- **Expected Outcome**: A simulated response offering feedback on aspects like thesis clarity, use of literary devices, or suggestions for improvement.

4. **Rubric Development**:

Design rubrics for various types of assessments.

- **Prompt**: "Create a rubric for assessing oral presentations in a college-level 'Business Communication' course using ChatGPT."

- **Expected Outcome**: A rubric with categories like content, delivery, organization, and audience engagement, along with scoring criteria.

5. **Customized Quiz Generator**:

Leverage ChatGPT to generate customized quizzes based on the learning objectives.

- **Prompt**: "Generate a set of quiz questions for a middle school history lesson on 'The American Civil War'."

- **Expected Outcome**: A set of questions covering key topics, events, and figures related to the American Civil War.

6. **Essay Topic Suggestions**:

Use ChatGPT to provide students with essay topic ideas for research assignments.

- **Prompt**: "Suggest three research topics related to 'Artificial Intelligence in Healthcare' for college-level students."

- **Expected Outcome**: A list of thought-provoking research topics along with brief descriptions.

7. **Peer Assessment Guidance**:

Provide instructions for peer assessment activities.

- **Prompt**: "Design guidelines for students conducting peer assessments of each other's 'Creative Writing' assignments using ChatGPT."

- **Expected Outcome**: A step-by-step guide outlining how to assess peers' writing, what to focus on, and how to offer constructive feedback.

8. **Timely Progress Checks**:

Show how ChatGPT can facilitate regular progress checks.

- **Prompt**: "Suggest methods for educators to use ChatGPT to conduct weekly progress checks in an online 'Programming' course."

- **Expected Outcome**: Ideas like weekly quizzes, coding challenges, or self-assessment exercises.

9. **Feedback Analysis Tools**:

Highlight tools and techniques for educators to analyze and use feedback effectively.

- **Prompt**: "Explain how educators can use ChatGPT to analyze and extract actionable insights from students' feedback on a 'Psychology' project."

- **Expected Outcome**: Recommendations such as sentiment analysis, thematic categorization of feedback, and identifying common misconceptions.

10. **Individual Learning Plans**:

Demonstrate how ChatGPT can help create personalized learning plans based on assessment

results.

- **Prompt**: "Design a learning plan for a student struggling with 'Statistics' after a ChatGPT assessment."

- **Expected Outcome**: A personalized plan that includes targeted resources, practice exercises, and recommended study techniques.

By implementing these ChatGPT modules for continuous assessment, educators can not only gauge students' progress but also provide personalized guidance and support, ensuring that each student has the opportunity to thrive in their learning journey.

Iterate & Improve Using ChatGPT:

1. **Understanding Iteration**:

Begin by grasping the essence and importance of iterative processes.

- **Prompt**: "ChatGPT, explain the principle of iterative improvement in the context of educational methodologies."

- **Expected Outcome**: A comprehensive understanding of the iterative process, emphasizing the continuous loop of implementation, feedback, analysis, and modification to enhance learning experiences.

2. **Feedback Collection**:

Use ChatGPT to help gather feedback after a module or lesson.

- **Prompt**: "Design a feedback questionnaire for students after completing a unit on 'Renaissance Literature'."

- **Expected Outcome**: A set of questions focusing on understanding, engagement, pace, resources used (including ChatGPT), and areas of improvement.

3. **Feedback Analysis**:

Analyze feedback to extract actionable insights.

- **Prompt**: "Given student feedback indicating difficulty in grasping poetic techniques in 'Shakespeare's Sonnets', how can the teaching approach be modified?"

- **Expected Outcome**: Recommendations like using modern parallels, interactive analysis sessions with ChatGPT, multimedia resources, or group discussions to break down complex techniques.

4. **Modifying Instructional Design**:

Rework lesson plans or modules based on feedback.

- **Prompt**: "Redesign a lesson plan on 'Quantum Mechanics' for high school students using ChatGPT, considering previous feedback about the content being too abstract."

- **Expected Outcome**: A revised plan incorporating more real-world applications, interactive Q&A with ChatGPT, analogies, and visual aids.

5. **Iterative Testing**:

Implement changes and test their efficacy.

- **Prompt**: "After revising a lesson on 'The French Revolution', suggest a method to gauge its effectiveness compared to the previous version using ChatGPT."

- **Expected Outcome**: Suggestions like a comparative pre-and-post test, student polls, or reflective assignments to evaluate understanding.

6. **Tailoring ChatGPT Interactions**:

Refine the way students interact with ChatGPT based on past experiences.

- **Prompt**: "Considering feedback that ChatGPT's answers were too lengthy in a 'History of Art' module, how can students be guided to get more concise responses?"

- **Expected Outcome**: Guidance like framing more specific questions, requesting summaries, or breaking queries into smaller parts.

7. **Continuous Professional Development**:

Educators can leverage ChatGPT for their own professional growth.

- **Prompt**: "Outline a plan for educators to use ChatGPT for continuous professional development in 'Digital Pedagogies'."

- **Expected Outcome**: A plan encompassing regular readings, ChatGPT-assisted research, online course suggestions, or peer collaboration techniques.

8. **Customized Learning Paths**:

Iteratively develop personalized learning paths for students.

- **Prompt**: "Based on a student's performance and feedback in a 'Calculus' course, suggest an iterative learning path using ChatGPT for further improvement."

- **Expected Outcome**: A customized plan with targeted practice problems, explanatory sessions, and periodic checks with ChatGPT.

9. **Updating Resources**:

Continuously update and refine educational resources.

- **Prompt**: "Given advancements in 'Neuroscience' over the past year, how can ChatGPT assist in updating a university curriculum to reflect these changes?"

- **Expected Outcome**: Recommendations for new topics, research areas, experts to consult, and methods to integrate updated content.

By integrating these modules, educators can develop a fluid and responsive teaching approach. Leveraging ChatGPT in the iterative improvement process ensures that educational experiences are always in tune with student needs, current knowledge, and best pedagogical practices.

Stay Updated Using ChatGPT:

1. **Understanding the Need to Update**:

Begin by understanding the essence and significance of staying updated.

- **Prompt**: "ChatGPT, explain the importance of staying updated in today's educational context."

- **Expected Outcome**: A detailed discussion highlighting the rapid pace of information change, the relevance of current events to curricula, and the need for educators to be aware of recent advancements in their fields.

2. **Current Events Discussions**:

Use ChatGPT to fetch and discuss recent events related to specific subjects.

- **Prompt**: "Provide a summary of the latest developments in 'Renewable Energy Technologies' over the past year."

- **Expected Outcome**: A concise overview of recent advancements, discoveries, or policies related to renewable energy.

3. **Trend Analysis**:

Leverage ChatGPT to analyze emerging trends in various fields.

- **Prompt**: "Highlight the current trends in 'Educational Technology' and their implications for classroom teaching."

- **Expected Outcome**: A list of trending technologies like AR/VR in education, adaptive learning platforms, and their potential benefits and challenges.

4. **Updating Curriculum**:

Continuously refine syllabi to integrate new knowledge and approaches.

- **Prompt**: "Given the rapid advancements in 'Genomic Editing', how can a biology curriculum be updated to include these changes?"

- **Expected Outcome**: Suggestions on topics to include, like CRISPR technology, ethical discussions, and practical applications, along with recommended resources.

5. **Resource Recommendations**:

Get updated resource suggestions for subjects from ChatGPT.

- **Prompt**: "Recommend the latest books and articles on 'Digital Marketing Strategies' for a college course."

- **Expected Outcome**: A curated list of recently published books, journals, or online resources that offer insights into modern digital marketing.

6. **Continuous Learning Activities**:

Design activities that foster a habit of continuous learning and staying updated.

- **Prompt**: "Propose an activity for high school students to stay updated about 'Space Exploration' using ChatGPT."

- **Expected Outcome**: An activity like monthly report generation where students ask ChatGPT about the latest space missions, discoveries, or technological advancements and present to the class.

7. **Feedback on Updates**:

Gather feedback after integrating updates to assess their effectiveness.

- **Prompt**: "After updating a module on 'Cybersecurity Practices' with the latest developments, how should feedback be collected to gauge its effectiveness?"

- **Expected Outcome**: Techniques like student surveys, assessment score comparisons, or group discussions to evaluate the update's relevance and clarity.

8. **Expert Collaboration**:

Use ChatGPT to facilitate collaborations with experts to stay informed.

- **Prompt**: "Suggest a method for educators to connect with leading experts in 'Artificial Intelligence Ethics' to stay updated on the subject."

- **Expected Outcome**: Recommendations for online forums, webinars, or AI ethics conferences, and suggestions for collaboration formats.

9. **Technology Integration**:

Stay updated on the latest educational tech tools, and learn how to integrate them.

- **Prompt**: "What are the emerging EdTech tools in 2023, and how can they be integrated into remote learning?"

- **Expected Outcome**: A list of current EdTech tools, with descriptions and potential use-cases for remote teaching scenarios.

By integrating these ChatGPT modules, educators can ensure they remain at the forefront of knowledge in their domain. It's not just about accumulating facts; it's about modeling a commitment to lifelong learning and showing students the value of staying informed in an ever-changing world.

Chapter 6: ChatGPT for Marketers

Leveraging ChatGPT for an online marketing campaign can provide a competitive edge in the market by offering personalized experiences to users, answering queries in real-time, and automating certain processes. Below is a step-by-step strategy to establish a successful online marketing campaign using ChatGPT, complete with examples.

1. Set Clear Objectives

- **Example:** To generate 200 leads from the campaign in one month.

2. Define the Target Audience

- **Example:** Millennial and Gen Z consumers interested in sustainable fashion.

3. Integration with Marketing Platforms

- Integrate ChatGPT with marketing platforms, such as a website, landing pages, social media, etc.

- **Example:** Add a chatbot on the landing page promoting a sustainable fashion product launch.

4. Personalize Conversations with User Data

- Use data analytics to fetch user preferences and tailor the conversation.

- **Example:** If a user previously searched for "vegan leather jackets," ChatGPT can start a conversation mentioning the latest collection of vegan leather jackets.

5. Design a Flow for the Chatbot

- Script typical conversation flows to guide users to a desired action.

- **Example:**

  - User: "Tell me about your new collection."

- ChatGPT: "Sure! Our latest collection focuses on sustainable fashion. Are you interested in clothing, accessories, or footwear?"

6. Offer Incentives through the Bot

- Encourage users to take desired actions by offering special discounts or promotions.

- **Example:** "By subscribing to our newsletter through this chat, you'll receive an exclusive 10% discount on your next purchase!"

7. Frequently Update the Chatbot's Knowledge Base

- As with any other marketing tool, ensure that the information is up-to-date.

- **Example:** Update the bot with the latest product releases, discount codes, and FAQs.

8. Incorporate Feedback Mechanism

- At the end of interactions, seek feedback on the user experience.

- **Example:** "On a scale of 1-10, how would you rate your chat experience?"

9. Monitor & Optimize

- Regularly check chat logs to understand user queries, preferences, and drop-offs.

- **Example:** If multiple users drop off after asking about the shipping charges, perhaps it's a point to reconsider or clarify in your marketing.

10. Drive Traffic to Your Platform

- Promote the chatbot's unique capabilities on social media, emails, and other channels.

- **Example:** A social media post saying, "Got questions about our new collection? Our AI chatbot is ready to guide you 24/7!"

11. Engage Users with Interactive Content

- Use ChatGPT's capabilities to host quizzes, polls, or games.

- **Example:** "Want to find your perfect outfit? Answer these 5 questions and our AI will make a personalized recommendation!"

12. Ensure GDPR Compliance & Transparency

- Ensure that users know they are interacting with a bot and that their data is protected.

- **Example:** "Hello! I'm a virtual assistant. I'm here to help you. We value your privacy. Click here to know how we handle your data."

13. Measure Success Metrics

- Track metrics like engagement rate, lead generation, conversion rate, and user satisfaction.

- **Example:** "In the past month, 70% of users who interacted with our chatbot subscribed to the newsletter."

14. Refine Strategy Based on Results

- Learn from metrics and feedback to refine the strategy continuously.

- **Example:** If users mostly interact during the evening, consider launching evening-specific promotions via the chatbot.

Remember, while ChatGPT is an incredibly powerful tool, the success of your campaign will still largely depend on the quality of your offer, the effectiveness of your marketing channels, and how well you understand and cater to your target audience.

ChatGPT Prompts and Modules for Marketers:
Set Clear Objectives:

Setting clear objectives is a cornerstone of any successful marketing campaign. Using ChatGPT, you can establish modules and prompts to help your team and your target audience understand and align with these objectives. Let's delve deeper into this:

1. User Engagement Prompts

These are meant to engage the user initially and probe them to think about their objectives or guide them toward understanding the objectives of your campaign.

Example Prompts:

- "Before we proceed, what would you like to achieve with our products/services?"

- "On a scale of 1-10, how important is [specific objective, e.g., sustainability] to you when purchasing a product?"

- "What's your primary goal when searching for [a product/service]?"

2. Clarification Modules

This module will help clarify the user's objectives or provide further clarity about your campaign's objectives.

Example Prompts:

- "To better serve you, could you specify what you mean by '[user's previous input]'?"

- "When you say you're looking for sustainable fashion, are you referring to environmental, ethical, or both aspects?"

- "Our primary objective is to offer sustainable fashion that doesn't compromise on style. Would you like to see some examples?"

3. Alignment Modules

After understanding the user's objective, these prompts will help align your offerings with the user's goals.

Example Prompts:

- "Based on your interest in [user's objective], we recommend [specific product/service]."

- "Many of our customers with similar goals found [specific product/service] to be beneficial. Would you like more information?"

- "Aligning with our objective of promoting sustainable fashion, we've launched a new eco-friendly line. Interested in exploring?"

4. Confirmation Prompts

To ensure that the user's objectives align with what you're offering or to confirm their understanding of your campaign objectives.

Example Prompts:

- "Just to confirm, you're looking to achieve [user's objective], correct?"

- "From our conversation, it seems you're keen on [specific objective, e.g., reducing your carbon footprint with sustainable fashion choices]. Is that right?"

- "Do you feel our new line aligns with your objective of [user's objective]?"

5. Feedback and Iteration Modules

Post-interaction, gauge user feedback to refine and iterate for future engagements.

Example Prompts:

- "On a scale of 1-10, how well do you feel our offerings align with your objectives?"

- "Do you feel more informed about our objective of [specific campaign objective] after this chat?"

- "Any suggestions on how we can better serve your goals in the future?"

By integrating such modules and prompts, you can:

1. Engage your users and understand their objectives.

2. Clearly convey your campaign's objectives.

3. Efficiently align user goals with your offerings.

4. Continuously refine your approach based on feedback.

It's worth noting that these prompts should be tailored further based on the specifics of your campaign, target audience, and offerings.

Define the Target Audience:

Defining the target audience is a pivotal step in any marketing strategy. Using ChatGPT, you can employ modules and prompts to help identify and understand this audience more clearly. Here's a detailed guide:

1. Initial Query Modules

The goal here is to start a conversation and gather preliminary data about the user.

Example Prompts:

- "Which age range best describes you? (a) Below 20, (b) 20-30, (c) 30-40, (d) Above 40."

- "What's the primary reason you're exploring our products/services today?"

- "Which of the following best describes your current occupation? (List options)"

2. Interest and Preference Exploration Modules

A deeper dive into the user's interests, preferences, and habits, providing clearer insights into their persona.

Example Prompts:

- "How often do you shop for [specific product] in a month?"

- "Which brands or products have you used in the past for [specific requirement]?"

- "What are your top three priorities when selecting [a product/service]?"

3. Pain Points and Challenges Modules

Understanding the challenges or issues faced by the user can help refine your audience definition further.

Example Prompts:

- "What challenges have you faced with [similar products/services] in the past?"

- "If there's one thing you could change about your current [product/service], what would it be?"

- "What's stopping you from making a purchase today?"

4. Behavioral Insight Modules

These are designed to understand user behaviors, providing hints about their lifestyle, spending habits, or how they consume content.

Example Prompts:

- "Where do you usually learn about new products or trends? Social media, blogs, friends, magazines?"

- "How often do you engage with online content related to [industry/niche]?"

- "When shopping online, do you (a) make impulse purchases, (b) research extensively before buying, or (c) rely on recommendations?"

5. Value and Motivation Modules

Aims to determine what drives the user's decisions – understanding this can help in more precise targeting.

Example Prompts:

- "What's more important to you: quality, price, brand reputation, or sustainability?"

- "If you had to choose between a premium product that lasts longer and a cheaper one that might need replacement soon, which would you pick?"

- "How important is a brand's environmental or ethical stance when you make a purchase decision?"

6. Feedback and Iteration Modules

Post-interaction, gather feedback on the user's experience, which can be insightful for audience definition.

Example Prompts:

- "Did you feel the products/services shown were tailored to your preferences?"

- "On a scale of 1-10, how relevant was the content we shared with you today?"

- "Would you prefer more personalized product recommendations in the future?"

Benefits of Using These Modules:

1. **Data Collection**: Gathering quantitative and qualitative data to create accurate user personas.

2. **Personalization**: Tailoring future interactions based on insights from previous engagements.

3. **Refinement**: Continuously improving the audience definition based on ongoing interactions.

When using ChatGPT for defining your target audience, remember to adhere to data privacy regulations and always inform users if and how their data will be used. Transparency is key to maintaining trust.

Integration with Marketing Platforms:

Integrating ChatGPT with various marketing platforms can enhance the overall user experience, provide real-time responses, and seamlessly combine the strengths of AI with existing marketing infrastructures. Let's delve into how this can be achieved across different platforms:

1. Website Integration

Purpose: To assist, guide, or convert website visitors.

Prompts & Modules:

- **Navigation Assistant**: "Looking for something specific? Let me guide you!"

- **Product Inquiry**: "Have questions about our product range? Ask away!"

- **Checkout Assistance**: "Facing issues during checkout? Let me help!"

Example: If a user spends more than 2 minutes on a checkout page, trigger the chatbot with, "Having trouble checking out? Let me assist you."

2. Email Marketing Integration

Purpose: Enhance email campaigns by providing interactive assistance and responses.

Prompts & Modules:

- **Survey Assistance**: "Need help with the survey? Ask me anything!"

- **Product Feedback**: "Have thoughts about our latest product? Share them with me!"

- **Subscription Inquiry**: "Questions about your subscription? I'm here to clarify!"

Example: In an email showcasing a new product range, include a link saying, "Have questions about this range? Chat with our AI assistant now!"

3. Social Media Integration

Purpose: Engage followers and answer queries directly from social platforms.

Prompts & Modules:

- **New Launches**: "Hey there! 👋 Check out our latest collection. Want a sneak peek?"

- **Event Queries**: "Interested in our upcoming webinar? Let me provide the details."

- **Support Issues**: "Sorry to hear about your issue. Describe it, and I'll do my best to help."

Example: For a Facebook ad about an upcoming sale, integrate a Messenger chatbot that says, "Want to know the best deals for you? Chat with me!"

4. E-Commerce Platforms

Purpose: Offer personalized shopping experiences and recommendations.

Prompts & Modules:

- **Personal Shopper**: "Describe your style, and I'll find the best matches for you!"

- **Size Assistant**: "Not sure about the size? Share your preferences, and I'll recommend."

- **Stock Inquiry**: "Looking for a specific item? I can check its availability."

Example: On a product page, have ChatGPT pop up with, "Need help with sizing or color choices? Ask me!"

5. CRM Integration

Purpose: Assist sales teams by providing instant information or taking over routine interactions.

Prompts & Modules:

- **Lead Qualification**: "Can you describe what you're looking for in our service? This will help me guide you better."

- **Appointment Setting**: "Want to talk to our sales team? Give me a time, and I'll schedule it."

- **Service History**: "Looking for your service history? Let me fetch that."

Example: If a lead interacts with a demo request form but doesn't complete it, trigger ChatGPT with, "Facing issues with the demo request? I can assist."

6. Content Platforms (Blogs, Forums)

Purpose: Engage readers and provide additional resources or support.

Prompts & Modules:

- **Content Suggestions**: "Interested in this topic? I have more articles for you!"

- **Clarifications**: "Have questions about what you just read? Let's discuss."

- **Subscription Assistance**: "Want regular updates? Let me help you subscribe."

Example: At the end of a blog post, integrate ChatGPT with, "Want a deep dive into this topic? Ask me for more resources."

Implementation Considerations:

1. **User Privacy**: Always ensure user data is handled with care and transparency.

2. **Mobile Responsiveness**: Ensure that the ChatGPT integration works seamlessly on mobile devices.

3. **Limitations**: Be clear about the bot's capabilities and guide users to human representatives when necessary.

Incorporating ChatGPT into your various marketing platforms provides an opportunity to engage and assist users dynamically, creating a more tailored and interactive experience.

Personalize Conversations with User Data:

Personalizing conversations using user data can be a game-changer in creating a dynamic and tailored experience for your users. Let's explore how you can create intricate modules and prompts for ChatGPT to make these personalizations:

1. Returning User Identification

Purpose: Recognize users who've interacted with your platform before.

Prompts & Modules:

- **Welcome Back**: "Hello again! Would you like to continue where we left off?"

- **Previous Inquiries**: "Last time, you were curious about our summer collection. Would you like updates on that?"

Example: If a user previously checked out winter boots but didn't make a purchase, you might prompt: "Still interested in winter boots? We have new arrivals!"

2. Purchase History Analysis

Purpose: Recommend new items or provide support based on previous purchases.

Prompts & Modules:

- **Recommendations**: "You bought our eco-friendly running shoes last time. How about checking out our sustainable workout gear?"

- **Post-Purchase Support**: "Having issues with the smartphone model you bought last month? Let's troubleshoot."

Example: For someone who bought a laptop, you could suggest, "Looking for compatible accessories for your new laptop?"

3. Cart Analysis

Purpose: Address items left in a cart or make additional recommendations.

Prompts & Modules:

- **Cart Reminder**: "I noticed you've left items in your cart. Need more information before purchasing?"

- **Complementary Products**: "Those sunglasses in your cart pair well with our new range of summer hats."

Example: If someone has skincare products in their cart: "Want to explore some new moisturizers to complement your skincare routine?"

4. Behavioral Analysis

Purpose: Personalize interactions based on user browsing behavior.

Prompts & Modules:

- **Browsing Specifics**: "You've been exploring a lot of our vegan recipes. Need any specific ingredients?"

- **Content Personalization**: "Based on your reading history, here's an article on 'Advanced Digital Marketing Strategies.'"

Example: If a user often reads travel blogs: "Planning your next trip? Check out our guides on top destinations for 2023!"

5. User Feedback Analysis

Purpose: Adjust interactions based on previous feedback or ratings.

Prompts & Modules:

- **Improvement Suggestions**: "You mentioned our checkout process was slow last time. We've made updates. Care to give it another try?"

- **Tailored Assistance**: "Last time, you seemed unsatisfied with our product range. Can I help you find something specific today?"

Example: If a user gave a low rating to a music album: "We've got new tracks from different genres. Want to explore?"

6. Profile Preferences Analysis

Purpose: Customize conversations based on explicit preferences set by users in their profiles.

Prompts & Modules:

- **Tailored News**: "Hello [Name]! Based on your preference for tech news, here are the top stories for today."

- **Event Notifications**: "You've mentioned an interest in web development. We have a webinar on that next week. Interested?"

Example: For a user who set their location as "New York": "Looking for local events in New York this weekend?"

Implementation Considerations:

1. **User Privacy**: Always ensure you handle user data with utmost care, informing users how their data is used and ensuring compliance with privacy laws like GDPR or CCPA.

2. **Relevance**: Make sure that the personalization is relevant. Misinterpreting data can lead to irrelevant suggestions, which might turn users off.

3. **Avoid Over personalization**: Too much personalization can come off as creepy or invasive. Strike the right balance.

By integrating detailed personalization into ChatGPT's interactions, businesses can offer a more curated experience, increasing user engagement and potentially boosting conversions. However, it's always crucial to prioritize user trust and data privacy.

Design a Flow for the Chatbot:

Creating a comprehensive chatbot flow is crucial for guiding users smoothly through their journey and ensuring they get the information or assistance they need. Let's break down how to design complex chatbot flows using ChatGPT:

1. Greeting & Introduction

Purpose: Welcome the user and set the tone for the interaction.

Prompts & Modules:

- **Standard Greeting**: "Hello! How can I assist you today?"

- **Time-based Greeting**: "Good morning! Ready to start your day with some exciting deals?"

Example: For an e-commerce site: "Hey there! Looking for something specific or just browsing?"

2. User Inquiry & Intent Recognition

Purpose: Understand the user's needs or questions.

Prompts & Modules:

- **Open-ended**: "Tell me what you're looking for, and I'll guide you."

- **Option-based**: "Are you here for (a) Product Information, (b) Support, or (c) Feedback?"

Example: For a tech support site: "Facing an issue with a product? Please describe the problem or provide the error code."

3. Deep Dive & Clarification

Purpose: Get more details about the user's inquiry or intent.

Prompts & Modules:

- **Specifics Gathering**: "Which model of the product are you inquiring about?"

- **Problem Details**: "Can you specify what's happening when you try to turn it on?"

Example: For a travel booking site: "Got it! You want to book a flight. One-way or round trip?"

4. Guided Actions & Responses

Purpose: Provide information, support, or guide users based on their identified intent.

Prompts & Modules:

- **Direct Answer**: "The product has a 2-year warranty covering manufacturing defects."

- **Guided Process**: "To reset your password, first click on 'Forgot Password', then enter your registered email."

Example: For an online course platform: "You can access all your purchased courses under the 'My Courses' tab."

5. Follow-up & Cross-sell

Purpose: Check if the user has further questions or offer additional related services/products.

Prompts & Modules:

- **Satisfaction Check**: "Did that answer your question?"

- **Additional Offers**: "You might also be interested in our premium warranty package."

Example: For a bookstore: "Since you bought a fantasy novel, you might love our new collection of fantasy bookmarks!"

6. Feedback & Closing

Purpose: End the interaction positively and gather feedback for improvement.

Prompts & Modules:

- **Feedback Request**: "On a scale of 1-10, how helpful was this chat?"

- **Goodbye Message**: "Thank you for chatting! If you have more questions in the future, don't hesitate to ask."

Example: For a restaurant: "Hope you found our menu enticing! If you have any dietary preferences for next time, let us know."

7. Error Handling & Escalation

Purpose: Manage situations where the bot can't comprehend the user or if the user needs human assistance.

Prompts & Modules:

- **Misunderstanding Apology**: "I'm sorry, I didn't quite catch that. Can you rephrase?"

- **Human Escalation**: "It seems I can't help with this specific request. Would you like to speak with a human representative?"

Example: For a bank: "Sorry for the inconvenience. For sensitive queries, I recommend speaking directly to our support team."

Implementation Considerations:

1. **User-Friendly Language**: Ensure the chatbot's language is clear, relatable, and doesn't come across as too robotic.

2. **Limitation Recognition**: If ChatGPT doesn't know an answer, it's essential to guide the user to alternative resources or human support.

3. **Testing & Iteration**: Regularly test the chatbot flow with real users and iterate based on feedback to ensure a seamless user experience.

A well-designed chatbot flow ensures users don't feel lost or frustrated during interactions, leading to higher user satisfaction and better conversion rates.

Offer Incentives through the Bot:

Offering incentives through a chatbot can be a strategic move to enhance user engagement, drive sales, or encourage certain user actions. Let's explore detailed chatbot flows using ChatGPT to offer these incentives:

1. User Engagement Incentives

Purpose: Reward users for interacting with the chatbot, making them more likely to continue the conversation.

Prompts & Modules:

- **Initial Engagement Reward**: "Thanks for chatting with us! Here's a 10% discount on your next purchase."

- **Loyalty Bonus**: "You've been with us for a year! Here's a special reward just for you."

Example: For a music streaming platform: "For sharing your favorite genres, enjoy a free month of our premium subscription!"

2. Referral Incentives

Purpose: Encourage users to refer friends or share content in exchange for rewards.

Prompts & Modules:

- **Referral Code Generation**: "Invite friends and get $10 credit for each one who signs up!"

- **Sharing Bonus**: "Share our latest collection on your social media and claim a special discount."

Example: For a fitness app: "Invite a workout buddy and both of you get a free personalized training plan!"

3. Purchase or Action-based Incentives

Purpose: Drive sales or specific user actions, such as completing a profile, writing a review, or attending a webinar.

Prompts & Modules:

- **Bulk Purchase Discount**: "Add one more item to your cart, and we'll slash 15% off your total!"

- **Review Reward**: "Share your feedback on this purchase, and get a voucher for your next one."

- **Webinar Attendance**: "Join our upcoming webinar, and you could win a free course!"

Example: For an online course platform: "Complete this course within the week, and get a 50% discount on the next one!"

4. Time-limited Incentives

Purpose: Create urgency and prompt quick decision-making.

Prompts & Modules:

- **Flash Sale Alert**: "Only for the next 2 hours: Get any product at half price!"

- **Early Bird Bonus**: "First 100 users to make a purchase get an exclusive gift."

Example: For a ticket booking site: "Book within the next hour and upgrade to premium seating at no extra cost!"

5. Gamified Incentives

Purpose: Make user interaction fun and rewarding through games or challenges.

Prompts & Modules:

- **Spin the Wheel**: "Try your luck! Spin the wheel for a chance to win exclusive discounts."

- **Quiz Rewards**: "Answer three quick questions about our brand, and win a surprise!"

Example: For a coffee shop chain: "Guess our flavor of the month, and get one for free on your next visit!"

6. Feedback and Data Collection Incentives

Purpose: Encourage users to provide valuable feedback or additional data.

Prompts & Modules:

- **Survey Completion Bonus**: "Help us improve by completing this short survey and get a $5 voucher."

- **Profile Completion**: "Fill out your profile and enjoy a curated gift, tailored just for you."

Example: For a reading app: "Share your top 5 favorite books and unlock a month of premium reading!"

Implementation Considerations:

1. **Clear Communication**: Ensure that terms and conditions related to incentives are clearly stated to avoid misunderstandings.

2. **Genuine Value**: Offer incentives that provide real value to the user.

3. **Avoid Over-Promotion**: Too many incentives can sometimes overwhelm or seem desperate. It's crucial to find a balance.

4. **User Behavior Analysis**: Regularly analyze the effectiveness of incentives and adjust strategies accordingly.

By integrating incentives within ChatGPT conversations, businesses can drive specific actions, improve user satisfaction, and potentially increase sales and loyalty.

Frequently Update the Chatbot's Knowledge Base:

Maintaining an updated knowledge base for ChatGPT is essential to ensuring that users receive accurate and timely information. This requires both an understanding of the underlying technology and a strategy for content management. Let's delve into how this can be executed:

1. Monitor User Interactions

Purpose: Identify gaps in the chatbot's knowledge or new queries that are frequently asked.

Prompts & Modules:

- **Feedback Loop**: "Was this answer helpful? (Yes/No)"

- **Missed Questions Log**: Automatically log questions ChatGPT couldn't answer adequately for review.

Example: If users frequently ask about a new product variant but ChatGPT provides information about an older model, it signals an update is needed.

2. Integrate with Dynamic Data Sources

Purpose: Ensure ChatGPT has access to the latest data or product catalogs.

Prompts & Modules:

- **Latest Inventory Check**: "Let me check our latest inventory for that item."

- **Product Updates**: "We've recently updated our product range. Would you like the latest details?"

Example: If ChatGPT is integrated with an e-commerce platform, it should regularly sync with the latest product availability data.

3. Scheduled Knowledge Refresh

Purpose: Regularly update the bot with new information, FAQs, or industry updates.

Prompts & Modules:

- **New Product Launches**: "We've just launched our summer collection! Would you like to explore?"

- **Industry News Update**: "There have been some recent developments in our sector. Would you like an overview?"

Example: If a tech company releases a new software update, ChatGPT should be prepped with details and potential troubleshooting tips.

4. Handling Outdated Information

Purpose: Ensure that old or outdated information is flagged and updated.

Prompts & Modules:

- **User Flagging**: "If you believe any information provided is outdated, please let us know."

- **Auto-Review Triggers**: Set triggers to review content after a specific duration or event.

Example: For tax-related queries, ChatGPT should be updated annually after tax laws are revised.

5. Feedback Analysis & Iteration

Purpose: Use feedback to refine answers and improve the chatbot's accuracy.

Prompts & Modules:

- **Rating System**: "On a scale of 1-5, how accurate was the provided information?"

- **Suggestion Collection**: "If you have suggestions for improving this answer, please share!"

Example: If a user finds a step-by-step guide confusing, they can suggest clearer instructions or highlight the problematic step.

6. Integrate with Change Management Tools

Purpose: Streamline the process of updating the bot by integrating with CMS or other change management tools.

Prompts & Modules:

- **Change Logs**: Maintain logs of all updates made to the chatbot's knowledge.

- **Versioning**: "You're interacting with version 3.5. For older version details, please specify."

Example: If ChatGPT is linked to a company's internal wiki, any changes made to the wiki could automatically prompt a review for chatbot content relevancy.

7. Periodic Testing & Validation

Purpose: Regularly test the chatbot to ensure it provides accurate and updated information.

Prompts & Modules:

- **Scenario-Based Testing**: Design test cases simulating real user queries to check the chatbot's responses.

- **Test Feedback Loop**: After testing, have a system in place for immediate updates based on findings.

Example: After updating shipping policies, simulate a user query about shipping durations to validate ChatGPT's response.

Implementation Considerations:

1. **User Trust**: Providing outdated or inaccurate information can erode user trust. Regular updates are crucial.

2. **Collaboration**: Collaborate with different departments to ensure that all relevant updates are communicated to the team responsible for the chatbot.

3. **Change Management**: Implement robust change management practices to track and validate all updates made to the chatbot's knowledge base.

By maintaining an updated knowledge base for ChatGPT, you ensure that users get the most accurate, timely, and relevant information, thereby improving user satisfaction and trust.

Monitor & Optimize:

Monitoring and optimizing ChatGPT's interactions can provide enhanced user experiences, ensure the accuracy of information, and keep user engagement high. Let's explore strategies and modules to implement this effectively:

1. User Feedback Collection

Purpose: Obtain direct feedback on ChatGPT's performance and user satisfaction.

Prompts & Modules:

- **Rating System**: "On a scale of 1-5, how helpful was this conversation?"

- **Open-Ended Feedback**: "Do you have any suggestions or comments about our chat today?"

Example: After resolving a support ticket, "Were you satisfied with the solution provided? Kindly share feedback to help us improve."

2. Track Engagement Metrics

Purpose: Measure user interaction levels with the chatbot.

Prompts & Modules:

- **Session Duration Monitor**: Calculate the average time users spend interacting with the bot.

- **Query Resolution Time**: Measure the time taken to resolve or answer user queries.

Example: If users generally spend only 15 seconds on average, it might indicate that they're dropping off quickly due to dissatisfaction or confusion.

3. Error & Dropout Rate Monitoring

Purpose: Identify frequent errors or points where users tend to end their interactions.

Prompts & Modules:

- **Error Logging**: Automatically log unrecognized queries or instances where ChatGPT couldn't provide an answer.

- **Dropout Point Tracker**: Mark points in the conversation where users frequently end the chat.

Example: If many users drop out after asking about shipping fees, there might be an issue with the clarity or accuracy of the bot's response.

4. A/B Testing

Purpose: Test different versions of responses to determine which one resonates better with users.

Prompts & Modules:

- **Variant Responses**: Set up two or more versions of an answer to a common query.

- **Performance Metrics**: Measure which variant leads to better user satisfaction or higher engagement.

Example: For a product recommendation query, test whether users prefer a detailed description versus a brief one with visual aids.

5. Integration with Analytics Platforms

Purpose: Use third-party analytics tools to get detailed insights on user interactions.

Prompts & Modules:

- **User Journey Mapping**: Visualize the paths users take during interactions.

- **Demographic Analysis**: Understand the profiles of users interacting with the chatbot.

Example: By integrating with Google Analytics, monitor which geographical regions have the highest chatbot interactions and tailor content accordingly.

6. Continuous Learning Loop

Purpose: Adapt and refine ChatGPT's responses based on the collected data and insights.

Prompts & Modules:

- **Adaptive Responses**: Update answers based on frequent user feedback or error logs.

- **Regular Training**: Continuously train ChatGPT with new data sets to improve its accuracy and relevance.

Example: If users frequently ask about a term the bot isn't familiar with, include it in the next training iteration.

7. Human Escalation Monitoring

Purpose: Identify when users request human assistance and analyze the reasons.

Prompts & Modules:

- **Human Request Tracker**: Log instances when users ask to speak to a human representative.

- **Reason Collection**: "May I know the reason you prefer human assistance? This helps us improve."

Example: If users dealing with payment issues always prefer human help, it might indicate a trust or complexity issue with the bot's responses.

Implementation Considerations:

1. **User Privacy**: Always ensure that monitoring respects user privacy and adheres to data protection regulations.

2. **Actionability**: It's not just about collecting data; it's crucial to act on the insights to improve user experience.

3. **Iterative Process**: Monitoring and optimization should be continuous processes, adapting to changing user needs and business objectives.

Effectively monitoring and optimizing ChatGPT ensures that it remains a valuable tool for users, effectively meeting their needs while driving business objectives.

Drive Traffic to Your Platform:

Using ChatGPT to drive traffic to your platform can be an innovative approach, leveraging conversational marketing to engage users and direct them to your content, products, or services. Here's how you can design intricate chatbot flows and modules to achieve this:

1. Share Featured Content

Purpose: Highlight specific content or promotions to draw users to your platform.

Prompts & Modules:

- **Latest Content**: "Have you checked out our latest article on sustainable living? Here's the link!"

- **Trending Topics**: "Our post on 'Top Tech Gadgets of 2023' is getting a lot of attention. Don't miss out!"

Example: For a news platform: "Breaking: Major events unfolding in the tech industry. Click here to get the latest updates."

2. Personalized Recommendations

Purpose: Offer tailored suggestions based on user profiles or past interactions.

Prompts & Modules:

- **User History Analysis**: "You've shown interest in adventure travel before. Here's our new guide on 'Top Adventure Destinations'."

- **Curated Lists**: "Based on your reading habits, I've curated a list of articles you might find intriguing."

Example: For an e-commerce platform: "Your last purchase was a digital camera. How about some bestselling camera accessories to enhance your photography?"

3. Exclusive Offers & Deals

Purpose: Entice users with special deals or promotions available on your platform.

Prompts & Modules:

- **Limited-Time Discounts**: "Exclusive for chat users: Get 20% off on your next purchase! Click here."

- **Special Bundles**: "Bundle Alert! Combine your current cart items with this and get an extra discount."

Example: For a subscription service: "Enjoy a premium subscription at half the price for your first month! Offer ends soon."

4. Events & Webinar Promotions

Purpose: Drive traffic by promoting upcoming events, webinars, or online sessions.

Prompts & Modules:

- **Event Alerts**: "We have an upcoming webinar on digital marketing trends. Interested?"

- **Reminder Settings**: "Would you like a reminder for our product launch event next week?"

Example: For a training platform: "Join our free workshop on 'Advanced Data Analytics'. Limited slots available!"

5. Engage with Interactive Content

Purpose: Use quizzes, polls, or interactive stories to encourage users to explore your platform.

Prompts & Modules:

- **Topic Quizzes**: "Test your knowledge on sustainable fashion with our quick quiz!"

- **Opinion Polls**: "We're debating the best movies of the decade. Cast your vote and see the results on our site!"

Example: For a movie streaming platform: "Discover movies tailored for you! Answer these 5 quick questions."

6. Share User Testimonials & Reviews

Purpose: Build trust and interest by showcasing real user feedback.

Prompts & Modules:

- **Success Stories**: "Many users found value in our premium services. Read their stories here."

- **Product Reviews**: "Not sure about this product? Here are reviews from customers who bought it."

Example: For an online course: "See how our course transformed careers! Check out these testimonials."

7. Seamless Navigation Assistance

Purpose: Help users navigate to your platform's relevant sections.

Prompts & Modules:

- **Direct Links**: "Looking for tech articles? Here's our tech section: [link]."

- **Search Assistance**: "Can't find what you're looking for? Let me help you search."

Example: For a multi-category blog: "We have sections ranging from travel to finance. Which one would you like to explore?"

Implementation Considerations:

1. **User-Centricity**: Ensure that the traffic-driving modules are designed with users' interests and convenience in mind.

2. **Not Too Pushy**: Be cautious not to overwhelm users with too many promotional prompts, which can deter them.

3. **Mobile Optimization**: Ensure that all links and platforms are mobile-friendly, considering a significant portion of users might access them via mobile devices.

By integrating these modules into ChatGPT, businesses can engage users in meaningful conversations that not only provide value but also guide them to explore the platform further.

Engage Users with Interactive Content:

Engaging users through interactive content via ChatGPT can provide an immersive experience that not only captures attention but also fosters a deeper connection with your platform or brand. Let's delve into the details:

1. Quizzes & Trivia

Purpose: Test user knowledge and offer insights or recommendations based on their answers.

Prompts & Modules:

- **Knowledge Quiz**: "Want to test your knowledge about renewable energy? Answer these five questions!"

- **Product Recommendation Quiz**: "Tell us about your skin type and preferences, and we'll suggest the perfect skincare routine!"

Example: For a movie platform: "Guess the director of these iconic movies and get personalized film suggestions."

2. Polls & Surveys

Purpose: Gather user opinions and make them feel a part of a larger community or decision-making process.

Prompts & Modules:

- **Opinion Polls**: "Which of these upcoming features excites you the most? Vote now!"

- **Feedback Surveys**: "Help us improve by rating our latest update on a scale of 1 to 10."

Example: For a fashion brand: "Which color palette would you love to see in our next collection? Earthy tones or Pastel shades?"

3. Choose Your Own Adventure

Purpose: Offer narrative-based interactions where users dictate the flow of the story or scenario.

Prompts & Modules:

- **Story Progression**: "You're lost in a forest. Do you (a) call for help or (b) try to find your way back?"

- **Scenario-based Learning**: "You're a manager dealing with a team conflict. How do you approach it?"

Example: For a travel agency: "You're on a global adventure! Choose a continent to start your journey."

4. Puzzles & Brain Teasers

Purpose: Challenge users and offer them a break from conventional content.

Prompts & Modules:

- **Riddles**: "I'm tall when I'm young and short when I'm old. What am I?"

- **Problem-solving Challenges**: "Here's a math puzzle for you. Solve it to get a discount!"

Example: For a book store: "Decode this book title from emojis: 🚂 ➡️ ⛰️. Guess correctly for a special deal!"

5. Interactive Tutorials & Demos

Purpose: Provide a hands-on understanding of products, services, or concepts.

Prompts & Modules:

- **Step-by-step Guides**: "Want to set up your new device? Let's walk through it step by step."

- **Product Demonstrations**: "Let me show you how our new software feature works. Choose a module to begin!"

Example: For a cooking platform: "Ready to bake a cake? Follow along with our interactive recipe."

6. Gamified Challenges

Purpose: Engage users through game elements, offering rewards or badges for achievements.

Prompts & Modules:

- **Progress Tracking**: "You've completed 5 challenges! 3 more to unlock a premium badge."

- **Reward-based Tasks**: "Participate in our daily challenge and earn points towards exclusive discounts."

Example: For a fitness app: "Complete this 7-day workout streak and unlock a special workout routine!"

7. Dynamic Visual Content Integration

Purpose: Integrate interactive visuals, such as infographics or videos, to enhance engagement.

Prompts & Modules:

- **Visual Explainers**: "Here's an infographic breaking down the concept for you."

- **Video Playlists**: "Based on your interests, we've curated this video playlist. Dive in!"

Example: For a science platform: "Want to understand how photosynthesis works? Here's an interactive animation."

Implementation Considerations:

1. **User Preferences**: Not every user might enjoy interactive content, so always provide an option to skip or proceed in a conventional manner.

2. **Platform Limitations**: Ensure that your platform supports the interactive modules you're integrating. Not all chat platforms may support highly interactive content.

3. **Feedback Mechanism**: Always provide users with an avenue to give feedback on interactive content, allowing you to refine and improve over time.

By incorporating interactive content through ChatGPT, you not only make the user experience more engaging but also encourage deeper exploration and understanding of your platform or offerings.

Ensure GDPR Compliance & Transparency:

Ensuring GDPR (General Data Protection Regulation) compliance when using a tool like ChatGPT is pivotal, especially when interacting with users from the European Union. Here's a detailed overview of modules and prompts to ensure compliance and transparency:

1. Explicit Consent Gathering

Purpose: Obtain clear and affirmative consent from users before collecting or processing their personal data.

Prompts & Modules:

- **Initial Interaction**: "Before we proceed, we need your consent to process your data for this chat. Do you agree?"

- **Data Collection Consent**: "Can we store this information to assist you better in the future?"

Example: For a survey: "To participate in this survey, we'll need to process your responses. Do you consent to proceed?"

2. Inform About Data Usage

Purpose: Clearly state why you're collecting data and how it will be used.

Prompts & Modules:

- **Usage Clarity**: "We use this data solely to improve our services and support. Your personal data won't be shared with third parties."

- **Data Retention Info**: "Your chat data will be stored for 30 days, after which it will be automatically deleted."

Example: For user feedback: "Your feedback helps us improve. We'll use this data internally to enhance our services."

3. Provide Data Access & Control

Purpose: Allow users to view, modify, or delete their data.

Prompts & Modules:

- **Data Access Request**: "Want to view the data we have stored about you? Please click here."

- **Data Modification**: "To update or correct your data, follow this link."

- **Data Deletion**: "If you wish to delete all your data from our system, please confirm."

Example: "Not satisfied with our service? You have the right to request data deletion at any time."

4. Third-party Data Sharing Transparency

Purpose: Inform users if their data is shared with any third-party or external service.

Prompts & Modules:

- **Third-party Sharing Alert**: "We use [Third-party Service] for analytics. Do you consent to share this chat data for analysis purposes?"

- **Opt-out Option**: "If you'd prefer not to have this chat analyzed, you can opt-out here."

Example: "We collaborate with [Payment Gateway] to process transactions. Your payment data will be securely handled by them."

5. Data Breach Notification

Purpose: Ensure users are informed in case of any data breaches, as per GDPR requirements.

Prompts & Modules:

- **Breach Notification**: "We regret to inform you that there's been a security incident involving user data. Here are the details and the measures we're taking."

6. Inform About Data Protection Officer (DPO)

Purpose: Provide users with a point of contact regarding all data protection queries.

Prompts & Modules:

- **DPO Introduction**: "For any concerns regarding your data, you can reach out to our Data Protection Officer at [DPO Email Address]."

7. Integration of Cookie Policies

Purpose: Inform users about tracking cookies and get their consent if your chatbot sets any.

Prompts & Modules:

- **Cookie Consent**: "We use cookies to enhance your chat experience. Do you agree to accept cookies?"

- **Cookie Policy Link**: "To learn more about how we use cookies, check our Cookie Policy here."

Example: "To remember your preferences, we'd like to set a cookie. Is that okay?"

Implementation Considerations:

1. **Regular Audits**: Regularly review and audit your chatbot interactions to ensure GDPR compliance.

2. **Training & Updates**: Ensure that ChatGPT's training data doesn't contain personally identifiable information and is regularly updated with GDPR-compliant interactions.

3. **Clear Opt-Outs**: Always provide users with clear pathways to opt-out of data processing or withdraw their consent.

By integrating these GDPR-focused modules into ChatGPT, businesses can ensure that they remain compliant while providing a transparent and trustable user experience. It's also wise to consult with legal professionals when handling GDPR matters to ensure full compliance.

Measure Success Metrics:

Measuring success metrics for ChatGPT or any chatbot is crucial to understand its effectiveness, user satisfaction, and areas of improvement. Detailed monitoring can help refine the bot's functionality and optimize user interactions. Here's how you can implement this:

1. User Satisfaction Rate

Purpose: Measure how satisfied users are with their chatbot interactions.

Prompts & Modules:

- **Post-interaction Rating**: "On a scale of 1-5, how would you rate this chat experience?"

- **Feedback Collection**: "Please provide any suggestions to improve our chat service."

Example: After resolving a query: "Did I help address your concern effectively? Please rate your experience."

2. Engagement Metrics

Purpose: Understand how often and how long users interact with the chatbot.

Prompts & Modules:

- **Session Duration Monitor**: Measure the average time users spend in a chat session.

- **Number of Interactions**: Track the total number of interactions per user.

Example: If users consistently engage in lengthy sessions, it could indicate they find the chat valuable or, conversely, they might be struggling to get the information they need.

3. Resolution Rate

Purpose: Determine how often the chatbot successfully resolves user queries without escalation.

Prompts & Modules:

- **Resolution Confirmation**: "Did this answer resolve your query? (Yes/No)"

- **Escalation Count**: Monitor how often users need to be transferred to human agents or other support channels.

Example: If a user asks about refund policies and later escalates to a human agent, it might indicate the bot's response was inadequate.

4. Retention Rate

Purpose: Measure how frequently users return to interact with the chatbot.

Prompts & Modules:

- **Return User Detection**: Identify returning users and the frequency of their interactions.

- **Feedback on Return**: "Welcome back! What brings you back to our chat today?"

Example: If users frequently return to the chatbot, it could signify a reliable and useful tool or recurring issues that aren't being resolved.

5. Top Queries & Missed Queries

Purpose: Identify the most common topics users ask about and where the chatbot might be lacking.

Prompts & Modules:

- **Query Categorization**: Classify user questions into predefined categories to see trends.

- **Missed Queries Log**: Automatically record and categorize questions the chatbot couldn't answer.

Example: If many users ask about international shipping but get inadequate answers, that area needs enhancement.

6. Conversion Rate

Purpose: For chatbots aimed at sales or specific user actions, measure the conversion effectiveness.

Prompts & Modules:

- **Action Completion Check**: Monitor and track if users completed the desired action post-chat (e.g., made a purchase, signed up).

- **Follow-up on Drop-offs**: "We noticed you didn't complete your purchase. How can we assist further?"

Example: If a user inquires about a product's specifics and later adds it to the cart, the bot played a role in that conversion.

7. Active Users vs. Drop-offs

Purpose: Determine how many users actively engage with the chatbot versus those who leave without meaningful interactions.

Prompts & Modules:

- **Engagement Depth Measurement**: Classify interactions based on depth (e.g., superficial greetings vs. in-depth queries).

- **Drop-off Point Identification**: Analyze at which point users typically end their chat.

Example: If users frequently drop off after the chatbot's initial greeting, the introduction might need to be more engaging.

Implementation Considerations:

1. **Integration with Analytics Tools**: Tools like Google Analytics can offer deeper insights into user behavior and chatbot performance.

2. **Regular Reviews**: Continuously review the metrics and adapt based on insights. A quarterly or monthly review can highlight trends and areas of improvement.

3. **User Privacy**: Ensure that while collecting and analyzing data, user privacy and data protection regulations are respected.

Measuring these success metrics for ChatGPT or any chatbot platform provides valuable insights that can drive improvements, enhance user experience, and ensure the bot aligns with organizational objectives.

Refine Strategy Based on Results:

Refining a strategy based on results is an ongoing process that involves interpreting the collected metrics, understanding user behavior, and adapting the chatbot to better meet user needs and business objectives. Here's a detailed guide:

1. Analyzing Metrics & Trends

Purpose: Understand patterns, anomalies, and standout results in the collected data.

Prompts & Modules:

- **Automated Reports**: "Provide a monthly performance report of the chatbot."

- **Metric Analysis**: "Highlight any metric that's deviated by more than 10% from the previous month."

Example: If there's a sudden spike in drop-offs at a specific chat stage, it could signal a confusing or unhelpful bot response.

2. Feedback Collection & Analysis

Purpose: Collect and evaluate user feedback to derive actionable insights.

Prompts & Modules:

- **Open-ended Feedback**: "Please share any specific issues or suggestions you have for our chat service."

- **Feedback Categorization**: Automate categorizing feedback into buckets like 'Usability', 'Accuracy', 'Speed', etc.

Example: If multiple users mention that the bot doesn't understand certain phrases, a language model update or more training data might be needed.

3. A/B Testing Iterations

Purpose: Continuously test different versions of bot responses or flows to determine the most effective one.

Prompts & Modules:

- **Version Comparisons**: "Version A of the response has a 20% higher satisfaction rate than Version B."

- **Ongoing Tests Alert**: Inform users, "We're currently testing new features. Feel free to share your feedback!"

Example: Testing two greetings – a simple "Hello!" versus a dynamic "Good [morning/afternoon/evening]!" – to see which one engages users more effectively.

4. Implementing User Behavior Insights

Purpose: Adapt the chatbot based on observed user behavior, preferences, and common paths.

Prompts & Modules:

- **Popular Topics Highlight**: "Our analysis indicates users frequently inquire about pricing. Consider adding a detailed pricing FAQ section."

- **Path Optimization**: Identify and smooth out common paths users take for a more streamlined experience.

Example: If users often ask about a product's warranty after purchase, proactively provide this information in post-purchase interactions.

5. Refining Data Collection & Analysis Tools

Purpose: Enhance the precision and scope of data collection to capture richer insights.

Prompts & Modules:

- **Advanced Analytics Integration**: "Integrate with [Advanced Analytics Tool] for deeper user journey mapping."

- **Data Visualization**: "Provide a visual dashboard of monthly chatbot metrics."

Example: Using heatmaps to understand where users spend the most time or frequently drop off in the chat flow.

6. Regular Strategy Reviews

Purpose: Establish routine evaluations of the chatbot's strategy and performance.

Prompts & Modules:

- **Quarterly Review Reminders**: "Schedule a chatbot strategy review for the end of the quarter."

- **Performance Summaries**: "Generate a performance summary highlighting key achievements and areas of improvement."

Example: A bi-annual deep dive into all metrics, feedback, and technological advancements to reassess and realign the chatbot's role and strategy.

7. Adaptation to External Changes

Purpose: Keep the chatbot relevant amid changing industry standards, technological advancements, and market shifts.

Prompts & Modules:

- **Trend Analysis**: "Identify any new chatbot trends or technologies emerging in the market."

- **Competitive Benchmarking**: Compare your chatbot's performance and features against market leaders or direct competitors.

Example: If there's a rising trend in integrating voice capabilities into chatbots, consider if this feature aligns with your user needs and business objectives.

Implementation Considerations:

1. **Stakeholder Collaboration**: Engage with various teams – customer support, IT, marketing – to gather diverse insights and feedback.

2. **User-Centric Approach**: Prioritize changes that enhance user experience and satisfaction.

3. **Technological Scalability**: Ensure the underlying technology and infrastructure can support the refinements and changes.

By continuously refining the strategy based on results, businesses can ensure that ChatGPT or any chatbot remains relevant, effective, and continues to provide value to both users and the organization.

Chapter 7: ChatGPT for Social Networking

Establishing a successful social network using ChatGPT can be a fascinating endeavor, given that it harnesses AI's capabilities to enrich users' interactions. Here's a step-by-step strategy to achieve this:

1. Define Your Niche: Identify a specific target audience or a unique selling proposition for your social network.

Example: A social network focused on connecting language learners with native speakers, using ChatGPT to facilitate real-time translations and language corrections.

2. Develop the MVP (Minimum Viable Product): Begin with a basic version of your platform. This includes:

- User registration and profile creation.

- Basic chat functionality with ChatGPT integration.

- Relevant features that cater to your niche.

3. ChatGPT Integration: Make sure you integrate ChatGPT in a way that enhances user experience.

Examples:

- For language learners, ChatGPT can correct grammar in real-time.

- For a business networking site, ChatGPT can provide industry news updates or brief users about specific industries during interactions.

4. Beta Testing: Before the full-scale launch, roll out your platform to a limited number of users to gather feedback and identify bugs.

5. Data Privacy & Security: Ensure that user data is protected. Inform users about the use of AI in chats and give them options to opt-out if needed. This builds trust and ensures GDPR and other data privacy regulations compliance.

6. Enhance UX/UI: Based on beta testing feedback, refine your user interface and experience to make it as intuitive and engaging as possible.

7. Launch & Promotion: Once you've refined your platform:

- Announce a launch date.

- Promote through relevant channels (e.g., language learning blogs for a language-focused network).

- Engage in partnerships to increase your user base.

8. Continuous Feedback Loop: Always engage with your users. Gather feedback, understand their needs, and make the necessary changes.

9. Monetization: After you've established a loyal user base:

- Introduce premium features (e.g., advanced language lessons, AI-based content suggestions).

- Consider ad placements, affiliate marketing, or partnerships with related businesses.

10. Expansion & Scaling: Look for opportunities to grow. This can be:

- Introducing new features.

- Expanding to new markets or demographics.

- Collaborating with educational institutions or businesses for a language-focused site.

11. Community Building: Foster a sense of community among users.

Examples:

- Host virtual events or challenges.

- Feature 'User of the Month' or success stories.

- Provide forums or groups for users to share their experiences.

12. Continuous AI Training: As user interactions grow, consider retraining or fine-tuning ChatGPT with the data (ensuring privacy) to improve its effectiveness and relevance.

13. Updates & Evolution: Stay updated with the latest AI advancements. Implement new features that benefit your platform and users.

14. Crisis Management: Be prepared for potential issues:

- Misunderstandings caused by ChatGPT.

- Data breaches or security threats.

- User conflicts.

Having a plan in place for such scenarios will help maintain your platform's reputation.

15. Review & Iterate: The digital landscape evolves rapidly. Regularly review your strategy, analyze user behavior and platform metrics, and make the necessary pivots.

By following these steps and focusing on your users' needs and the unique value proposition that ChatGPT integration can bring, you can establish a successful and engaging social network.

ChatGPT Prompts and Modules for Social Networking:

Define Your Niche:

Defining Your Niche is a crucial step in establishing any venture. Using ChatGPT effectively requires crafting complex prompts and modules that specifically cater to the chosen niche. Let's delve deeper:

Complex ChatGPT Prompts and Modules for "Define Your Niche":

1. Interactive Questionnaires for Niche Identification: *Module:* An AI-driven survey system that helps prospective social network founders to pinpoint their niche.

Example Prompt: "Please describe the primary audience you're hoping to target with your social network." Depending on the answer, ChatGPT can ask more in-depth questions, guiding the user towards a precise niche.

2. Analysis of Current Market Trends: *Module:* A system where ChatGPT pulls in (from pre-set datasets) and analyzes current trends in the social networking space.

Example Prompt "ChatGPT, provide an overview of the top trending niches in social networking for the last year."

3. SWOT Analysis Guidance: *Module:* Guiding users to perform a SWOT analysis (Strengths, Weaknesses, Opportunities, Threats) for their potential niche.

Example Prompt: "I'm considering a social network for pet lovers. Can you guide me through a SWOT analysis?"

4. Niche Validation: *Module:* Once a niche is proposed, ChatGPT can provide feedback on its potential viability by comparing it with available data or based on logic and trends.

Example Prompt: "I want to create a network for vintage car enthusiasts. What's your take on its potential success?"

5. Brainstorming Sessions: *Module:* A system to brainstorm related sub-niches or specific features that cater to the main niche.

Example Prompt: "I'm set on creating a platform for travel bloggers. Can we brainstorm specific features that would cater to them?"

6. Competitor Analysis: *Module:* ChatGPT could guide the user in identifying potential competitors in the chosen niche, even if not directly.

Example Prompt: "Given that my niche is 'sustainable living communities', who are the major players in this space?"

7. User Persona Creation: *Module:* Help users define potential user personas for their chosen niche.

Example Prompt: "For a social network focused on indie game developers, what might the user personas look like?"

8. Feedback Loop: *Module:* After defining a niche, use ChatGPT to collect and analyze feedback from a small target audience to refine the niche further.

Example Prompt: "I've gathered feedback from 50 potential users about 'a platform for remote workers to share co-working spaces'. Can you analyze and provide insights?"

By effectively utilizing these complex modules and prompts, one can not only define a precise niche for their social networking platform but also validate its potential, understand its challenges, and brainstorm ways to cater specifically to the intended audience. It's all about making informed decisions based on the intelligence and insights offered by tools like ChatGPT.

Develop the MVP (Minimum Viable Product):

Developing a Minimum Viable Product (MVP) is about creating a product with just enough features to be usable by early customers who can then provide feedback for future product development. Incorporating ChatGPT in the MVP development process can greatly enhance and streamline this stage. Let's look at detailed modules and prompts for this:

Complex ChatGPT Prompts and Modules for "Develop the MVP":

1. Feature Prioritization: *Module:* Use ChatGPT to help sort and prioritize the features based on their importance and feasibility.

Example Prompt: "Given these features: [list of features], which ones should be prioritized for a social network targeting digital artists?"

2. User Flow Mapping: *Module:* Use ChatGPT to design an ideal user flow, from sign-up to key interactions within the platform.

Example Prompt: "Help me design a user flow for a user signing up and posting their first artwork on our digital artists' platform."

3. Prototype Feedback: *Module:* After creating a basic prototype, ChatGPT can be used to simulate user interactions and provide feedback.

Example Prompt: "I've designed this [prototype link] for our fitness enthusiasts' social network. Can you provide feedback on user experience and potential pitfalls?"

4. Database Design Guidance: *Module:* ChatGPT can guide in designing the basic database structure, considering the chosen niche and features.

Example Prompt: "Considering our platform is for book lovers, how should we structure our database to manage user profiles, book reviews, and reading lists?"

5. Initial Content Creation: *Module:* If your platform relies on content (e.g., posts, articles), ChatGPT can help generate or suggest initial content to populate the platform.

Example Prompt: "We need introductory posts for our 'freelancer financial advice' social network. Can you generate three sample posts?"

6. User Onboarding Experience: *Module:* ChatGPT can assist in scripting an intuitive onboarding experience for new users.

Example Prompt: "Outline a step-by-step onboarding experience for new users joining our 'virtual reality enthusiasts' network."

7. Feature Explanation and Tutorials: *Module:* Create guided tutorials or explanations for features, leveraging ChatGPT's explanatory capabilities.

Example Prompt: "Can you explain how the 'collaborative design' feature would work on our platform for DIY crafters?"

8. Integration Testing Simulations: *Module:* Once features are developed, use ChatGPT to simulate integration tests, highlighting possible integration issues.

Example Prompt: "Given the feature set for our 'indie musician collaboration' platform, can you simulate a user journey and identify any integration pain points?"

9. Gathering Initial Feedback: *Module:* Implement a ChatGPT-driven feedback collection system for the initial set of users, categorizing and analyzing their feedback.

Example Prompt: "Analyze the feedback received from our beta testers for the 'home chefs network' and identify the top 3 areas for improvement."

10. Continuous Iteration: *Module:* Use ChatGPT to assist in regularly analyzing user behavior, feedback, and other data to suggest feature iterations.

Example Prompt: "Based on the usage stats of our 'travel bloggers platform', what features should we consider adding or refining in the next iteration?"

By using these modules and prompts, developers can harness ChatGPT's capabilities to drive MVP development more efficiently. Not only can they prioritize and refine features but also anticipate potential user needs, ensuring that the MVP resonates well with the target audience and has a smooth user experience.

ChatGPT Integration:

Integrating ChatGPT into a platform involves not just embedding the AI, but also making it a seamless part of the user experience. Depending on the niche and the nature of the platform, the way in which ChatGPT is integrated can vary widely. Here are some complex modules and prompts for the "ChatGPT Integration" phase:

Complex ChatGPT Prompts and Modules for "ChatGPT Integration":

1. Customization Based on User Profiles: *Module:* ChatGPT adjusts its responses based on user profiles, tailoring interactions according to user data.

Example Prompt: "Given user profile data of [Age: 25, Interests: Music, Coding], tailor the ChatGPT responses to match their interests."

2. Real-time User Assistance: *Module:* Use ChatGPT to help users navigate the platform, answering queries about features, or guiding them through tasks.

Example Prompt: "A user on our book exchange platform is struggling to list a book. Guide them through the process."

3. Content Enhancement: *Module:* ChatGPT aids in improving the quality of user-generated content by suggesting edits or providing additional information.

Example Prompt: "A user has written a review for 'The Great Gatsby'. Provide additional trivia or insights they might want to add."

4. Behavior-based Customization: *Module:* ChatGPT's interactions are adjusted based on a user's past behavior on the platform.

Example Prompt: "Given that a user frequently interacts with sci-fi content on our platform, tailor your responses to reflect a preference for sci-fi."

5. Multi-lingual Support: *Module:* ChatGPT translates or offers support in multiple languages to cater to a diverse user base.

Example Prompt: "Translate the following user query to Spanish: 'How do I change my profile picture?'"

6. Integration with Platform's Notification System: *Module:* ChatGPT sends personalized notifications or reminders to users based on their activities.

Example Prompt: "A user hasn't completed their profile on our professional networking platform. Send a reminder with tips on optimizing their profile."

7. Content Moderation: *Module:* ChatGPT aids in moderating user-generated content, flagging inappropriate content, or suggesting edits.

Example Prompt: "Review the following user post for any inappropriate content or language: 'I just watched this amazing movie!'"

8. Contextual Understanding: *Module:* ChatGPT recognizes the context of user interactions on the platform, offering more relevant responses.

Example Prompt: "Given the context that a user is on our 'recipe sharing page', provide suggestions for popular dessert recipes."

9. Feedback Collection: *Module:* ChatGPT facilitates feedback collection, asking users about their experiences or specific features.

Example Prompt: "Ask the user about their experience using our new 'virtual travel tour' feature and gather detailed feedback."

10. Tutorial and Learning Modules: *Module:* ChatGPT assists in teaching or guiding users, especially if the platform has educational components.

Example Prompt: "A user wants to learn about the basics of digital photography. Guide them through the key concepts."

By strategically integrating these modules and crafting detailed prompts, you ensure that ChatGPT doesn't just act as a separate tool on the platform but becomes an integral part of the user experience. Its potential is realized best when it can adapt, assist, and enhance user interactions seamlessly within the context of the platform's goals and user needs.

Beta Testing:

Beta testing is a critical phase in the development of any product or platform. It allows you to identify bugs, receive feedback, and make necessary refinements before a full-scale launch. Integrating ChatGPT can streamline this process, gather detailed feedback, and even simulate certain user interactions. Let's explore complex modules and prompts for the "Beta Testing" phase:

Complex ChatGPT Prompts and Modules for "Beta Testing":

1. User Simulation: *Module:* ChatGPT can be programmed to simulate a variety of user behaviors, aiding in initial stress and integration tests.

Example Prompt: "Simulate a user journey for a first-time visitor on our e-commerce platform, including browsing products, adding items to the cart, and initiating a checkout."

2. Feedback Collection: *Module:* Use ChatGPT to gather nuanced feedback from beta testers in real-time.

Example Prompt: "Ask beta testers about their experience navigating our new forum feature and if they found any elements confusing."

3. Bug Reporting Assistance: *Module:* ChatGPT aids beta testers in reporting bugs, ensuring that all necessary details are captured.

Example Prompt: "Guide the user in providing a detailed bug report for an issue they encountered with our video playback feature."

4. A/B Testing Analysis: *Module:* ChatGPT can assist in analyzing results from A/B tests, comparing different versions of a feature.

Example Prompt: "Given data from two layout variants of our landing page, analyze which had better user engagement and why."

5. Real-time Solution Suggestion: *Module:* If beta testers encounter common issues, ChatGPT can provide immediate troubleshooting solutions.

Example Prompt: "A user is having difficulty with the registration process. Provide step-by-step guidance to resolve common registration issues."

6. Feature Understanding Assessment: *Module:* ChatGPT quizzes beta testers on specific features to assess how intuitive they are.

Example Prompt: "Quiz the user on the functionalities of our new 'collaborative playlist' feature to see if they understood its purpose and usage."

7. Data Integrity Checks: *Module:* ChatGPT can be utilized to verify the integrity of user data after certain interactions.

Example Prompt: "Verify that user data remains consistent after they use our 'import contacts' feature."

8. Sentiment Analysis: *Module:* Analyze feedback to gauge user sentiment regarding the platform or specific features.

Example Prompt: "Analyze beta tester feedback comments to determine overall sentiment towards our redesigned user interface."

9. Suggestion Aggregation: *Module:* ChatGPT groups and categorizes feedback and suggestions, highlighting the most common or critical ones.

Example Prompt: "From the feedback received, list the top 5 most frequently suggested improvements for our messaging system."

10. Documentation and FAQs: *Module:* Based on beta tester interactions and queries, ChatGPT can assist in creating documentation, FAQs, or help articles.

Example Prompt: "Generate a FAQ section based on the most common questions asked by beta testers about our calendar integration."

Incorporating these modules and prompts during the beta testing phase can not only make the process more efficient but can also extract more actionable insights from the feedback and interactions of beta testers. This ensures that the platform is more refined, user-friendly, and robust when it proceeds to a full-scale launch.

Data Privacy & Security:

Ensuring data privacy and security is of utmost importance, especially when integrating AI models like ChatGPT. Here's a detailed exploration of the modules and prompts related to "Data Privacy & Security":

Complex ChatGPT Prompts and Modules for "Data Privacy & Security":

1. User Consent Verification: *Module:* Before ChatGPT accesses or processes any user-specific data, it verifies and logs the user's consent.

Example Prompt: "Before we proceed, do you give consent for ChatGPT to access your profile data for a personalized experience? (Yes/No)"

2. Data Masking and Anonymization: *Module:* ChatGPT anonymizes user information and interactions to prevent any personally identifiable information (PII) from being stored or used inappropriately.

Example Prompt: "I noticed you mentioned your email in the previous message. For security reasons, this information has been redacted."

3. GDPR and CCPA Adherence: *Module:* ChatGPT provides information on user rights and assists with requests concerning data protection regulations like GDPR or CCPA.

Example Prompt: "Would you like to know more about how we handle your data under GDPR guidelines or request data deletion?"

4. Data Retention Policy: *Module:* ChatGPT informs users about how long their data is stored and offers options for data deletion.

Example Prompt: "Our platform retains user chat logs for 30 days for quality purposes. If you'd like to delete this chat immediately after ending, please let us know."

5. Encrypted Data Transmission: *Module:* Ensure that any data transferred between ChatGPT and the platform is encrypted. Although this process occurs in the backend, users can be informed about it.

Example Prompt: "Rest assured, all interactions with ChatGPT are encrypted for your security."

6. Monitoring Suspicious Activities: *Module:* ChatGPT can be trained to recognize and alert users or administrators about potential phishing attempts or malicious links.

Example Prompt: "The link you've shared seems suspicious and might be harmful. For safety, please refrain from sharing or clicking such links."

7. User Data Access Logs: *Module:* Maintain logs of when and how ChatGPT accessed user data, ensuring transparency.

Example Prompt: "Would you like a log of all instances when ChatGPT accessed your data during this session?"

8. Opt-Out and Data Control: *Module:* Users can easily opt-out from ChatGPT accessing their data or any personalized features.

Example Prompt: "If at any point you wish for ChatGPT to stop using your data for customization, just type 'Opt-out', and your preferences will be respected."

9. Regular Security Audits: *Module:* Periodically remind administrators or developers to conduct security audits and check for potential vulnerabilities.

Example Prompt for Admins: "It's been three months since the last security audit. We recommend conducting an audit soon to ensure data protection measures are intact."

10. Continuous Learning and Updates: *Module:* ChatGPT, while not directly responsible for software updates, can remind users/admins about the importance of keeping all software up to date for security reasons.

Example Prompt: "Keeping software up-to-date is crucial for security. Ensure all associated platforms and interfaces with ChatGPT are regularly updated."

By integrating these modules and prompts, platform owners can uphold the highest standards of data privacy and security. It's essential to continually review and update these measures, especially as technology and regulations evolve.

Enhance UX/U:

Enhancing User Experience (UX) and User Interface (UI) is pivotal to the success of any digital product. ChatGPT can play a vital role in gathering insights, providing real-time assistance, and optimizing user interactions. Here's a deep dive into the modules and prompts tailored for "Enhance UX/UI":

Complex ChatGPT Prompts and Modules for "Enhance UX/UI":

1. Real-time Feedback Collection: *Module:* As users navigate the platform, ChatGPT can solicit real-time feedback about their experience.

Example Prompt: "How would you rate your experience with our new dashboard layout on a scale of 1-10?"

2. Interface Navigation Assistance: *Module:* ChatGPT aids users in finding features or understanding UI elements.

Example Prompt: "I'm here to help! If you're looking for the settings, click on the gear icon in the top right corner."

3. A/B Testing Feedback: *Module:* When A/B testing different UI elements, ChatGPT can gather detailed feedback from users about their preferences.

Example Prompt: "Which version of our homepage do you prefer: the one with the large banner or the one with segmented categories?"

4. Error Troubleshooting: *Module:* When users encounter errors or UI glitches, ChatGPT can provide immediate solutions or alternative actions.

Example Prompt: "It seems you're having trouble loading the images. Try refreshing the page or check your internet connection."

5. Accessibility Recommendations: *Module:* ChatGPT can provide accessibility suggestions to users, such as enabling a dark mode or increasing font size.

Example Prompt: "Do you want to enable 'High Contrast Mode' for better visibility?"

6. Personalized UI Suggestions: *Module:* Based on user behavior and preferences, ChatGPT can suggest UI customizations.

Example Prompt: "I've noticed you frequently use the 'collaborate' feature. Would you like to add it to your main toolbar for quicker access?"

7. Onboarding Experience Enhancement: *Module:* ChatGPT can guide new users through platform features, ensuring they understand the platform's functionalities.

Example Prompt: "Welcome aboard! Let's take a quick tour of the main features. Ready to start?"

8. Intuitive Search Assistance: *Module:* When users are looking for something specific, ChatGPT can assist in refining search queries or directing them to the relevant sections.

Example Prompt: "Looking for vintage posters? Head to our 'Art & Collectibles' section or try searching with the keywords 'vintage art prints'."

9. Usability Testing Assistance: *Module:* ChatGPT can guide selected users through specific tasks to test usability, collecting feedback after each task.

Example Prompt: "For our usability test, please try creating a new playlist. Once done, share your experience about the process."

10. User Behavior Analysis: *Module:* By analyzing user interactions and dwell times (while ensuring privacy), ChatGPT can suggest UI improvements to administrators.

Example Prompt for Admins: "Users seem to spend a lot of time on the 'Profile' page, but many don't complete their profiles. Consider simplifying the profile creation process."

Incorporating these prompts and modules ensures that users not only find the platform easy and intuitive to use but also feel that their feedback is valued, leading to continuous UX/UI improvements. The integration of ChatGPT in this aspect bridges the gap between users and developers, making refinements more targeted and efficient.

Launch & Promotion:

Launching and promoting a new product, especially a digital platform, is a multi-faceted process. Utilizing ChatGPT can provide unique ways to generate buzz, gather insights, and streamline user interactions. Here's an in-depth look at the modules and prompts geared towards "Launch & Promotion":

Complex ChatGPT Prompts and Modules for "Launch & Promotion":

1. Event Registration & Reminders: *Module:* Use ChatGPT to facilitate registration for launch events or webinars and send reminders.

Example Prompt: "Would you like to attend our launch event on the 15th? Register now and I'll send you a reminder a day before."

2. Promotion Explanation: *Module:* ChatGPT explains ongoing promotions, offers, or early bird benefits to users.

Example Prompt: "Hello! As part of our launch, the first 100 sign-ups get a premium subscription for a month. Would you like more details?"

3. Feedback on Marketing Materials: *Module:* ChatGPT can solicit feedback on promotional content, ads, or trailers.

Example Prompt: "We've just released our launch trailer. Watch it [here]. What are your thoughts on it?"

4. Referral Program Assistance: *Module:* ChatGPT guides users through referral programs, explaining benefits and processes.

Example Prompt: "Refer a friend and both of you get extra storage space. Would you like to know how to refer?"

5. Social Media Engagement: *Module:* ChatGPT can provide updates on social media campaigns or encourage users to engage with posts for greater visibility.

Example Prompt: "Have you seen our latest post on Twitter? Engage with it to help spread the word!"

6. Survey on Promotion Effectiveness: *Module:* ChatGPT conducts surveys to understand which promotional channels are most effective.

Example Prompt: "How did you hear about us? a) Social Media b) Search Engine c) Friend's Recommendation d) Other"

7. Launch Special Features or Easter Eggs: *Module:* Introduce unique features or "easter eggs" during launch as a promotional tactic and use ChatGPT to hint or guide users towards them.

Example Prompt: "Want a hint about a special feature? Try shaking your device when on the homepage!"

8. Collaborations & Partnerships Announcements: *Module:* ChatGPT can inform users about collaborations, partnerships, or endorsements relevant to the launch.

Example Prompt: "Exciting news! We've partnered with [Brand Name] for exclusive content. Stay tuned!"

9. User-generated Content Promotions: *Module:* Encourage users to create and share content related to the platform, offering incentives or features in return.

Example Prompt: "Share your experience with our platform using #OurLaunchDay and stand a chance to win exclusive merchandise."

10. Post-Launch Analysis: *Module:* After the initial promotion period, ChatGPT assists in gathering data on the success of different promotional strategies.

Example Prompt for Admins: "Based on user interactions, the email campaign had a 15% conversion rate, while the social media ads had a 7% conversion rate."

By integrating these prompts and modules during the "Launch & Promotion" phase, platform creators can ensure they're engaging their audience effectively, gauging the success of their strategies, and swiftly adapting to feedback. ChatGPT can not only enhance user experience but also provide actionable insights for further promotional activities.

Continuous Feedback Loop:

Establishing a continuous feedback loop is essential to iterative development and ensuring that your platform stays aligned with user needs and expectations. ChatGPT can be a vital tool in facilitating this loop, given its capabilities to engage in real-time dialogue. Here's a breakdown for "Continuous Feedback Loop":

Complex ChatGPT Prompts and Modules for "Continuous Feedback Loop":

1. Periodic User Satisfaction Surveys: *Module:* ChatGPT can prompt users at regular intervals to rate their experience or provide feedback.

Example Prompt: "On a scale of 1-10, how satisfied are you with the recent updates to our platform?"

2. Feature-specific Feedback: *Module:* After users engage with a newly released feature, ChatGPT can solicit feedback specifically about that feature.

Example Prompt: "I noticed you tried out our new 'Collaboration Tool'. How was your experience? Any suggestions for improvement?"

3. Issue Reporting: *Module:* ChatGPT facilitates users to report bugs, glitches, or any issues they face.

Example Prompt: "Sorry to hear you're facing an issue. Can you describe the problem so we can help resolve it?"

4. Feedback Tagging and Categorization: *Module:* As feedback is received, ChatGPT automatically categorizes and tags it for easier analysis by the development team.

Example Prompt: "Thank you for your feedback on the 'Chat Interface'. We've tagged it under 'UI/UX Feedback'. Our team will review it soon."

5. Idea Solicitation: *Module:* Encourage users to provide suggestions or ideas for future features or improvements.

Example Prompt: "We're always looking to improve! Do you have any feature suggestions or ideas you'd like to see in the next update?"

6. Real-time User Assistance based on Feedback: *Module:* If users provide feedback about difficulties or confusion, ChatGPT can offer immediate guidance.

Example Prompt: "You mentioned difficulty with the 'Search' function. Would you like a quick tutorial on how to use it effectively?"

7. Feedback Incentivization: *Module:* Encourage detailed feedback by offering incentives or rewards for comprehensive reviews.

Example Prompt: "Thank you for your feedback! As a token of appreciation, here's a 10% discount for your next subscription month."

8. User Journey Analysis: *Module:* ChatGPT can ask users about their typical journey or use-case scenarios, providing insights into user behavior and needs.

Example Prompt: "Can you describe your typical process when using our platform? Understanding your journey helps us improve."

9. Change Log Communication: *Module:* Whenever there are updates or changes based on previous feedback, ChatGPT can inform users, emphasizing the value of their input.

Example Prompt: "Good news! Based on user feedback, we've made updates to the 'Notifications' feature. Check it out and let us know your thoughts."

10. Feedback Appreciation and User Engagement: *Module:* Always express gratitude for feedback and engage users in the platform's development journey.

Example Prompt: "Your feedback has been invaluable in our recent update. Thank you for helping shape our platform! We hope you enjoy the improvements."

Incorporating these modules and prompts fosters a sense of collaboration and trust between users and developers. Users feel heard and valued, leading to increased loyalty, while developers gain crucial insights to continually refine and enhance the platform.

Monetization:

Monetization is a key aspect of ensuring sustainability and profitability for digital platforms, especially those offering services for free or at a subsidized rate initially. Integrating ChatGPT can streamline monetization efforts by educating users, promoting premium services, and facilitating transactions. Let's dive into the modules and prompts for "Monetization":

Complex ChatGPT Prompts and Modules for "Monetization":

1. Premium Feature Promotion: *Module:* ChatGPT introduces and promotes premium features to users, highlighting their benefits.

Example Prompt: "Have you tried our premium 'Advanced Analytics' feature? It offers deeper insights into your data. Would you like a free trial?"

2. Subscription Renewal Reminders: *Module:* ChatGPT reminds users of upcoming subscription renewals, offering seamless renewal options.

Example Prompt: "Your premium subscription expires in 7 days. Renew now and get a 10% discount!"

3. Upselling and Cross-selling: *Module:* Based on user behavior, ChatGPT can suggest related premium services or products.

Example Prompt: "Given your frequent use of our 'Image Editor', you might benefit from our 'Pro Image Toolkit'. Interested in upgrading?"

4. Advertisement Interaction: *Module:* If the platform uses ads for monetization, ChatGPT can encourage users to engage with these ads or provide feedback.

Example Prompt: "Please check out this ad from our partner. Let us know your thoughts and earn 50 bonus points!"

5. Referral Programs: *Module:* Promote referral programs, explaining benefits and guiding users on how to refer and earn.

Example Prompt: "Invite friends to our platform and for each successful referral, both you and your friend get a month of premium access for free!"

6. In-app Purchases Assistance: *Module:* ChatGPT can guide users through in-app purchase processes, ensuring smooth transactions.

Example Prompt: "Looking to purchase additional storage space? Let me guide you through the process."

7. Feedback on Pricing Models: *Module:* Solicit user feedback regarding pricing, packages, or any monetary aspects to optimize pricing strategies.

Example Prompt: "How do you feel about our current subscription pricing? Do you believe it offers good value for the features provided?"

8. Exclusive Deals and Promotions: *Module:* ChatGPT can notify users about exclusive deals, discounts, or promotions related to premium services.

Example Prompt: "Exclusive deal alert! Upgrade to our yearly subscription today and get 3 months extra for free."

9. Affiliate Product Recommendations: *Module:* If the platform has affiliate partnerships, ChatGPT can recommend related products, earning commission on successful referrals.

Example Prompt: "Based on your interests, you might like this book from our affiliate partner. Check it out [link] and enjoy a special discount."

10. Microtransaction Encouragements: *Module:* For platforms relying on microtransactions (like game platforms), ChatGPT can promote in-game items or limited-time offers.

Example Prompt: "Limited time offer! Purchase the exclusive 'Golden Armor' for your character at a 20% discount now."

Using these modules and prompts ensures that monetization efforts are seamlessly integrated into the user experience without being overly intrusive. By providing value, clear benefits, and facilitating smooth transactions, ChatGPT can play a significant role in optimizing the revenue streams of a digital platform.

Expansion & Scaling:

Expansion and scaling are critical phases for a successful platform or service. It's about growing your user base, entering new markets, or offering new features. Integrating ChatGPT into this phase can assist in gathering market insights, facilitating new feature rollouts, and enhancing user onboarding in new territories. Here's a breakdown for "Expansion & Scaling":

Complex ChatGPT Prompts and Modules for "Expansion & Scaling":

1. Market Research Surveys: *Module:* ChatGPT conducts surveys to understand user preferences in potential markets or regions.

Example Prompt: "We're considering expanding to Southeast Asia. How often do you use digital platforms for shopping in this region?"

2. Language and Localization Assistance: *Module:* As you enter new territories, ChatGPT aids in translations and provides information respecting local customs and nuances.

Example Prompt: "Welcome! Would you prefer assistance in English or Spanish? ¡Hola! ¿Prefieres asistencia en inglés o español?"

3. New Feature Testing: *Module:* ChatGPT introduces and gathers feedback on new features tailored for specific markets.

Example Prompt: "We've introduced a 'Group Collaboration' feature, specially designed for team projects. Try it out and share your feedback!"

4. User Education in New Markets: *Module:* ChatGPT educates new users about platform functionalities, ensuring smooth onboarding in new regions.

Example Prompt: "Welcome to our platform! Let's take a quick tour to get you started. Are you ready?"

5. Collaboration and Partnership Announcements: *Module:* ChatGPT informs users about collaborations or partnerships that are part of the expansion strategy.

Example Prompt: "Exciting news! We've partnered with [Local Brand] to offer you exclusive content and deals. Check them out!"

6. Cultural Nuance Guidance: *Module:* As you scale, ChatGPT can provide insights and guidelines about cultural nuances to ensure respectful and effective communication.

Example Prompt: "In Japan, it's customary to address users with their last name followed by '-san'. Ensure your communications respect this norm."

7. Feedback on Expansion Efforts: *Module:* Solicit user feedback regarding the platform's performance and user experience in newly entered markets.

Example Prompt: "We've recently launched in Brazil. How has your experience been with our platform in this region?"

8. Scaling Support Systems: *Module:* As the user base grows, ChatGPT can provide real-time support, reducing the load on human customer support teams.

Example Prompt: "Facing an issue? Describe your problem, and I'll do my best to assist you immediately."

9. Promote Regional Features or Offers: *Module:* ChatGPT promotes features, offers, or content specifically designed for a particular region.

Example Prompt: "For our users in Australia, we've introduced local news updates. Click here to activate this feature."

10. Resource Allocation Insights: *Module:* Based on user interactions, ChatGPT can provide insights on where to allocate resources during expansion.

Example Prompt for Admins: "Considering user interactions, it's advisable to increase server capacities in Eastern Europe due to increased traffic."

Incorporating these prompts and modules during the "Expansion & Scaling" phase can ensure that growth is managed effectively, with user experience remaining at the forefront. Tailoring interactions to cater to specific regions and understanding their unique needs is pivotal, and tools like ChatGPT can play a significant role in this endeavor.

Community Building:

Community building is a cornerstone for platforms that thrive on user interaction, content generation, and shared experiences. A strong, engaged community can be a huge asset, promoting organic growth, fostering loyalty, and providing valuable feedback. Leveraging ChatGPT can significantly assist in community management, growth, and engagement. Here's a breakdown for "Community Building":

Complex ChatGPT Prompts and Modules for "Community Building":

1. Community Onboarding: *Module:* Use ChatGPT to welcome new members and guide them through community norms, guidelines, and features.

Example Prompt: "Welcome to our community! Let me guide you through our community guidelines and introduce you to some popular discussion threads."

2. Moderation Assistance: *Module:* ChatGPT can aid moderators by flagging inappropriate content or behaviors based on community guidelines.

Example Prompt: "This comment seems to violate our community guidelines. Moderators have been notified."

3. Community Event Promotion: *Module:* Use ChatGPT to notify users of upcoming community events, AMAs, webinars, or meetups.

Example Prompt: "Reminder: Our monthly community meetup is this Friday. Click here to RSVP!"

4. User Recognition & Rewards: *Module:* Recognize active users or contributors and inform them about rewards or badges they've earned.

Example Prompt: "Congratulations! You've been recognized as a 'Top Contributor' this month. Thank you for your valuable insights!"

5. Facilitate User Interaction: *Module:* Encourage users to engage in discussions, respond to polls, or participate in community challenges.

Example Prompt: "Our 'Photo of the Month' challenge is on! Share your best shot and get a chance to be featured."

6. Community Feedback Collection: *Module:* Solicit feedback on community features, events, or guidelines.

Example Prompt: "How did you find our recent AMA session with [Guest Name]? Your feedback helps us organize better events."

7. Promote Community-Centric Features: *Module:* Introduce and promote features that foster community interactions, like group chats, collaborative boards, or shared playlists.

Example Prompt: "Have you tried our new 'Group Discussion' feature? It's a space to deep dive into topics with like-minded members."

8. Address Community Concerns: *Module:* ChatGPT can provide real-time responses to common community concerns or questions, ensuring members feel heard and valued.

Example Prompt: "Concerned about privacy? Here's how our community ensures your data is protected."

9. Spotlight Community Content: *Module:* Periodically spotlight or highlight high-quality content or contributions from community members.

Example Prompt: "Check out this insightful article by [User Name], one of our community members. It's a must-read!"

10. Cultivate Community Ambassadors: *Module:* Identify and engage active or influential members, encouraging them to take on ambassador or mentor roles.

Example Prompt: "Your contributions have been outstanding! Interested in becoming a community ambassador? Here's what it entails."

Utilizing these modules and prompts, platforms can foster a sense of belonging, respect, and mutual growth among community members. By actively facilitating interactions, recognizing contributions, and addressing concerns, ChatGPT can play a pivotal role in nurturing vibrant, engaged, and loyal communities.

Continuous AI Training:

The efficiency and effectiveness of AI platforms, like ChatGPT, depend on their ability to learn continuously. This involves processing new information, adapting to changing user behavior, and refining responses. Given that AI models can't learn in real-time from individual interactions (to maintain user privacy and data security), they need structured mechanisms to integrate new learning. Let's dive deep into the "Continuous AI Training" phase:

Complex ChatGPT Prompts and Modules for "Continuous AI Training":

1. Feedback on AI Responses: *Module:* After ChatGPT provides a response, users can be prompted to rate the relevance or accuracy of its answer.

Example Prompt: "Was this response helpful? Rate on a scale from 1-5."

2. Scenario-based Training: *Module:* Users can be presented with hypothetical or real-world scenarios to gauge AI's approach to diverse situations.

Example Prompt: "Imagine you're a tourist in Paris. Ask me any questions you might have about your trip!"

3. Data Augmentation Queries: *Module:* Generate prompts that encourage users to provide diverse answers, enhancing the model's understanding of varied expressions.

Example Prompt: "In your own words, how do you describe a 'sunset'?"

4. Addressing Edge Cases: *Module:* Periodically test the AI with edge cases or lesser-known queries to improve its handling of outliers.

Example Prompt for Admins/Developers: "Test Query: Explain the concept of 'quantum entanglement' in three sentences."

5. Multimodal Training Enhancements: *Module:* If ChatGPT or the AI model integrates other modalities (like images or sound), prompts can be crafted for training on these.

Example Prompt: "Describe the emotions conveyed in this [linked image]."

6. Handling Ambiguous Queries: *Module:* Train the AI to handle ambiguity better by prompting it with vague questions and refining its clarifying responses

Example Prompt: "What's the capital?" [Follow-up Training Prompt: "Can you specify the country you're referring to?"]

7. Cultural and Localized Training: *Module:* As the platform expands globally, train the AI on local cultures, slangs, and nuances.

Example Prompt: "Explain the significance of 'Diwali' in India."

8. Continuous Evaluation Metrics: *Module:* Regularly evaluate the AI's performance based on accuracy, response time, and user satisfaction metrics.

Example Prompt for Admins: "Generate a monthly report detailing the model's accuracy and areas of improvement."

9. Bias Detection and Correction: *Module:* Incorporate prompts to detect any unintentional biases in the AI's responses and refine them.

Example Prompt: "Describe the role of women in tech." [Ensure the response is unbiased and factual.]

10. Advanced Feature Integration Feedback: *Module:* As new features or integrations are added to the AI, solicit feedback specifically about them.

Example Prompt: "We've introduced a feature where you can ask for book recommendations. Try it out and let us know your thoughts."

Incorporating these modules and prompts ensures that the AI model remains dynamic, evolving, and most importantly, relevant to the changing needs and diversities of its user base. Continuous training isn't just about refining the AI but ensuring that it understands and respects the wide spectrum of its users, their cultures, and their contexts.

Updates & Evolution:

The lifecycle of any digital platform, especially one that's AI-driven, doesn't end after its initial launch or even after a series of iterations. Regular updates and evolution are crucial to stay relevant, effective, and aligned with user needs. With the integration of ChatGPT, the process can be more seamless, ensuring users are always in the loop and their feedback is integrated. Here's a breakdown for "Updates & Evolution":

Complex ChatGPT Prompts and Modules for "Updates & Evolution":

1. Change Log Notifications: *Module:* Whenever there's an update or a change, ChatGPT can proactively inform users about what's new or different.

Example Prompt: "We've recently updated our platform! Here are the latest features and improvements you can expect..."

2. Feedback on New Features: *Module:* Post updates, actively solicit user feedback on the newly introduced features or changes.

Example Prompt: "Have you tried our new 'Interactive Dashboard'? We'd love to hear your thoughts and any suggestions for improvement!"

3. User Adaptation Guidance: *Module:* As features evolve or change, ChatGPT aids in ensuring users can smoothly adapt, guiding them through any changes.

Example Prompt: "I noticed you're trying the old method to share a file. Let me guide you through our new and improved sharing process."

4. A/B Testing Engagement: *Module:* When testing new features or changes, ChatGPT can engage users in A/B tests, gauging preferences.

Example Prompt: "We're testing two different interfaces for our homepage. Would you like to try the new design and provide feedback?"

5. Deprecated Feature Notifications: *Module:* Inform users about features that are being deprecated or replaced, ensuring they're not caught off-guard.

Example Prompt: "Heads up! The 'Classic Editor' will be phased out next month. Here's how to transition to our new editing experience."

6. Evolution Surveys: *Module:* Periodically engage users in surveys about the platform's evolution, gathering insights on future development directions.

Example Prompt: "Where would you like to see our platform in the next year? Your insights shape our evolution. Please fill out this quick survey."

7. Proactive Problem Solving: *Module:* If an update introduces unforeseen issues, ChatGPT can offer immediate solutions or workarounds.

Example Prompt: "It seems there's a bug with the new update causing slow loading. While we fix it, try clearing your cache as a temporary solution."

8. Promoting Evolution Milestones: *Module:* Celebrate and inform users about milestones, such as platform anniversaries or major update rollouts.

Example Prompt: "It's our 5th anniversary! Here's a look at how our platform has evolved and what's coming next."

9. Continuous Learning Opportunities: *Module:* Offer users tutorials, webinars, or learning resources to understand the platform's evolving features better.

Example Prompt: "Join our webinar next week to deep dive into all the new features we introduced this month."

10. Integration of External Feedback: *Module:* Showcase how feedback from external platforms (like review sites or social media) has been integrated into updates.

Example Prompt: "Based on popular feedback on [ReviewSite], we've enhanced our search functionality. Try it out!"

By incorporating these modules and prompts, platforms can ensure that the evolution of their services or features is a collaborative process with their user base. It fosters trust, reduces friction during transitions, and most importantly, ensures that the platform remains user-centric throughout its lifecycle.

Crisis Management:

Crisis management is essential for businesses to maintain trust, prevent significant brand damage, and ensure the wellbeing of their stakeholders. Digital platforms are not exempt from crises, which could range from data breaches to misinformation spread. Incorporating ChatGPT can provide immediate, clear, and consistent responses during such situations. Here's an in-depth look into the "Crisis Management" phase:

Complex ChatGPT Prompts and Modules for "Crisis Management":

1. Immediate Notification: *Module:* In the event of a crisis, ChatGPT can inform users immediately, providing essential details.

Example Prompt: "We're aware of a technical issue causing slow platform responses. Our team is actively working on a resolution. We appreciate your patience."

2. FAQ During Crises: *Module:* ChatGPT can offer real-time answers to commonly asked questions during a crisis, ensuring users have accurate information.

Example Prompt: "If you have questions about the recent data incident, please ask. We're here to provide clarity."

3. Directing to Official Statements: *Module:* Point users to official press releases, statements, or information hubs detailing the nature of the crisis and the steps taken.

Example Prompt: "For detailed information on our recent security update, please read our official statement [here]."

4. Misinformation Correction: *Module:* Actively correct any misinformation or misconceptions that may arise during a crisis.

Example Prompt: "Contrary to some circulating information, no personal data was accessed during the recent incident. Please refer to our official channels for accurate updates."

5. Regular Updates: *Module:* Continuously update users on the status of the crisis resolution.

Example Prompt: "Update on the technical issue: We've identified the cause and are expecting a resolution within the next 2 hours."

6. User Guidance on Protective Actions: *Module:* If a crisis demands user action (e.g., during a data breach), ChatGPT can guide users on protective steps.

Example Prompt: "For safety, we recommend changing your password and enabling two-factor authentication. Click here for a step-by-step guide."

7. Gathering User Concerns: *Module:* Actively solicit user concerns or questions related to the crisis to ensure they feel heard and supported.

Example Prompt: "We understand this is concerning. Please let us know if you have any specific questions or worries, and we'll address them."

8. Rebuilding Trust: *Module:* Post-crisis, engage with users to rebuild trust, informing them of preventive measures taken for the future.

Example Prompt: "We've taken rigorous steps to prevent future incidents, including [specific measure]. Your trust is paramount to us."

9. Crisis Feedback Collection: *Module:* Gather feedback on how the crisis was managed, ensuring continuous improvement in crisis response.

Example Prompt: "We value your feedback. How do you feel about our response to the recent situation? Your input helps us serve you better."

10. Escalation Channels: *Module:* If users need immediate human intervention or further clarification, ChatGPT can escalate or direct them to appropriate channels.

Example Prompt: "If you'd like to discuss this matter further with our support team, click here, and we'll connect you immediately."

Integrating these modules and prompts ensures that during a crisis, users receive timely, accurate, and clear information. Addressing concerns proactively and transparently can help in reducing panic, maintaining trust, and ensuring the platform's reputation remains intact even during challenging situations.

Review & Iterate:

Review & Iterate is an integral phase in the lifecycle of digital platforms and services. Continuous improvement is achieved by assessing current performance, gathering feedback, and then refining features or strategies based on this feedback. Leveraging ChatGPT in this process can offer valuable insights and facilitate seamless iteration. Here's a detailed breakdown for "Review & Iterate":

Complex ChatGPT Prompts and Modules for "Review & Iterate":

1. Periodic Review Reminders: *Module:* Remind platform administrators or team members to conduct regular reviews of platform performance and user feedback.

Example Prompt for Admins: "It's been a month since the last platform review. Consider conducting a comprehensive assessment to ensure optimal performance."

2. User Satisfaction Surveys: *Module:* ChatGPT initiates surveys post-interactions or at regular intervals to gauge user satisfaction.

Example Prompt: "On a scale of 1-10, how satisfied are you with our latest feature update?"

3. Detailed Feedback Collection: *Module:* Dive deeper into specific areas by soliciting detailed feedback from users.

Example Prompt: "You mentioned some concerns with our new interface. Could you elaborate on what improvements you'd like to see?"

4. Performance Metric Analysis: *Module:* For platform administrators, offer insights into user interactions, dwell times, and other metrics to assist in reviews.

Example Prompt for Admins: "User engagement time on the 'Profile' page has decreased by 15% since the last update. It might warrant a closer look."

5. A/B Testing Feedback: *Module:* After A/B testing sessions, ChatGPT can gather detailed feedback to inform which version to finalize.

Example Prompt: "We're testing two layouts for our homepage. Which do you prefer, and why?"

6. Change Impact Analysis: *Module:* Post major updates or changes, solicit feedback to analyze the impact of these changes on the user experience.

Example Prompt: "We recently revamped our notification system. Have you noticed a positive difference in your experience?"

7. Iteration Suggestions: *Module:* Encourage users to provide suggestions on how existing features or content can be improved.

Example Prompt: "We're planning the next update for our chat feature. Do you have any suggestions for enhancements?"

8. Error and Bug Reports: *Module:* Make it easier for users to report any errors, bugs, or issues they encounter, thereby helping in iterative refinements.

Example Prompt: "Experiencing any glitches? Describe the issue, and we'll work on resolving it."

9. Comparative Feedback: *Module:* Gather feedback comparing the current version of a feature or platform with previous iterations.

Example Prompt: "Compared to our previous design, how do you rate our new homepage layout?"

10. Implementation Feedback: *Module:* After iterating based on feedback, reach out to users to understand how well the changes have been received.

Example Prompt: "You previously suggested improvements to our search function. We've made some updates based on feedback. How do you find it now?"

Incorporating these modules and prompts ensures that the iterative process is user-centric, and the platform continually evolves in alignment with user needs and expectations. The aim is to make each iteration better than the last, and tools like ChatGPT can play a crucial role in gathering insights and guiding improvements.

Chapter 8: ChatGPT for Search Engine Optimization (SEO)

Utilizing ChatGPT for SEO optimization can be a strategic move, especially given the capabilities of the model in generating quality, relevant content, and answering diverse questions. Below is a step-by-step strategy to establish successful SEO optimization using ChatGPT:

1. **Keyword Research:**

   - Start by identifying target keywords for your website. Tools like Google's Keyword Planner, SEMrush, or Ahrefs can help.

   - **ChatGPT Example:** Ask ChatGPT, "What are some trending keywords for organic skincare in 2023?" or "Suggest some long-tail keywords for digital marketing courses."

2. **Content Creation:**

   - Once you've identified keywords, generate quality content around them. Remember, content should not only be keyword-focused but also provide genuine value to readers.

   - **ChatGPT Example:** "Write a 500-word article on the benefits of organic skincare in 2023."

3. **Meta Descriptions and Titles:**

   - Create compelling meta titles and descriptions for your content.

   - **ChatGPT Example:** "Suggest a meta title and description for an article about the benefits of organic skincare."

4. **Content Updates:**

   - SEO isn't a one-time task. Regularly update content to keep it relevant and fresh.

   - **ChatGPT Example:** "Review this article and suggest updates for current SEO trends."

5. **Link Building:**

   - Generate ideas for guest posting, collaborations, or other link-building strategies.

   - **ChatGPT Example:** "List some potential websites where I can guest post about organic skincare."

6. **On-Page SEO Optimization:**

   - This involves optimizing individual pages for SEO, which includes header tags, image alt tags, internal linking, etc.

   - **ChatGPT Example:** "Review this webpage's content and suggest on-page SEO improvements."

7. **Technical SEO:**

   - Make sure your site loads quickly, is mobile-friendly, and has an XML sitemap, among other technical aspects.

   - **ChatGPT Example:** "List technical SEO best practices for an e-commerce website."

8. **Local SEO (if applicable):**

   - Optimize for local search if you have a physical location or serve a specific geographic area.

   - **ChatGPT Example:** "Provide tips for optimizing a bakery's website for local SEO."

9. **Voice Search Optimization:**

   - As voice searches become more common, optimize content to answer voice search queries.

   - **ChatGPT Example:** "How can I optimize my content for voice search?"

10. **Monitor and Analyze:**

- Use tools like Google Analytics and Google Search Console to monitor website traffic, rankings, and user behavior.

- **ChatGPT Example:** "List key performance indicators for SEO I should monitor regularly."

11. **Iterate and Improve:**

- Based on the analysis, make necessary changes, and keep improving.

- **ChatGPT Example:** "Suggest ways to improve organic traffic for a website that sells digital courses."

12. **Stay Updated:**

- SEO trends change frequently. Always stay updated with the latest trends and algorithms.

- **ChatGPT Example:** "What are the latest SEO trends and updates for 2023?"

By using ChatGPT in conjunction with your SEO strategy, you can ensure that your content remains fresh, relevant, and optimized for search engines. Remember to maintain ethical standards and not to over-optimize or spam, as quality and authenticity are crucial for lasting SEO success.

ChatGPT Prompts, Formulas and Modules for SEO: Keyword Research:

keyword research is fundamental in SEO, and having advanced prompts for ChatGPT can be beneficial. Here's a deeper dive into complex prompts, formulas, and modules for keyword research using ChatGPT:

1. Detailed Keyword Ideas:

Prompt: "Provide detailed keyword ideas for [Topic/Niche]." **Example:** "Provide detailed keyword ideas for vegan footwear."

Output:

- vegan leather shoes

- sustainable footwear

- cruelty-free shoes

- eco-friendly sneakers

- vegan shoe brands

2. Long-tail Keyword Suggestions:

Prompt: "Suggest long-tail keywords related to [Seed Keyword]."
Example: "Suggest long-tail keywords related to digital marketing."

Output:

- digital marketing strategies for startups

- benefits of digital marketing in e-commerce

- digital marketing trends in 2023

- online marketing tools for small businesses

- how to measure digital marketing ROI

3. Question-based Keywords:

Prompt: "What are common questions people ask about [Topic]?"
Example: "What are common questions people ask about solar energy?"

Output:

- How do solar panels work?

- Are solar panels worth the investment?

- How long do solar panels last?

- What's the difference between monocrystalline and polycrystalline panels?

- How much can I save with solar energy?

4. Local Keyword Suggestions:

Prompt: "Provide local keywords for [Service] in [City/Location]."
Example: "Provide local keywords for dental clinics in Seattle."

Output:

- best dental clinics in Seattle

- Seattle pediatric dentistry

- emergency dental care Seattle

- teeth whitening services in Seattle

- top-rated Seattle orthodontists

5. Keywords by User Intent:

Prompt: "List buying-intent keywords for [Product/Service]." **Example:** "List buying-intent keywords for fitness trackers."

Output:

- best fitness trackers 2023

- fitness trackers on sale

- top-rated heart rate monitors

- buy waterproof fitness trackers

- fitness tracker deals and discounts

6. Seasonal Keyword Research:

Prompt: "Provide keywords related to [Product/Event] for the upcoming [Season/Holiday]." **Example:** "Provide keywords related to fashion for the upcoming summer."

Output:

- summer fashion trends 2023

- beachwear essentials

- lightweight summer dresses

- must-have summer footwear

- breathable fabrics for summer

7. Keyword Difficulty Estimation:

Prompt: "Based on a hypothetical scenario, estimate the difficulty for ranking the keyword [Keyword]." **Example.** "Based on a hypothetical scenario, estimate the difficulty for ranking the keyword 'organic skincare brands'."

Output:

- Given the high demand for organic products and the vast number of established brands in the market, ranking for "organic skincare brands" would be moderately difficult. It would require consistent content marketing, backlink strategies, and possibly some PPC campaigns.

8. LSI (Latent Semantic Indexing) Keyword Suggestions:

Prompt: "Provide LSI keywords related to [Primary Keyword]." **Example:** "Provide LSI keywords related to 'web development'."

Output:

- website design principles

- front-end development tools

- responsive web layouts

- coding languages for web

- user experience and web navigation

Using the above complex prompts and formulas, ChatGPT can be a handy tool in the keyword research process. You can customize these prompts according to your niche and requirements to unearth valuable keywords for your SEO campaigns.

Content Creation:

Content creation is a central part of SEO and digital marketing. Using ChatGPT can significantly streamline the process by generating topic ideas, outlines, and even complete articles. Here's a detailed breakdown of advanced prompts, formulas, and modules for content creation with ChatGPT:

1. Topic Ideation:

Prompt: "Generate content topic ideas related to [Niche/Industry]." **Example:** "Generate content topic ideas related to sustainable living."

Output:

- The Rise of Zero-Waste Living: A Comprehensive Guide

- 10 Eco-Friendly Alternatives for Everyday Products

- How Sustainable Living Benefits Both You and the Planet

- A Beginner's Journey to Minimalist Living

- The Environmental Impact of Fast Fashion

2. Content Outline Creation:

Prompt: "Create a detailed outline for an article titled '[Article Title]'."
Example: "Create a detailed outline for an article titled 'The Benefits of Remote Work'."

Output:

- **Introduction**

    - Brief overview of the rise of remote work

- **The Environmental Benefits**

    - Reduction in commuter carbon footprints

    - Decrease in office energy consumption

- **The Personal Advantages**

    - Flexibility in scheduling

    - Work-life balance

- **Economic Upsides for Companies**

    - Decreased overhead costs

    - Access to a global talent pool

- **Challenges and Solutions**

    - Addressing feelings of isolation

    - Maintaining productivity

- **Conclusion**

    - Summing up the long-term benefits and the future of remote work

3. Full Article Production:

Prompt: "Write a 500-word article on [Topic]." **Example:** "Write a 500-word article on the health benefits of meditation."

Output: *Beginnings of an article about the health benefits of meditation, covering areas like stress reduction, improved concentration, and potential reductions in blood pressure.*

4. Content Expansion:

Prompt: "Expand on this topic: [Brief Content or Point]." **Example:** "Expand on this topic: The relationship between gut health and mental well-being."

Output: A detailed paragraph or series of paragraphs discussing how gut health can influence mental well-being, possibly mentioning the gut-brain axis, the role of gut microbiota, and how certain foods or probiotics can impact mood and mental health.

5. Data Interpretation for Content:

Prompt: "Translate these data points into a user-friendly blog paragraph: [Data Points]." **Example:** "Translate these data points into a user-friendly blog paragraph: 70% of users prefer videos over text, 20% feel neutral, 10% favor text."

Output: "In a recent survey, a staggering 70% of participants expressed a clear preference for video content over traditional text. While 20% of the audience felt indifferent, a mere 10% stated that they lean towards text-based content. This showcases the growing dominance of video as the preferred content medium."

6. Infographic Descriptions:

Prompt: "Describe the key points for an infographic about [Topic]." **Example:** "Describe the key points for an infographic about the lifecycle of a butterfly."

Output:

- **Egg**: The beginning stage, where the butterfly lays eggs on leaves.

- **Caterpillar (Larva)**: The growth phase, where it feeds aggressively.

- **Pupa (Chrysalis)**: The transformation stage, wrapped in a protective casing.

- **Adult Butterfly**: Emergence as a full-grown butterfly, ready to reproduce.

7. Interactive Content Ideas:

Prompt: "Suggest interactive content formats for [Topic]." **Example:** "Suggest interactive content formats for teaching kids about the solar system."

Output:

- VR Tours of each planet

- Interactive quizzes on planet facts

- Drag and drop games to order planets by size

- Clickable infographics with sounds and animations

- Storytelling sessions with animated characters from each planet

By utilizing the above complex prompts and formulas, ChatGPT can serve as a robust content creation tool. The prompts can be tailored for any niche or topic, and the resulting content can be used as is or further refined to match specific brand tones and styles.

Meta Descriptions and Titles:

Crafting meta descriptions and titles is crucial for SEO, as they act as a first impression of your content in search results. Using ChatGPT, you can generate or refine these elements efficiently. Here's a detailed guide on using ChatGPT for creating meta descriptions and titles:

1. Meta Title Generation:

Prompt: "Create a compelling meta title for an article about [Topic]." **Example:** "Create a compelling meta title for an article about the rise of electric vehicles."

Output: "The Electric Revolution: Unraveling the Surge of Electric Vehicles"

2. Meta Description Generation:

Prompt: "Craft a concise meta description for an article titled '[Article Title]' which covers [Brief Content Overview]." **Example:** "Craft a concise meta description for an article titled 'The Electric Revolution: Unraveling the Surge of Electric Vehicles' which covers the history, benefits, and future trends of electric cars."

Output: "Dive into the transformative journey of electric cars. Explore their historic milestones, undeniable benefits, and a glimpse into a sustainable, electric future."

3. Meta Title Refinement:

Prompt: "Refine this meta title for better SEO and user engagement: '[Existing Meta Title]'." **Example:** "Refine this meta title for better SEO and user engagement: 'Electric Vehicles and Their Popularity'."

Output: "Electric Vehicles in 2023: Why They're Dominating the Roads"

4. Meta Description Refinement:

Prompt: "Optimize this meta description for better clarity and SEO: '[Existing Meta Description]'." **Example:** "Optimize this meta description for better clarity and SEO: 'A look at electric vehicles and their growth'."

Output: "Explore the dynamic rise of electric vehicles, understanding the key factors driving their unprecedented growth and adoption."

5. Meta Title for Product Pages:

Prompt: "Generate a meta title for a product page that sells [Product Description]." **Example:** "Generate a meta title for a product page that sells organic green tea sourced from the Himalayas."

Output: "Premium Organic Himalayan Green Tea: Experience Pure Wellness"

6. Meta Description for Product Pages:

Prompt: "Craft a meta description for a product page featuring [Product Description] that highlights its [Unique Selling Points]." **Example:** "Craft a meta description for a product page featuring organic green tea sourced from the Himalayas that highlights its antioxidants and authentic flavor."

Output: "Savor the authentic flavor of our Himalayan Green Tea, packed with potent antioxidants. Go organic, embrace health and taste in every sip."

7. Meta for Local Business:

Prompt: "Create a meta title and description for a local [Business Type] in [Location]." **Example:** "Create a meta title and description for a local bakery in Brooklyn."

Output:

- **Title:** "Brooklyn's Finest Bakery: Fresh, Artisanal Baked Delights"

- **Description:** "Discover Brooklyn's hidden gem! Experience freshly baked goods, from classic croissants to artisanal pastries, right in the heart of the city."

8. Character Count Adherence:

Remember that search engines have character limits for meta titles (usually 50-60 characters) and descriptions (usually 150-160 characters). While ChatGPT doesn't automatically count characters in its output, you can prompt it to stay within limits.

Prompt: "Craft a meta description under 160 characters for an article about sustainable fashion trends." **Output:** "Unveil 2023's top sustainable fashion trends. Embrace style that cherishes the planet."

By leveraging the above prompts and formulas, you can utilize ChatGPT effectively to craft or refine meta titles and descriptions that are both SEO-friendly and engaging for potential readers.

Content Updates:

Refreshing content to keep it updated is an essential aspect of SEO. As industries evolve, content becomes outdated and needs to be revamped to remain relevant. Utilizing ChatGPT can be a smart way to tackle content updates. Here's a deeper dive into using ChatGPT for this purpose:

1. Reviewing Content Relevance:

Prompt: "Review the following excerpt and suggest updates to make it current for 2023: [Content Excerpt]" **Example:** "Review the following excerpt and suggest updates to make it current for 2023: 'In 2018, mobile browsing surpassed desktop for the first time.'"

Output: "In recent years, mobile browsing has solidified its dominance over desktop, with 2018 being a pivotal turning point."

2. Fact-checking and Updating Data Points:

Prompt: "Update the data points in this content to reflect the current scenario: [Content with Data Points]" **Example:** "Update the data points in this content to reflect the current scenario: 'As of 2019, there are 2 billion active Android users.'"

Output: "As of 2023, there are over 3 billion active Android users."

3. Incorporating New Industry Trends:

Prompt: "Given the topic '[Topic]', suggest new trends or updates to incorporate into an existing article." **Example:** "Given the topic 'Digital Marketing', suggest new trends or updates to incorporate into an existing article."

Output:

- Rise of AI and machine learning in personalized marketing.

- Growing importance of voice search optimization.

- Surge in video content, especially short-form videos.

- Increased focus on user privacy and data protection.

- Evolution of omnichannel marketing strategies.

4. Content Expansion Ideas:

Prompt: "What sections or topics can be added to enrich an article about [Topic]?" **Example:** "What sections or topics can be added to enrich an article about 'Vegan Diets'?"

Output:

- Health benefits of a vegan diet.

- Environmental impact of plant-based diets.

- Common myths and misconceptions debunked.

- Tips for transitioning to a vegan lifestyle.

- Vegan recipe suggestions and resources.

5. Improving Content Structure:

Prompt: "Review the structure of this content and suggest improvements: [Content Outline/Excerpt]" **Example:** "Review the structure of this content and suggest improvements: 'Introduction, Benefits of Vegan Diets, Recipe Ideas, Myths about Veganism'."

Output:

- Introduction

- Benefits of Vegan Diets

- Debunking Myths about Veganism

- Vegan Recipe Ideas and Inspiration

- Conclusion and Additional Resources

6. Updating External and Internal Links:

Prompt: "Suggest updated or more relevant links for a topic on [Subject]." **Example:** "Suggest updated or more relevant links for a topic on 'Cybersecurity Best Practices'."

Output:

- [Link to a 2023 article on cybersecurity trends]

- [Link to a recent case study on a major security breach]

- [Link to an updated guide on personal online safety]

- [Internal link to a related post on the importance of regular software updates]

7. Revamping Visual Content:

Prompt: "Provide ideas for visual content or infographics for an article about [Topic]." **Example:** "Provide ideas for visual content or infographics for an article about 'Benefits of Yoga'."

Output:

- An infographic showcasing different yoga poses and their specific benefits.

- A flowchart illustrating the mental and physical progression of a regular yoga practitioner

- Before-and-after visuals showcasing posture improvements.

- A visual timeline of the history of yoga.

By using these complex prompts and formulas, ChatGPT can assist content creators in ensuring that their existing content remains fresh, updated, and in line with current industry trends, facts, and data.

Link Building:

Link building remains a cornerstone of SEO, playing a vital role in establishing domain authority, trustworthiness, and driving organic traffic. Leveraging ChatGPT can provide insights and strategies for effective link building. Here's a detailed guide on using ChatGPT for link building:

1. Guest Posting Opportunities:

Prompt: "Suggest websites or platforms where I can guest post about [Topic/Niche]." **Example:** "Suggest websites or platforms where I can guest post about digital marketing trends."

Output:

- MarketingLand

- HubSpot's Blog

- Search Engine Journal

- Content Marketing Institute

- Digital Marketer Blog

2. Content Collaboration Ideas:

Prompt: "Generate collaboration content ideas for [Your Website/Brand] and [Potential Partner Brand/Website]." **Example:** "Generate collaboration content ideas for a fitness blog and a health supplement brand."

Output:

- Joint webinar on "Nutrition and Exercise: The Perfect Balance."

- An in-depth article featuring the science behind popular supplements and their fitness benefits.

- Collaborative video content on "A Day in a Fitness Enthusiast's Life" with product integration.

- An interview series with nutritionists discussing the role of supplements in fitness.

3. Backlink Audit:

Prompt: "Given the following backlinks to our website, identify potential low-quality or spammy links: [List of Links]." **Example:** "Given the following backlinks to our website, identify potential low-quality or spammy links: link1.com, qualitysite2.com, spamlink3.net, unknownsource4.biz."

Output: Potential low-quality or spammy links to review:

- spamlink3.net

- unknownsource4.biz

4. Competitor Backlink Opportunities:

Prompt: "Suggest a strategy to identify and leverage backlink opportunities from competitors in the [Industry/Niche]." **Example:** "Suggest a strategy to identify and leverage backlink opportunities from competitors in the SaaS industry."

Output:

- Begin by using tools like Ahrefs or SEMrush to analyze the backlink profile of top competitors.

- Identify industry-relevant websites linking to multiple competitors but not to you.

- Reach out to these websites with a value proposition or unique content idea.

- Regularly monitor competitors' new backlinks and identify emerging industry platforms or blogs.

- Engage in industry forums, comment sections, or guest posting to create organic backlink opportunities.

5. Broken Link Building:

Prompt: "Describe the broken link building strategy for the [Industry/Niche]." **Example:** "Describe the broken link building strategy for the health and wellness niche."

Output:

- Start by using tools like Ahrefs or Broken Link Checker to identify broken links on high-authority websites within the health and wellness niche.

- Once identified, create or offer an existing piece of content from your website as a replacement for the broken link.

- Reach out to the website owner or webmaster, informing them of the broken link and suggesting your content as a valuable replacement.

- Ensure that your replacement content is of high quality and provides genuine value to the audience.

6. Resource Link Building:

Prompt: "Provide a strategy for resource link building in the [Industry/Niche]." **Example:** "Provide a strategy for resource link building in the educational sector."

Output:

- Identify authoritative "resource pages" in the educational sector that list valuable links and resources for students, teachers, or institutions.

- Create comprehensive, high-quality content or tools that cater to this audience.

- Reach out to the owners of these resource pages, introducing your content/tool and highlighting its unique value.

- Ensure regular follow-ups and foster relationships with educational websites for future link-building opportunities.

7. Local Link Building Ideas:

Prompt: "Suggest local link building opportunities for a [Type of Local Business] in [City/Location]." **Example:** "Suggest local link building opportunities for a bakery in San Francisco."

Output:

- Partner with San Francisco-based food bloggers for reviews and features.

- Engage with local events or farmers' markets and get featured on their websites.

- Collaborate with nearby restaurants or cafes for special promotions, leading to mutual website mentions.

- Get listed on San Francisco local business directories and review sites.

- Participate in community initiatives or sponsor local events for backlink opportunities on event pages.

By implementing the above complex prompts and strategies, ChatGPT can assist in amplifying the link-building efforts for any website, helping to bolster SEO and drive organic growth.

On-Page SEO Optimization:

On-page SEO optimization encompasses all the tactics applied directly to a webpage to improve its position in search rankings. It includes content quality, keyword placements, headers, meta tags, and more. ChatGPT can be a valuable tool to guide and enhance these efforts. Here's a detailed guide for using ChatGPT in the realm of on-page SEO:

1. Keyword Placement Recommendations:

Prompt: "For optimal on-page SEO, where should I place the keyword '[Your Keyword]' in my article?" **Example:** "For optimal on-page SEO, where should I place the keyword 'sustainable fashion' in my article?"

Output:

- In the meta title and description.

- Within the first 100 words of the content.

- In at least one subheading (H2 or H3).

- Naturally throughout the content, aiming for a keyword density of 1-2%.

- In the ALT text of relevant images.

2. Header (H1, H2, H3) Suggestions:

Prompt: "Based on the topic '[Your Topic]', suggest a hierarchy of headers and subheaders." **Example:** "Based on the topic 'Benefits of Green Tea', suggest a hierarchy of headers and subheaders."

Output:

- **H1**: The Remarkable Benefits of Green Tea
    - **H2**: Historical Context of Green Tea Consumption
    - **H2**: Key Health Benefits
        - **H3**: Boosting Metabolism and Weight Loss
        - **H3**: Rich in Antioxidants and Reducing Inflammation
        - **H3**: Improving Brain Function
    - **H2**: How to Integrate Green Tea into Your Diet

3. Meta Description Enhancement:

Prompt: "Optimize this meta description for the keyword '[Your Keyword]': '[Existing Meta Description]'." **Example:** "Optimize this meta description for the keyword 'vegan leather boots': 'Find high-quality boots that match your style.'"

Output: "Discover high-quality vegan leather boots that blend sustainability with impeccable style."

4. Image ALT Text Recommendations:

Prompt: "Suggest ALT text for an image showing [Image Description], keeping SEO in mind." **Example:** "Suggest ALT text for an image showing a group of people practicing yoga in a park, keeping SEO in mind."

Output: "Group of individuals practicing yoga outdoors in a serene park setting."

5. Content Structure & Readability:

Prompt: "Review this excerpt and suggest improvements for better readability and on-page SEO: [Content Excerpt]" **Example:** "Review this excerpt and suggest improvements for better readability and on-page

SEO: 'Green tea is good. It has many benefits. People have been drinking it for years because it's beneficial.'"

Output: "Green tea has been cherished for generations due to its myriad of health benefits. From ancient times to the modern era, its therapeutic properties have made it a preferred choice for many."

6. Internal Linking Recommendations:

Prompt: "Given an article about '[Your Topic]', suggest potential internal linking opportunities to other articles or topics." **Example:** "Given an article about 'Mediterranean Diet', suggest potential internal linking opportunities to other articles or topics."

Output:

- Benefits of Olive Oil: A Mediterranean Staple

- Exploring the Role of Fish in a Balanced Diet

- Heart Health: Foods and Diets to Consider

- Traditional Mediterranean Recipes to Try at Home

7. URL Structure Suggestions:

Prompt: "Suggest an SEO-friendly URL structure for a page about [Topic/Subject]." **Example:** "Suggest an SEO-friendly URL structure for a page about beginner's guide to digital photography."

Output: "https://[yourdomain].com/guides/digital-photography-for-beginners"

8. Page Speed Optimization Tips:

Prompt: "Provide recommendations to improve webpage loading speed." **Output:**

- Compress images to reduce file sizes without sacrificing quality.

- Use browser caching for recurring visitors.

- Minimize HTTP requests by reducing the number of items loading (like scripts and plugins).

- Use a Content Delivery Network (CDN) to distribute the load.

- Minify CSS, JavaScript, and HTML files.

By leveraging these complex prompts and guidelines with ChatGPT, you can get insightful recommendations and guidance to enhance your on-page SEO efforts, ensuring your web pages are well-optimized for both users and search engines.

Technical SEO:

Technical SEO refers to the optimizations made to a website and server that help search engine spiders crawl and index your site more effectively. Properly executing technical SEO ensures that your website has a solid foundation and can help in improving organic rankings. Here's how you can use ChatGPT to assist with technical SEO aspects:

1. XML Sitemap Creation Guidance:

Prompt: "Provide a step-by-step guide on creating an XML sitemap for a website." **Output:**

- List all URLs on your website.

- Use tools like Screaming Frog or Yoast SEO to automatically generate an XML sitemap.

- Validate the XML sitemap using a Sitemap Validator.

- Upload the sitemap to the root directory of your site (e.g., www.yoursite.com/sitemap.xml).

- Submit the sitemap through Google Search Console and Bing Webmaster Tools.

2. Robots.txt File Recommendations:

Prompt: "Provide best practices for setting up a robots.txt file for an e-commerce website." **Output:**

- Place the robots.txt file in the root directory of your site.

- Allow major search engine bots (e.g., Googlebot, Bingbot).

- Disallow sensitive user data directories or private sections.

- Disallow cart and checkout pages to prevent indexing.

- Specify the location of your XML sitemap using **Sitemap: https://www.yourdomain.com/sitemap.xml**.

3. Site Structure and URL Optimization:

Prompt: "Suggest an optimized URL structure for a multi-category e-commerce store." **Output:**

- Home: **https://www.yourstore.com/**

- Categories: **https://www.yourstore.com/category-name/**

- Subcategories: **https://www.yourstore.com/category-name/subcategory-name/**

- Products: **https://www.yourstore.com/category-name/product-name/**

- Blog: **https://www.yourstore.com/blog/post-title/**

4. Mobile Optimization Tips:

Prompt: "List best practices for ensuring a mobile-friendly website in 2023." **Output:**

- Implement a responsive design that adjusts to different screen sizes.

- Avoid using Flash and prioritize HTML5.

- Optimize images to load quickly on mobile.

- Ensure clickable elements are adequately spaced.

- Use readable font sizes.

- Implement Accelerated Mobile Pages (AMP) for faster loading.

5. Website Speed Enhancement:

Prompt: "Provide advanced techniques for improving website loading speed." **Output:**

- Use browser caching to store resources.

- Optimize and compress images with tools like TinyPNG or WebP format.

- Implement lazy loading for images and scripts.

- Minimize the number of redirects.

- Use a Content Delivery Network (CDN) like Cloudflare or Akamai.

- Optimize CSS and JS files (minification and concatenation).

6. Schema Markup Recommendations:

Prompt: "Suggest appropriate schema markup types for a recipe blog."
Output:

- **Recipe** schema for individual recipe posts.

- **Person** or **Organization** schema for the blog author or brand.

- **BreadcrumbList** schema for navigational breadcrumbs.

- **Video** schema if recipes include video demonstrations.

- **Review** schema for user-generated recipe ratings.

7. Hreflang Tags for Multilingual Sites:

Prompt: "Explain the proper implementation of hreflang tags for a website available in English, Spanish, and French." **Output:**

- Use the hreflang attribute to specify language and regional targeting.

- For English (generic): **<link rel="alternate" hreflang="en" href="https://www.example.com/en/" />**

- For Spanish: **<link rel="alternate" hreflang="es" href="https://www.example.com/es/" />**

- For French: **<link rel="alternate" hreflang="fr" href="https://www.example.com/fr/" />**

- Ensure each page with a specific language variant points to all other language versions, including itself.

8. Core Web Vitals Insights:

Prompt: "What are Core Web Vitals, and how do they impact SEO?"
Output: Core Web Vitals are a set of metrics introduced by Google that focus on user experience. They consist of:

- **Largest Contentful Paint (LCP):** Measures loading performance. Ideal time is 2.5 seconds or faster.

- **First Input Delay (FID):** Gauges interactivity. Ideal time is less than 100 milliseconds.

- **Cumulative Layout Shift (CLS):** Evaluates visual stability. Ideal score is less than 0.1. These metrics are crucial as they directly impact the user experience on a website. Since Google aims to deliver high-quality and user-friendly results, they've incorporated Core Web Vitals as ranking signals in their algorithm.

Using these prompts and guidelines, ChatGPT can guide and assist webmasters and SEO professionals in enhancing the technical health of their websites, ensuring better crawlability, indexation, and user experience.

Local SEO (if applicable):

Local SEO is all about optimizing a business to be found in local search results. It's especially important for brick-and-mortar businesses that serve specific towns, cities, regions, or even states. Here's a detailed guide on utilizing ChatGPT for various aspects of local SEO:

1. Google My Business (GMB) Optimization:

Prompt: "Provide a checklist for optimizing a Google My Business listing for a local bakery." **Output:**

- Ensure the business name, address, and phone number (NAP) are accurate and consistent across all online platforms.

- Choose the correct business category and sub-categories.

- Add high-quality images of the bakery, products, and staff.

- Write a compelling business description including keywords related to "bakery" and the local area.

- Encourage satisfied customers to leave reviews.

- Respond promptly and professionally to all reviews, both positive and negative.

- Update business hours, including special hours for holidays.

- Use the GMB posts feature to announce promotions, events, or news.

2. Local Keyword Suggestions:

Prompt: "Suggest local SEO keyword ideas for a dental clinic in Austin, Texas." **Output:**

- Austin dental clinic
- Best dentist in Austin
- Teeth whitening Austin TX
- Emergency dental care Austin
- Pediatric dentist in Austin Texas
- Austin dental implants services
- Denture clinics in Austin

3. Local Citation Recommendations:

Prompt: "List key platforms or websites where a local restaurant should ensure they have citations." **Output:**

- Yelp
- TripAdvisor
- Foursquare
- YellowPages
- Local chamber of commerce website
- Zomato
- Local business directories (specific to the city or region)
- Google Maps

4. Local Content Ideas:

Prompt: "Generate content ideas to boost local SEO for a fitness center in Seattle." **Output:**

- A guide to staying fit in Seattle's rainy season.
- Top local trails in Seattle for outdoor workouts.

- Highlighting health and fitness events in Seattle.

- Profile pieces on local Seattle residents who transformed their health at the fitness center.

- An article on the best post-workout eateries around Seattle.

5. Optimizing Local Reviews:

Prompt: "Provide a strategy to encourage more local reviews for a boutique hotel." **Output:**

- Ask guests during check-out if they had a positive experience and encourage them to leave a review.

- Send post-stay emails with direct links to review platforms.

- Run a promotion or contest incentivizing reviews.

- Respond to every review to show engagement and appreciation.

- Train staff to provide exceptional service and mention the importance of reviews.

6. Local Backlink Building Ideas:

Prompt: "Suggest backlink building strategies for a veterinarian clinic in San Diego." **Output:**

- Collaborate with local pet shops for mutual website features or promotions.

- Contribute guest posts to San Diego pet blogs or magazines.

- Get featured or listed in local business directories or community pages.

- Sponsor or host local pet-related events and ensure a backlink from the event page.

- Engage in local forums or community discussions and provide expert advice.

7. Technical Aspects for Local SEO:

Prompt: "What are the technical on-site elements to optimize for local SEO?" **Output:**

- Ensure NAP (Name, Address, Phone Number) information is consistent across the website.

- Embed a Google Map on the site, preferably on the contact page.

- Use schema markup (LocalBusiness Schema) to provide search engines detailed local business information.

- Optimize meta titles and descriptions with local keywords.

- Make sure the website is mobile-responsive, as many local searches come from mobile devices.

8. Local SEO Audit Questions:

Prompt: "What questions should I ask when conducting a local SEO audit for a car repair service in Chicago?" **Output:**

- Is the Google My Business listing claimed, verified, and fully optimized?

- Are there any inconsistencies in NAP information across online platforms?

- Is the website optimized with local Chicago-related keywords?

- Are there any local citations missing or are there opportunities to build more?

- Is the business receiving regular reviews on platforms like Yelp and Google?

- Are there backlinks from local Chicago websites or directories?

Leveraging ChatGPT with these prompts and guidelines can significantly aid businesses in optimizing their local SEO strategy, ensuring they stand out in local search results and reach their target audience effectively.

Voice Search Optimization:

Voice search optimization focuses on improving online content to enhance the likelihood of it being picked up by voice search results. As more users turn to voice-activated assistants like Google Assistant, Siri, Alexa, and Cortana, ensuring your content is voice-search friendly is vital. Here's a guide on using ChatGPT for various aspects of voice search optimization:

1. Question-Based Keyword Suggestions:

Voice searches are often in the form of questions. **Prompt:** "Provide question-based keyword suggestions for the topic 'homemade pizza'." **Output:**

- How do I make homemade pizza?

- What are the best toppings for homemade pizza?

- How long does it take to cook a homemade pizza?

- Why is my homemade pizza crust not crispy?

- Can I freeze homemade pizza dough?

2. Optimizing for Conversational Tone:

Prompt: "Revise this content to be more conversational, suitable for voice search: 'The annual rainfall in Seattle is 37.49 inches.'" **Output:** "On average, Seattle gets about 37.5 inches of rain every year."

3. Local Voice Search Optimization:

Prompt: "Suggest ways to optimize a local coffee shop's online presence for voice searches." **Output:**

- Ensure the coffee shop's Google My Business listing is accurate and comprehensive.

- Encourage customers to leave reviews, as voice assistants often recommend places with higher ratings.

- Create content answering common questions like "What time does [coffee shop name] open?" or "Does [coffee shop name] have almond milk?"

- Make sure the website is mobile-responsive, as many voice searches are made on mobile devices.

4. Creating Voice Search Optimized FAQs:

Prompt: "Generate voice-search optimized FAQ questions for a brand selling eco-friendly cleaning products." **Output:**

- How eco-friendly are [brand's] cleaning products?

- Where can I buy [brand's] green cleaning items?

- Are [brand's] products safe for kids and pets?

- How does [brand] ensure its products are sustainable?

- Can I get a discount on my first order from [brand]?

5. Voice Search User Intent Insights:

Prompt: "Explain the difference in user intent between text and voice searches." **Output:** Text searches are often brief and might be more transactional, while voice searches tend to be longer, more conversational, and might be informational in nature. For example, a user might type "weather NYC" on a search engine, but ask their voice assistant, "What's the weather going to be like in New York City tomorrow?"

6. Technical Optimization for Voice Search:

Prompt: "What technical aspects should be considered for voice search optimization?" **Output:**

- Ensure website speed is optimized; voice search users expect quick answers.

- Structured data (Schema Markup) helps voice search engines understand the context of content.

- Create a robust FAQ section to directly answer common queries.

- Ensure the website is HTTPS, as voice search gives preference to secure sites.

- Optimize for mobile, since many voice queries come from mobile devices.

7. Content Structure for Voice Search:

Prompt: "Recommend a content structure to maximize the chance of being picked up by voice search for the topic 'benefits of solar energy'." **Output:**

- Start with a concise answer that directly responds to the main query.

- Follow with detailed subsections:

  - Environmental Benefits of Solar Energy.

  - Cost Savings Over Time.

  - Energy Independence and Reliability.

  - Boost in Property Value.

- End with a CTA or related resources.

- Consider creating an infographic summarizing the benefits, as visual content can support voice search optimization efforts.

8. Optimizing Existing Content for Voice Search:

Prompt: "Review this excerpt for voice search optimization and suggest improvements: 'Solar energy reduces electricity bills. It's derived from the sun's rays.'" **Output:** A more voice-search friendly version might be: "Using solar energy can help you save on your electricity bills because it harnesses power directly from the sun's rays."

By employing these detailed prompts with ChatGPT, you can ensure your content is not just readable but also 'speakable', catering to the growing trend of voice search users and smart home devices.

Monitor and Analyze:

Monitor and Analyze is an essential phase in the SEO process. It involves tracking your website's performance, understanding user behavior, and adjusting strategies based on gathered data. Using ChatGPT, you can get insights, recommendations, and further clarifications on various analytics tools and metrics. Here's a guide for that:

1. Understanding Analytics Metrics:

Prompt: "Explain the significance of 'Bounce Rate' in website analytics and how it impacts SEO." **Output:** "Bounce rate represents the percentage of visitors who enter your site and then leave rather than continuing to view other pages within the same site. A high bounce rate might indicate that users aren't finding what they're looking for, which can affect user experience and, consequently, SEO rankings."

2. Traffic Source Insights:

Prompt: "Break down the various sources of website traffic and their implications." **Output:**

- **Organic Search:** Traffic coming from search engines due to SEO efforts. It indicates the health of your SEO strategy.

- **Direct:** Users directly typing in your URL or accessing through bookmarks. It's an indication of brand recall or loyalty.

- **Referral:** Traffic coming from links on other websites. High referral traffic can indicate successful off-page SEO or partnerships.

- **Social:** Visitors from social media platforms. It shows how effective your social media strategies are.

- **Paid Search:** Traffic from pay-per-click (PPC) campaigns, indicating the performance of your paid ads.

3. Keyword Ranking Analysis:

Prompt: "Suggest a strategy to monitor and improve keyword rankings for an e-commerce website selling sportswear." **Output:**

- Use tools like SEMrush, Ahrefs, or Google Search Console to track current keyword rankings.

- Identify high-performing and underperforming keywords.

- Optimize product descriptions, meta tags, and content around high-value keywords.

- Monitor competitors' performance for similar keywords.

- Create high-quality backlinks with anchor texts related to sportswear.

- Regularly refresh content and product listings with updated keyword research.

4. Monitoring Backlink Profile:

Prompt: "Recommend a method for monitoring and analyzing the backlink profile of a travel blog." **Output:**

- Use backlink analysis tools like Ahrefs or Majestic.

- Monitor the number of new backlinks and lost backlinks regularly.

- Check the domain authority of linking sites to ensure high-quality backlinks.

- Disavow any toxic or spammy backlinks that could harm SEO.

- Engage with high-authority travel sites or forums for guest posting or partnerships to improve the backlink profile.

5. User Behavior Analysis:

Prompt: "Describe the importance of 'Average Session Duration' in analyzing user behavior." **Output:** "Average Session Duration indicates the average amount of time a user spends on your site during a session. A longer session duration often suggests that your content is engaging and users are finding value, which can indirectly benefit SEO by signaling to search engines that your site provides quality content."

6. Content Performance Evaluation:

Prompt: "How can I evaluate which blog posts on my tech website are driving the most organic traffic?" **Output:**

- Use Google Analytics and navigate to Behavior > Site Content > All Pages.

- Filter or segment the traffic source to "organic."

- Analyze the page views, average time spent, and bounce rate for each blog post.

- Cross-reference with conversion metrics, if applicable, to understand not just traffic but also the quality of visitors each post is attracting.

7. Mobile Performance Analysis:

Prompt: "Recommend steps to assess and improve mobile performance for an online news portal." **Output:**

- Use Google's Mobile-Friendly Test to see if the site meets basic mobile optimization standards.

- Analyze mobile traffic metrics on Google Analytics to understand user behavior on mobile devices.

- Implement Accelerated Mobile Pages (AMP) for faster loading on mobile.

- Regularly test the site on various mobile devices and screen sizes to ensure consistent user experience.

- Pay attention to mobile UX/UI, ensuring that buttons, links, and CTAs are touch-friendly.

8. Conversion Rate Optimization (CRO) Insights:

Prompt: "Explain the connection between SEO and CRO and why they should be optimized together." **Output:** "While SEO focuses on driving traffic to the site, CRO aims to convert that traffic into tangible actions, be it sales, sign-ups, or other desired outcomes. By optimizing both simultaneously, businesses ensure not only higher traffic but also that visitors take meaningful actions, leading to better ROI."

Using these prompts with ChatGPT can aid in the interpretation and strategic evolution of your SEO efforts, ensuring they align with performance metrics and adapt based on analytic insights.

Iterate, improve and stay updated:

SEO is a continually evolving field, and staying current while iteratively improving your strategies is key. The ability to iterate and stay updated ensures that you not only keep up with algorithm changes but also with shifts in user behavior and technological advancements. Here's how you can use ChatGPT for these aspects:

Iterate and Improve:

1. **SEO Strategy Review**:

Prompt: "Analyze the following SEO strategy and suggest areas for improvement: [Brief of Your SEO Strategy]." **Example:** "Analyze the following SEO strategy: 'Focusing primarily on short-tail keywords, not actively pursuing backlinks, and updating content semi-annually.'" **Output:** "Consider integrating long-tail keywords to capture more specific queries, actively pursue high-quality backlinks to boost authority, and update content more frequently to stay relevant."

2. **Content Refresh**:

Prompt: "Based on the latest trends in [Industry/Topic], suggest updates for the following article excerpt: [Article Excerpt]." **Example:** "Based on the latest trends in digital marketing, suggest updates for the following article excerpt: 'Facebook and Twitter are the leading platforms for social media marketing.'" **Output:** "While Facebook and Twitter remain significant, platforms like Instagram, TikTok, and LinkedIn have gained immense popularity in digital marketing."

3. **Technical SEO Re-evaluation**:

Prompt: "Suggest a quarterly checklist to review and improve technical SEO for an e-commerce site." **Output:**

- Re-crawl the site for broken links or 404 errors.

- Check site speed and optimize any lagging pages.

- Review mobile optimization and improve any UI/UX discrepancies.

- Update XML sitemaps as new products or pages are added.

- Regularly check and renew SSL certificates.

4. **Backlink Profile Iteration**:

Prompt: "Given a decline in organic traffic, recommend a backlink analysis and improvement plan." **Output:**

- Use tools like Ahrefs or SEMrush to analyze current backlinks.

- Identify and disavow toxic or low-quality backlinks.

- Strategize new backlink opportunities, focusing on high-authority domains.

- Engage in guest blogging, collaborations, or partnerships.

- Monitor backlink growth and correlate with traffic trends.

Stay Updated:

1. **Algorithm Updates**:

Prompt: "Provide a summary of Google's most recent algorithm update as of [Month, Year]." (Note: While ChatGPT can't provide real-time updates after its last training data in September 2021, it can guide on where to look or how to stay updated.) **Output:** "I recommend checking Google's official blog, SEO news sites like Search Engine Journal or Search Engine Land, and forums like WebmasterWorld for the latest updates."

2. **Emerging SEO Trends**:

Prompt: "Based on current industry shifts, predict potential SEO trends for the upcoming year." **Output:** "Voice search optimization might grow with the rise of smart assistants, user experience signals could gain more weight in ranking, and video content could become even more vital for online visibility."

3. **Competitor Benchmarking**:

Prompt: "Recommend a monthly routine to analyze and stay updated with competitors' SEO activities." **Output:**

- Use tools like SEMrush to monitor competitors' keyword rankings.

- Analyze their content updates and new blog posts.

- Check for new backlinks they've acquired.

- Monitor any shifts in their site structure or user experience.

- Stay updated with any new products, services, or offerings they announce.

4. **Staying Updated with Tools**:

Prompt: "List resources or platforms to stay updated with new SEO tools and technologies." **Output:**

- Attend conferences like SMX or BrightonSEO.

- Follow platforms like Moz Blog, Ahrefs Blog, and Yoast SEO Blog.

- Engage in SEO communities on Reddit, Stack Exchange, and other forums.

- Take online courses or webinars on platforms like Udemy or Coursera.

By integrating these prompts and guidelines into your SEO process, ChatGPT can assist in ensuring that your strategies remain agile, current, and effective in an ever-evolving digital landscape.

Chapter 9: ChatGPT for Professional Business Emails

Writing professional business emails is essential for effective communication. Here's a step-by-step strategy using ChatGPT, along with examples.

Step 1: Determine Your Objective

Before you start, be clear about the purpose of your email. This will guide the tone, content, and structure.

Example Objectives:

1. To schedule a meeting.
2. To introduce a new product.
3. To follow up after a meeting.

Step 2: Use a Suitable Salutation

Depending on your relationship with the recipient, use an appropriate greeting.

Examples:

1. Formal: "Dear Dr. Smith,"
2. Semi-formal: "Hello John,"
3. Informal (known colleague/friend): "Hey John,"

Step 3: Start With a Polite Introduction (if necessary)

If you're introducing yourself or if the recipient might not recognize your name, briefly explain your identity and context.

Example: "My name is Jane, and I'm the new project manager at XYZ Corp. We met briefly during last week's industry conference."

Step 4: Get to the Point

State the purpose of your email in a concise manner. Avoid fluff.

Example for scheduling a meeting: "I'm writing to propose a meeting next week to discuss our upcoming marketing campaign."

Step 5: Elaborate if Necessary

After stating the main point, provide details or expand on your reason for writing.

Example for introducing a new product: "Our new product, the ABC Widget, offers several features that align with your company's manufacturing needs, including..."

Step 6: Include a Call to Action (CTA)

Clearly state what you want the recipient to do after reading your email.

Example for follow-up: "Could you please share your feedback on the proposal I sent over by Friday?"

Step 7: Be Courteous and Professional

Use polite language and avoid jargon unless you're sure the recipient understands it.

Example: "Would it be possible for you to share the files by tomorrow?" **Instead of**: "Get me those files by tomorrow."

Step 8: Use a Professional Closing

Choose a sign-off that matches the tone and formality of your email.

Examples:

1. Formal: "Kind regards," or "Sincerely,"

2. Semi-formal: "Best wishes," or "Thank you,"

3. Informal: "Thanks," or "Cheers,"

Step 9: Proofread

Before hitting send, proofread for grammar, punctuation, and clarity. ChatGPT can assist by reviewing sentences or phrasings you're unsure about.

Example: "Please advice on the above." → "Please advise on the above."

Step 10: Use a Clear Subject Line

The subject line should reflect the main point of the email. It's what the recipient sees first, so make it clear and relevant.

Examples:

1. "Proposal for Marketing Campaign Discussion - Meeting Request"

2. "Introduction to Our New ABC Widget"

3. "Follow-Up on Yesterday's Meeting"

Sample Email:

Subject: Proposal for Marketing Campaign Discussion - Meeting Request

Dear Dr. Smith,

I hope this email finds you well. I'm writing to propose a meeting next week to discuss our upcoming marketing campaign. Given your expertise in digital strategies, your feedback would be invaluable. Could we potentially schedule this for Tuesday or Wednesday? Please let me know your availability. Thank you for considering my request.

Kind regards,

Jane Doe

Project Manager, XYZ Corp.

Incorporating these steps will ensure your emails are clear, professional, and effective. And always remember, with ChatGPT, you can draft, review, or refine your business emails anytime.

ChatGPT Prompts, Formulas and Modules for Business Emails: Determine Your Objective:

Developing complex prompts and modules for ChatGPT, specifically for the "Determine Your Objective" phase of email writing, requires a structured approach. These prompts can assist users in narrowing down their intent for the email, ensuring that the email's content remains relevant and concise.

1. Modules for Objective Determination:

a. Objective Categorization:

Prompt: "Please choose the main objective for your email from the following categories:

- Scheduling

- Information Sharing

- Request

- Feedback

- Introduction

- Other"

b. Objective Elaboration:

Prompt: "Please provide a brief 1-2 sentence summary of your specific objective."

2. Complex Prompts for Each Category:

a. Scheduling:

Prompt: "Are you trying to:

- Schedule a one-on-one meeting?

- Propose a team meeting?

- Reschedule an existing meeting?

- Confirm a meeting time?"

Example User Response: "Schedule a one-on-one meeting."

b. Information Sharing:

Prompt: "What type of information are you sharing:

- Updates on a project?

- Sharing files or resources?

- Announcing changes or news?

- Providing general updates?"

Example User Response: "Updates on a project."

c. Request:

Prompt: "What are you requesting:

196

- Assistance or support on a task?

- Resources or materials?

- Approval or feedback?

- Collaboration or input?"

Example User Response: "Approval or feedback."

d. Feedback:

Prompt: "Are you:

- Seeking feedback on a specific task or project?

- Providing feedback on a recent event or work product?

- Discussing feedback received from others?

- Soliciting general opinions or thoughts?"

Example User Response: "Seeking feedback on a specific task."

e. Introduction:

Prompt: "Is this introduction regarding:

- Introducing yourself to a new team or individual?

- Introducing someone else?

- Presenting a new product or service?

- Explaining a new concept or idea?"

Example User Response: "Introducing myself to a new individual."

f. Other:

Prompt: "Please specify the objective of your email in your own words."

Example User Response: "I am writing to inform my team about my upcoming vacation dates."

3. Compile and Construct:

Once the user's objective has been narrowed down, ChatGPT can construct a relevant introduction or first few sentences of the email based on the provided information.

Example:

User's Objective: Schedule a one-on-one meeting. ChatGPT's Suggested Start: "I hope this email finds you well. I'm reaching out to propose a one-on-one meeting to discuss our upcoming project's details. Your insights would be invaluable."

This methodical approach ensures that the email remains focused on the main objective, making the communication effective and to the point.

Use a Suitable Salutation:

The salutation sets the tone for your email, so it's crucial to get it right. The salutation should match the level of formality appropriate for the recipient and the purpose of the email. By using ChatGPT's prompts and modules for this, you can ensure the right choice every time.

1. Modules for Salutation Determination:

a. Relationship Assessment:

Prompt: "How would you describe your relationship with the recipient?

- Professional (e.g., superior, client, or external partner)

- Peer (e.g., colleague at the same level)

- Subordinate (e.g., someone you supervise)

- Personal acquaintance in a professional context"

b. Formality Level:

Prompt: "Choose the level of formality you believe is suitable for this email:

- Highly formal

- Moderately formal

- Casual

- Not sure"

c. Name & Title Confirmation:

Prompt: "Do you know the recipient's name and title?

- Yes, I know both

- I only know the name

- I only know the title

- I don't know either"

2. Complex Prompts Based on User Response:

a. Professional Relationship:

Prompt for Highly Formal: "Do you want to use their title and last name (e.g., 'Dear Dr. Smith') or only the title (e.g., 'Dear Sir/Madam')?"

Prompt for Moderately Formal: "Would you prefer to use their first name (e.g., 'Dear John') or title and last name (e.g., 'Dear Mr. Smith')?"

b. Peer Relationship:

Prompt for Moderately Formal: "Do you want to use 'Hello' or 'Dear' with their first name?"

Prompt for Casual: "Do you prefer a simple greeting like 'Hi' or 'Hey' followed by their name?"

c. Subordinate Relationship:

Prompt for Moderately Formal: "Would you like to start with 'Hello' followed by their first name?"

Prompt for Casual: "Do you want to use a simple greeting, like 'Hi'?"

d. Personal Acquaintance in Professional Context:

Prompt: "Given your personal acquaintance, would you prefer a:

- Standard professional greeting (e.g., 'Dear [Name]')

- Friendly, but still professional greeting (e.g., 'Hello [Name]')

- More casual tone (e.g., 'Hi [Name]')?"

3. Compilation Based on Responses:

Once ChatGPT has the required details, it can suggest a suitable salutation:

Example 1: User's Relationship: Professional Formality Level: Highly Formal Name & Title: Knows both

ChatGPT Suggestion: "Dear Dr. Smith,"

Example 2: User's Relationship: Peer Formality Level: Casual Name & Title: Knows name only

ChatGPT Suggestion: "Hey John,"

This approach provides users with a tailored salutation that respects the context and nuances of their relationship with the recipient, setting the right tone for the rest of the email.

Start With a Polite Introduction (if necessary):
Starting with a polite introduction can set a positive and respectful tone for the email, particularly if there's a chance the recipient doesn't remember you or isn't familiar with the context of your email.

1. Modules for Introduction Determination:

a. Recipient Memory Assessment:

Prompt: "Do you believe the recipient would remember you or the context of your email?

- They would definitely remember me.

- They might remember me.

- It's likely they don't remember me or the context.

- I've never interacted with them before."

b. Context Clarity:

Prompt: "How clear is the context of this email to the recipient?

- Highly clear: We've been consistently discussing this.

- Moderately clear: We've touched on this before.

- Not clear: This is a new topic or request.

- Not sure."

c. Relationship Detailing:

Prompt: "How would you describe your most recent interaction or relationship with the recipient?

- Met at an event or conference.

- Collaborated on a project.

- Had a formal meeting or discussion.

- No recent interaction."

2. Complex Prompts Based on User Response:

a. For Those They Might/Might Not Remember:

Prompt for Met at an Event: "Do you want to remind them of the specific event? If yes, please provide the event name and date."

Prompt for Collaborated on a Project: "Please provide a brief summary or name of the project you collaborated on."

b. For First-time Interactions:

Prompt: "Please provide a short background about yourself or your company to introduce yourself to the recipient."

c. For Unclear Context:

Prompt: "Provide a concise explanation or summary of the topic you're addressing to clarify the context for the recipient."

3. Compilation Based on Responses:

After obtaining the required details, ChatGPT can craft a suitable introduction:

Example 1: Recipient Memory: Might remember Context Clarity: Moderately clear Relationship: Met at an event Event Name: "Tech Innovators Conference 2023" on March 15th

ChatGPT Suggestion: "I hope this email finds you well. My name is [Your Name], and we met at the Tech Innovators Conference on March 15th. I wanted to follow up on a brief discussion we had about software solutions."

Example 2: Recipient Memory: Never interacted Context Clarity: Not clear Relationship: No recent interaction

ChatGPT Suggestion: "Good day, [Recipient Name]. My name is [Your Name] from [Company Name]. We specialize in [Brief Company Description]. I'm reaching out to discuss potential collaboration opportunities that might be beneficial for both of us."

This approach ensures that the introduction is both polite and informative, bridging any potential gaps in memory or context for the recipient and laying the groundwork for a productive conversation.

Get to the Point:

Getting to the point ensures that your email remains concise, focused, and relevant, allowing the recipient to quickly grasp the essence of the message. Complex prompts and modules can be designed for ChatGPT to assist users in constructing a direct and clear main point for their emails.

1. Modules for Determining the Main Point:

a. Content Type Assessment:

Prompt: "Which of the following best describes the main content of your email?

- Making a Request

- Providing Information

- Asking a Question

- Making an Announcement

- Sharing Feedback

- Other"

b. Detail Level:

Prompt: "How detailed do you want the main point to be?

- Succinct (one sentence)

- Moderate (a short paragraph)

- Detailed (a longer paragraph)

- Not sure"

-

c. Urgency Indicator:

Prompt: "How urgent is this matter?

- Highly Urgent
- Moderately Urgent
- Not Urgent
- Not sure"

2. Complex Prompts Based on User Response:

a. For Making a Request:

Prompt: "Please provide a brief summary of what you're requesting."

Example User Response: "I am requesting additional budget for the marketing campaign."

b. For Providing Information:

Prompt: "Summarize the key information you wish to convey."

Example User Response: "I wanted to update the team about changes in our project timeline."

c. For Asking a Question:

Prompt: "What main question do you want to pose to the recipient?"

Example User Response: "I want to ask if they're available for a meeting next week."

d. For Making an Announcement:

Prompt: "What is the main announcement you'd like to make?"

Example User Response: "Announcing the launch of our new product next month."

c. For Sharing Feedback:

Prompt: "Can you summarize the main feedback or topic you wish to address?"

Example User Response: "I'd like to provide feedback on the recent training session."

3. Compilation Based on Responses:

Once the required details are obtained, ChatGPT can craft a suitable main point:

Example 1 (Request + Moderate Detail + Highly Urgent): User's Response: "I am requesting additional budget for the marketing campaign."

ChatGPT Suggestion: "I'm writing to urgently request an increase in the budget for our marketing campaign. Given the recent market changes and opportunities, a modest budget boost will significantly enhance our campaign's effectiveness."

Example 2 (Announcement + Succinct + Not Urgent): User's Response: "Announcing the launch of our new product next month."

ChatGPT Suggestion: "I'm pleased to announce that our new product will officially launch next month."

This structured approach helps in forming the core message of the email with clarity and relevance, ensuring the recipient quickly understands the primary purpose of the communication.

Elaborate if Necessary:

Elaborating in your emails is essential when you need to provide context, clarify details, or offer supportive information to enhance the recipient's understanding. This section is where the depth and richness of content comes into play.

1. Modules for Elaboration Determination:

a. Requirement Assessment:

Prompt: "Based on your main point, do you think elaboration is required?

- Definitely required

- Might be helpful

- Not necessary

- Not sure"

b. Content Type Determination:

Prompt: "What type of additional information would you like to include?

- Contextual background
- Supportive data or statistics
- Personal experiences or observations
- Examples or illustrations
- Potential implications or consequences
- Other"

c. Length Determination:

Prompt: "How lengthy do you envision this elaboration to be?

- One to two sentences
- A short paragraph
- Multiple paragraphs
- Not sure"

2. Complex Prompts Based on User Response:

a. For Contextual Background:

Prompt: "Please provide key details or history that led to your main point."

Example User Response: "We've seen a 20% decrease in sales over the last quarter, which prompted our budget request."

b. For Supportive Data or Statistics:

Prompt: "Please share the specific data, figures, or statistics you'd like to include."

Example User Response: "According to our latest survey, 70% of our clients are demanding the feature we're about to launch."

c. For Personal Experiences or Observations:

Prompt: "Describe the personal experiences or observations you believe are pertinent."

Example User Response: "In my recent interactions with key clients, several expressed concerns about our software's speed."

d. For Examples or Illustrations:

Prompt: "Provide a concise example or illustration relevant to your main point."

Example User Response: "For instance, competitor X recently upgraded their software, making it twice as fast as ours."

e. For Potential Implications or Consequences:

Prompt: "Outline the implications or consequences related to your main point."

Example User Response: "If we don't allocate the requested budget, we risk falling behind our competitors."

3. Compilation Based on Responses:

After gathering the details, ChatGPT can craft an elaborative segment:

Example 1 (Contextual Background + One to two sentences): User's Response: "We've seen a 20% decrease in sales over the last quarter, which prompted our budget request."

ChatGPT Suggestion: "To provide some background, our sales dipped by 20% in the previous quarter, underscoring the urgency of our budget request."

Example 2 (Supportive Data + Personal Observations + Short paragraph): User's Responses: "According to our latest survey, 70% of our clients are demanding the feature we're about to launch." and "In my recent interactions with key clients, several expressed concerns about our software's speed."

ChatGPT Suggestion: "Our recent survey data indicates that a significant 70% of our clients are eagerly anticipating the feature we're poised to launch. Additionally, from my personal discussions with some key clients, it's become clear that there's growing concern regarding our software's speed."

Through this detailed method, ChatGPT can help users create an elaboration that reinforces their main point, provides clarity, and resonates with the recipient.

Include a Call to Action (CTA):

A Call to Action (CTA) is a critical component of any email, especially in a professional setting. It directs the recipient towards the desired next steps or outcomes. Crafting an effective CTA can increase engagement, promote understanding, and drive results.

1. Modules for CTA Determination:

a. Action Type Assessment:

Prompt: "What do you want the recipient to do after reading your email?

- Reply with specific information

- Schedule or attend a meeting

- Review a document or resource

- Give feedback or approval

- Take a particular action (e.g., make a payment, complete a task)

- Other"

b. Urgency Level:

Prompt: "How urgent is this action?

- Immediate

- By a specific deadline

- When convenient

- Not time-sensitive"

c. Specifics and Details:

Prompt: "Please provide any specific details you'd like to include in your CTA (e.g., deadline date, meeting preferences, specific questions)."

2. Complex Prompts Based on User Response:

a. For Reply with Specific Information:

Prompt: "What specific information or details are you seeking in the reply?"

Example User Response: "I need their feedback on the proposed design changes."

b. For Schedule or Attend a Meeting:

Prompt: "Do you have preferred dates or times for the meeting? Also, provide any other details such as format or platform."

Example User Response: "I prefer next Wednesday afternoon, using Zoom."

c. For Review a Document or Resource:

Prompt: "Briefly describe the document or resource and any specific aspects you'd like them to focus on."

Example User Response: "It's a draft of our new product proposal, and I'd particularly appreciate feedback on the budget section."

d. For Give Feedback or Approval:

Prompt: "Is there a particular aspect you're seeking feedback or approval on?"

Example User Response: "I want approval on the finalized marketing strategy."

3. Compilation Based on Responses:

After obtaining the necessary details, ChatGPT can craft a targeted CTA:

Example 1 (Reply with Information + Immediate): User's Response: "I need their feedback on the proposed design changes."

ChatGPT Suggestion: "Please review the attached design changes and provide your feedback as soon as possible."

Example 2 (Schedule a Meeting + Specific Deadline): User's Responses: "I prefer next Wednesday afternoon, using Zoom."

ChatGPT Suggestion: "Could we schedule a Zoom meeting for next Wednesday afternoon to discuss this in detail? Please confirm your availability by Friday."

By using these detailed prompts and modules, ChatGPT can assist in crafting clear and actionable CTAs, ensuring that recipients understand their next steps and the importance of their response or action.

Be Courteous and Professional:

Being courteous and professional in business emails is paramount, as it fosters respect, ensures clarity, and maintains a positive relationship between sender and recipient. By implementing a systematic approach with ChatGPT, users can be guided to express their message in a more polished manner.

1. Modules for Courtesy & Professionalism Determination:

a. Tone Assessment:

Prompt: "Which tone do you wish to convey in your email?

- Highly formal

- Professional yet friendly

- Neutral

- Informal (use with caution in a business setting)"

b. Intent Clarification:

Prompt: "In your own words, what is the main message or request you're trying to convey? This will help in framing it courteously."

c. Potential Sensitivity:

Prompt: "Does your message touch on any potentially sensitive or contentious topics?

- Yes

- No

- Not sure"

2. Complex Prompts Based on User Response:

a. For Highly Formal Tone:

Prompt: "Would you prefer to use traditional phrases (e.g., 'I hereby request') and more structured language?"

Example User Response: "Yes, it's a legal communication."

b. For Professional yet Friendly Tone:

Prompt: "Would you like to add expressions of gratitude or personal touches while maintaining professionalism (e.g., 'I appreciate your time on this')?"

Example User Response: "Yes, I'd like to show appreciation."

c. For Potential Sensitivity:

Prompt: "Please provide details on the sensitive or contentious topic so we can approach it with care."

Example User Response: "I have to address a missed deadline by the recipient's team."

3. Compilation Based on Responses:

After gathering the details, ChatGPT can craft or adjust the content to ensure it's courteous and professional:

Example 1 (Highly Formal + Legal Communication): User's Message: "We need the contract signed."

ChatGPT Suggestion: "I hereby request the prompt signing and return of the enclosed contract. Your timely attention to this matter is greatly appreciated."

Example 2 (Professional yet Friendly + Appreciation Expressed): User's Message: "Can you attend the meeting?"

ChatGPT Suggestion: "I hope you're well. Would you be able to attend the upcoming meeting? I genuinely appreciate your time and insights on this matter."

Example 3 (Potential Sensitivity + Missed Deadline): User's Message: "You missed the deadline."

ChatGPT Suggestion: "I hope this message finds you well. I noticed the deadline for our recent project was missed. Can we discuss how to proceed and ensure alignment for future timelines?"

Through this methodical approach, ChatGPT can help users convey messages in a way that is both professional and courteous, regardless of the subject matter or intended tone.

Use a Professional Closing:

The closing of an email, much like the salutation, sets a tone and can leave a lasting impression on the recipient. It's an opportunity to close the communication gracefully while ensuring alignment with the overall tone of the email.

1. Modules for Closing Determination:

a. Tone Consistency Check:

Prompt: "Considering the tone you've maintained throughout your email, how would you like to close it?

- Highly formal

- Professional yet friendly

- Neutral

- Informal (typically avoided in business settings)"

b. Future Interaction Indication:

Prompt: "Would you like to indicate any forthcoming interactions or meetings in your closing?

- Yes, we have a scheduled interaction.

- Yes, I'm expecting a reply or further communication.

- No specific future interactions.

- Not sure."

c. Expressing Gratitude:

Prompt: "Would you like to express gratitude or appreciation in your closing?

- Definitely

- Only if it fits the tone

- Not necessary

- Not sure"

2. Complex Prompts Based on User Response:

a. For Highly Formal Tone:

Prompt: "Choose your preference for a formal closing:

- 'Yours sincerely'

- 'Yours faithfully'

- 'Respectfully'

- Custom (please provide)"

b. For Professional yet Friendly Tone:

Prompt: "Choose your preference for a professional yet friendly closing:

- 'Best regards'

- 'Kind regards'

- 'Warm regards'

- 'Thank you'

- Custom (please provide)"

c. For Neutral Tone:

Prompt: "Choose your preference for a neutral closing:

- 'Regards'

- 'Best'

- Custom (please provide)"

d. For Future Interaction Indication:

Prompt: "Please specify the nature of the forthcoming interaction (e.g., 'Looking forward to our meeting next week.')."

3. Compilation Based on Responses:

Based on the user's inputs, ChatGPT can craft a suitable closing:

Example 1 (Highly Formal): User's Choice: "Yours faithfully"

ChatGPT Suggestion: "Yours faithfully, [Your Name]"

Example 2 (Professional yet Friendly + Expecting a Reply + Expressing Gratitude): User's Choices: "Thank you" and "Looking forward to your response."

ChatGPT Suggestion: "Thank you and looking forward to your response. Warm regards, [Your Name]"

Example 3 (Neutral + Scheduled Interaction): User's Choice: "Regards" and "Our scheduled call is on Friday."

ChatGPT Suggestion: "Looking forward to our call on Friday. Regards, [Your Name]"

By employing this systematic approach, ChatGPT ensures that the email's closing is in line with the intended tone, wrapping up the message coherently while addressing any future interactions or sentiments.

Proofread:

Proofreading is a critical step in email communication, ensuring clarity, professionalism, and minimizing errors. With ChatGPT's prompts and modules, users can be guided to effectively review and refine their emails.

1. Modules for Proofreading Determination:

a. Grammar and Syntax Check:

Prompt: "Would you like to review the email for grammatical and syntax errors?

- Yes

- No

- Not sure"

b. Tone and Politeness Review:

Prompt: "Do you want to ensure the tone is consistent and polite throughout the email?

- Yes

- No

- Not sure"

c. Content Clarity and Redundancy Review:

Prompt: "Would you like to check the email for clarity and eliminate any redundant information or phrases?

- Yes

- No

- Not sure"

d. Custom Review Point:

Prompt: "Are there specific aspects or sections of the email you're particularly concerned about and would like to focus on during the proofreading process?"

2. Complex Prompts Based on User Response:

a. For Grammar and Syntax Check:

Prompt: "Please paste the sections of the email you feel might contain grammatical or syntax errors."

Example User Response: "She have completed the task."

ChatGPT Suggestion: "She has completed the task."

b. For Tone and Politeness Review:

Prompt: "Please paste any sections of the email you're unsure about in terms of tone or politeness."

Example User Response: "You didn't send the files."

ChatGPT Suggestion: "I noticed the files haven't been sent yet. Could you please check?"

c. For Content Clarity and Redundancy Review:

Prompt: "Share sections of the email where you think the content might be unclear or redundant."

Example User Response: "I am writing to ask if you can send the report. Can you send it?"

ChatGPT Suggestion: "I am writing to ask if you can send the report."

d. For Custom Review Point:

Prompt based on user's initial query: "You mentioned being concerned about [specific aspect]. Please paste the relevant sections for a detailed review."

Example User Response: "I'm unsure about the introduction."

ChatGPT Suggestion after review: "The introduction is clear, but you could add a bit more context about your relationship with the recipient for better clarity."

3. Comprehensive Review:

After a series of focused checks, a general prompt can tie everything together:

Prompt: "Would you like a final review of the entire email to ensure cohesion and overall clarity? If yes, please paste the full content."

By employing this structured approach, ChatGPT can assist users in thoroughly proofreading their emails, ensuring that the communication is clear, polite, and free from errors.

Use a Clear Subject Line:

The subject line is a critical component of an email. It's the first thing the recipient sees and often determines if and when the email will be opened. A clear and relevant subject line can greatly improve the efficiency of communication. Let's explore a systematic approach with ChatGPT to craft impactful subject lines.

1. Modules for Subject Line Determination:

a. Main Purpose Identification:

Prompt: "What is the primary purpose or theme of your email?

- Scheduling or confirming an appointment

- Providing an update or information

- Making a request

- Seeking feedback or approval

- Announcing something

- Other"

b. Urgency Level:

Prompt: "How urgent is the content of your email?

- Immediate attention required

- Action needed, but not urgent

- Informative, no action required

- Not sure"

c. Specificity Indicator:

Prompt: "Would you like the subject line to be:

- General and broad

- Specific and detailed

- A mix of both"

2. Complex Prompts Based on User Response:

a. For Scheduling or Confirming an Appointment:

Prompt: "Please provide specifics, like the meeting topic or date."

Example User Response: "Project X review on 10th September."

b. For Providing an Update or Information:

Prompt: "Briefly describe the main update or information."

Example User Response: "Changes to the marketing strategy."

c. For Making a Request:

Prompt: "What are you requesting? Please be concise."

Example User Response: "Approval for budget increase."

d. For Seeking Feedback or Approval:

Prompt: "What specifically are you seeking feedback or approval on?"

Example User Response: "Design mockups for the new campaign."

e. For Announcing Something:

Prompt: "What is the main announcement?"

Example User Response: "New product launch next month."

3. Compilation Based on Responses:

After obtaining the necessary details, ChatGPT can suggest an apt subject line:

Example 1 (Scheduling + Specific + Urgent): User's Response: "Project X review on 10th September."

ChatGPT Suggestion: "URGENT: Confirmation Needed for Project X Review on 10th September."

Example 2 (Update + Mix of Both + Not Urgent): User's Response: "Changes to the marketing strategy."

ChatGPT Suggestion: "Strategy Update: Key Changes to Marketing Approach."

Example 3 (Announcement + General + Informative): User's Response: "New product launch next month."

ChatGPT Suggestion: "Exciting News: Upcoming Product Launch!"

This systematic approach ensures that the email's subject line is clear, relevant, and aligned with the content, increasing the likelihood of timely and appropriate responses.

DALL·E 3

Integrating DALL·E 3 into ChatGPT represents a groundbreaking advancement in the field of AI, blending the power of advanced natural language understanding with sophisticated image generation capabilities. This integration offers numerous benefits to users, fundamentally enhancing the interactive experience and broadening the scope of creative and practical applications. Here are some key aspects of this integration:

1. **Enhanced Creativity and Visualization**: Users can now not only discuss ideas and concepts but also visualize them. Whether it's for creative projects, educational purposes, or just for fun, the ability to generate images from text descriptions opens up a world of possibilities. This tool can be especially valuable for artists, designers, educators, and marketers.

2. **Immediate Visual Representation**: With DALL·E 3 integrated into ChatGPT, users receive instant visual representations of their ideas. This immediacy is crucial for brainstorming sessions, conceptual design, or when explaining complex ideas that are easier understood visually.

3. **Customization and Precision**: Users can provide detailed descriptions to generate highly specific images. This level of customization allows for precise alignment with the user's vision, which is particularly beneficial in fields like graphic design, architecture, and content creation.

4. **Educational Applications**: For educational purposes, this integration is a game-changer. It can help in creating custom illustrations for teaching materials, visual aids for complex academic concepts, or engaging content for e-learning platforms.

5. **Business Applications**: In the business realm, this tool can assist in product design, advertising, brand development, and creating visual content for social media or websites. It

streamlines the process of visual ideation and creation, saving time and resources.

In summary, the integration of DALL·E 3 into ChatGPT marks a significant step forward in AI-powered creativity and communication, offering users an unparalleled tool for visual expression and exploration alongside sophisticated language understanding capabilities.

The above points will be expanded and explained in details as follow:

Enhanced Creativity and Visualization:

The integration of DALL·E 3 into ChatGPT is a remarkable advancement in the realm of artificial intelligence, offering users an unprecedented level of enhanced creativity and visualization. This integration transforms the way we interact with AI, merging the power of sophisticated language models with advanced image generation technology. Here's a detailed look at how this integration amplifies creativity and visualization:

I. Visualization of Abstract Concepts:

One of the most striking benefits of integrating DALL·E 3 with ChatGPT is the ability to visualize abstract ideas and concepts. Users can describe scenarios, abstract art concepts, or theoretical ideas, and see them come to life in visual form. This feature is particularly useful for creative professionals, such as writers, artists, and designers, who often work with complex concepts that are difficult to articulate.

Integrating DALL·E 3 into ChatGPT marks a significant advancement in the realm of artificial intelligence, particularly in the field of Enhanced Creativity and Visualization. This integration is groundbreaking, especially in terms of visualizing abstract concepts, which traditionally has been a challenging area in both creative and analytical domains. Let's delve deeper into how this integration revolutionizes the visualization of abstract concepts:

1. **Bringing Abstract Ideas to Life**: One of the most powerful aspects of this integration is its ability to turn abstract ideas, which are often difficult to convey through words alone, into tangible visual representations. Whether it's a complex philosophical concept, a mood, an emotion, or a metaphor, DALL·E 3 can produce images that give form to these abstract notions, making them more comprehensible and relatable.

2. **Aiding Creative and Analytical Thinking**: For creative professionals, thinkers, and educators, this capability is

invaluable. It allows them to express and explore concepts that are often intangible or challenging to articulate. Visual representations can stimulate further creative thinking, offer new perspectives, and even lead to groundbreaking ideas and solutions.

3. **Enhancing Understanding and Retention**: From an educational standpoint, the ability to visualize abstract concepts can greatly enhance understanding and retention. Complex theories in physics, intricate patterns in mathematics, or nuanced themes in literature can be represented visually, making them easier for students to grasp and remember.

4. **Cross-Disciplinary Applications**: This feature finds applications across various disciplines. In psychology, it can help in visualizing emotions or mental states. In business, it can illustrate market trends or business strategies. In technology, it can represent data patterns or conceptual frameworks. The potential is vast and varied.

5. **Inspiring Artistic Exploration**: Artists and designers can use this tool to explore new realms of creativity. By inputting abstract artistic concepts or emotional states, they can generate visual art that may not have been conceivable using traditional methods. This opens up new avenues for artistic expression and experimentation.

6. **Facilitating Brainstorming and Ideation**: In brainstorming sessions, whether in business, academia, or creative fields, the ability to quickly visualize abstract ideas can stimulate discussion and ideation. It makes the process more dynamic and inclusive, allowing participants to build on visual concepts in real-time.

7. **Communication Aid for Abstract Thinking**: For individuals who naturally think in abstract terms, this integration offers a powerful communication aid. They can more easily share and articulate their ideas with others, bridging gaps in understanding and fostering more effective collaboration.

8. **Exploring the Unexplored**: The AI's capability to interpret and visualize abstract concepts can lead to the exploration of ideas and themes that have not been traditionally visualized. This can lead to unique and innovative art pieces or conceptual illustrations that push the boundaries of conventional thinking.

9. **Customizing Visual Interpretations**: Users have the flexibility to customize how abstract concepts are visualized. By tweaking their descriptions, they can guide the AI to produce images that align closely with their personal vision or the specific requirements of a project or study.

10. **Feedback Loop for Refinement**: As users interact with the AI and provide feedback on the images generated, the system learns and adapts. This continuous learning process enhances the AI's ability to accurately interpret and visualize increasingly complex abstract concepts.

In conclusion, the integration of DALL·E 3 into ChatGPT represents a monumental step in AI's ability to enhance creativity and visualization, particularly in the realm of abstract concepts. It opens up new possibilities for understanding, communicating, and exploring ideas that are difficult to capture in words, thereby enriching the landscape of human thought and creativity.

II. **Aiding Creative Processes**:

For individuals in creative fields, this integration serves as a powerful tool for inspiration and ideation. It allows for rapid prototyping of visual ideas and can significantly speed up the creative process. Artists can experiment with different styles, compositions, and color schemes, while designers can quickly visualize and iterate on product concepts.

The integration of DALL·E 3 with ChatGPT represents a significant leap in the field of artificial intelligence, particularly in enhancing creativity and aiding creative processes. This convergence of advanced image generation and sophisticated language understanding offers a plethora of opportunities for individuals across various creative domains. Let's explore how this integration is revolutionizing the way we approach creative processes:

1. **Instant Visual Realization of Ideas**: With DALL·E 3 integrated into ChatGPT, creators can instantly transform their verbal or written ideas into visual representations. This immediate conversion from thought to image accelerates the creative process, allowing for rapid exploration and iteration of ideas.

2. **Inspiration and Idea Generation**: Creatives often face the challenge of a blank canvas or writer's block. This integration offers a new avenue for inspiration, generating images that can spark new ideas or provide fresh perspectives on existing

projects. Whether it's for writing, designing, or conceptualizing, the AI can produce a range of visual stimuli to get the creative juices flowing.

3. **Exploring Multiple Concepts Quickly**: The ability to quickly generate a variety of visual interpretations of a single concept is invaluable in creative fields. Designers, artists, and writers can explore multiple angles or styles in a fraction of the time it would take manually, allowing for a more expansive exploration of creative possibilities.

4. **Enhanced Collaborative Creativity**: The integration facilitates collaboration among teams, especially in remote or distributed work environments. Teams can share and visualize ideas in real-time, making the collaborative process more dynamic and efficient.

5. **Prototyping and Mock-ups**: For designers and architects, the ability to create quick visual prototypes or mock-ups is a game changer. It enables them to present and refine their ideas more effectively, saving time and resources in the early stages of the design process.

6. **Visual Aid for Storytelling**: For writers and content creators, translating narrative elements into visuals can enrich storytelling. Character designs, settings, and plot elements can be visualized, providing a clearer picture of the narrative world and assisting in the development of more detailed and immersive stories.

7. **Customized Visual Content Creation**: Users can generate customized illustrations, graphics, and designs tailored to their specific needs. This not only enhances the uniqueness of their creative projects but also provides a level of customization that was previously difficult to achieve without specialized skills.

8. **Breaking Creative Boundaries**: The AI's ability to combine elements in novel ways can lead to unexpected and innovative visual outcomes. This pushes the boundaries of traditional creativity, encouraging users to explore beyond conventional norms and experiment with new artistic styles and concepts.

9. **Learning and Skill Development**: For those learning art or design, this integration serves as a tool for understanding and experimenting with different visual styles, compositions, and

color theories. It can serve as an educational aid, providing visual examples and inspiration.

10. **Feedback Loop for Creative Growth**: As users interact with the AI, providing feedback and refining their requests, they engage in a learning loop that enhances their own creative skills. Understanding how to effectively communicate ideas to produce desired visual outcomes can refine one's creative thought process and articulation skills.

In summary, integrating DALL·E 3 into ChatGPT is a transformative development for creative industries. It empowers creators with tools to visualize, experiment, and refine their ideas with unprecedented speed and flexibility. This synergy of AI-driven visual generation and natural language processing is not just a technological advancement; it's a catalyst for a new era of enhanced creativity and innovation.

III. **Educational Enhancement**:

In educational settings, the ability to generate images from textual descriptions can enhance learning and teaching experiences. Complex subjects, particularly in science and history, can be made more accessible and engaging through visual aids. Students can better grasp difficult concepts when they are accompanied by corresponding visual representations.

The integration of DALL.E 3 with ChatGPT heralds a transformative era in the educational landscape, significantly enhancing learning experiences through a blend of visual creativity and interactive dialogue. This synergistic combination opens up new dimensions in educational methodologies, catering to diverse learning styles and complex subjects. Here's an exploration of how this integration serves as a pivotal tool for educational enhancement:

1. **Visual Learning Enhancement**: Many learners absorb and retain information more effectively through visual means. The integration of DALL.E 3 with ChatGPT allows educators to instantly transform textual information into vivid imagery, catering to visual learners and making complex concepts more accessible and engaging.

2. **Interactive Educational Content**: The combination of conversational AI and image generation creates an interactive learning environment. Students can explore concepts through a

dialogue with ChatGPT, prompting DALL.E 3 to generate visual aids that complement the textual explanations, leading to a more immersive and engaging learning experience.

3. **Aiding in Conceptual Understanding**: Subjects that involve abstract or complex concepts, such as advanced mathematics, physics, or even art, can be challenging to convey through words alone. DALL.E 3 can visualize these concepts, aiding in deeper understanding and retention.

4. **Creativity in Learning**: This integration fosters creativity in students. They can experiment with generating images based on their interpretations of the study material, encouraging creative thinking and a deeper, more personal engagement with the content.

5. **Language and Literature Visualization**: In language and literature classes, DALL.E 3 can bring texts to life by visualizing scenes, historical contexts, or character portrayals. This not only enhances comprehension but also adds a layer of enjoyment and engagement in literature study.

6. **Enhanced Accessibility for Diverse Needs**: For students with learning disabilities or those who struggle with textual information, the ability to convert text to images can make learning more accessible and less daunting. It levels the playing field, allowing all students to access educational content in a format that suits their needs.

7. **Facilitating Global Education**: With its ability to translate and visualize educational content across languages, this integration bridges educational gaps globally. Students from different linguistic backgrounds can better understand and relate to educational material, breaking down language barriers.

8. **Encouraging Exploration and Curiosity**: Students can use ChatGPT with DALL.E 3 to explore topics beyond the curriculum, catering to their curiosity and interests. This self-directed learning approach fosters a love for learning and independent thinking.

9. **Support in STEM Education**: In STEM subjects, visual aids are crucial for understanding complex theories and data. DALL.E 3 can generate diagrams, models, and graphical representations of data, aiding in comprehension and analysis.

10. **Innovative Teaching Aids for Educators**: Educators can use this technology to create customized teaching materials that resonate with their teaching style and the needs of their students. It offers a way to refresh traditional teaching methods and make lessons more dynamic and impactful.

In conclusion, the integration of DALL.E 3 with ChatGPT is a groundbreaking development in the realm of education. It enriches the learning experience by blending visual creativity with interactive AI, offering a dynamic and customizable approach to education. This technology has the potential to transform traditional learning paradigms, making education more engaging, accessible, and effective for a diverse range of learners.

IV. **Storytelling and Narrative Development**:

For storytellers and content creators, the integration offers a unique way to develop narratives. Visual representations can add depth to written content, helping to convey emotions, settings, and character descriptions more vividly. This can be particularly beneficial in fields like journalism, scriptwriting, and children's literature.

The integration of DALL.E 3 with ChatGPT marks a groundbreaking advancement in the realm of storytelling and narrative development. This fusion of cutting-edge image generation and sophisticated language processing technologies has opened up new avenues for creators, writers, and storytellers, enhancing both the creative process and the storytelling experience. Let's delve into how this integration significantly enriches storytelling and narrative development:

1. **Visualizing Story Concepts**: The ability to instantly transform written narratives or story ideas into visual representations is revolutionary. Storytellers can now see their characters, settings, and scenes come to life, offering a new perspective and depth to their narrative crafting.

2. **Inspiring Creative Storytelling**: Sometimes, finding the right inspiration for a story can be challenging. With DALL.E 3, storytellers can generate images based on random or specific prompts, providing a wealth of visual stimuli that can spark new story ideas, plot twists, or character developments

3. **Aiding in World-Building**: For genres like fantasy or science fiction, creating unique and believable worlds is crucial. DALL.E 3 can visualize these fantastical elements – from otherworldly

landscapes to futuristic cities, aiding writers in developing rich, immersive worlds that captivate their audience.

4. **Character Development and Design**: Writers can use DALL.E 3 to create detailed visual representations of their characters. This not only aids in developing consistent and vivid character descriptions but also helps in understanding and portraying the characters' emotions and evolution throughout the story.

5. **Enhancing Scriptwriting and Screenplays**: For screenwriters, visualizing scenes can be a vital part of the writing process. DALL.E 3 can generate storyboard visuals or scene concepts, aiding in the visualization of how a scene might play out on screen.

6. **Interactive Storytelling**: Integrating DALL.E 3 with ChatGPT enables an interactive storytelling experience. Audiences can engage in stories where they can request visual elements or alterations, making the narrative experience more dynamic and personalized.

7. **Educational Storytelling**: In educational contexts, this integration can be used to create stories that are both informative and visually engaging, making learning more enjoyable for students and aiding in the retention of information.

8. **Cultural and Historical Narratives**: Writers focusing on historical or cultural narratives can use DALL.E 3 to generate accurate and period-specific visuals, helping to ensure authenticity and immersion in their storytelling.

9. **Enhancing Emotional Impact**: Visuals can amplify the emotional impact of a story. By generating images that complement the narrative's mood and tone, writers can create a more powerful and emotionally resonant storytelling experience.

10. **Streamlining the Creative Process**: The integration simplifies and accelerates the process of story development. Writers can quickly iterate through different visual ideas, refine their narratives, and achieve a more polished end product in a shorter time frame.

In essence, the integration of DALL.E 3 with ChatGPT offers storytellers an unprecedented tool to enhance creativity and visualization in their narrative processes. It not only provides new ways to imagine and visualize stories but also enriches the storytelling experience for both creators and audiences alike. This integration signifies a new era in narrative arts, blending the power of AI-driven visuals with the art of storytelling to create deeply engaging, innovative, and visually rich narratives.

V. **Bridging Communication Gaps**:

The visual element introduced by DALL·E 3 can help bridge communication gaps. For individuals who are visual learners or those who might struggle with language barriers, the ability to convey ideas through images can be invaluable. It creates a more inclusive environment where ideas can be shared and understood more universally.

The integration of DALL.E 3 with ChatGPT represents a significant leap forward in bridging communication gaps, leveraging the power of visual aids and advanced language processing. This fusion not only enhances creativity and visualization but also plays a pivotal role in overcoming barriers in communication. Let's explore the various dimensions of how this integration aids in bridging communication gaps:

1. **Visual Representation of Complex Ideas**: Often, complex or abstract ideas are challenging to convey through words alone. DALL.E 3's capability to create visual representations of such concepts can make them more comprehensible, facilitating better understanding and engagement in conversations.

2. **Overcoming Language Barriers**: In multilingual settings, the integration serves as a powerful tool to transcend language barriers. ChatGPT can interpret and translate text across languages, while DALL.E 3 provides visual accompaniments, ensuring that the message is conveyed effectively, irrespective of the linguistic proficiency of the audience.

3. **Aiding Non-Verbal Communication**: Visual imagery is a universal language in itself. For individuals who find verbal communication challenging, such as those with speech impairments or different language proficiencies, DALL.E 3's visuals can serve as an effective medium of expression, facilitating clearer and more effective communication.

4. **Enhancing Accessibility for Visual Learners**: People have diverse learning and communication styles. Visual learners, in particular, benefit greatly from the integration of DALL.E 3 with ChatGPT, as it allows for the conversion of text-based

information into images, aiding in better comprehension and retention.

5.   **Supporting Education for Diverse Needs**: In educational contexts, this integration can be particularly beneficial for students with special needs or learning difficulties. The combination of visual aids and interactive text can make learning more accessible and engaging for them.

6.   **Cultural Communication and Understanding**: Visuals can play a significant role in bridging cultural differences. By illustrating cultural concepts, traditions, or nuances visually, DALL.E 3 aids in fostering a better understanding and appreciation of diverse cultures.

7.   **Emotion and Sentiment Expression**: Visuals can convey emotions and sentiments more powerfully and subtly than text. Through the generation of images that capture the emotional tone of a conversation, this integration can add depth and empathy to digital communications.

8.   **Clarifying Ambiguous Concepts**: In situations where textual descriptions are open to interpretation or ambiguity, visual representations can provide clarity. DALL.E 3 can generate images that precisely depict specific ideas or scenarios, reducing misunderstandings in communication.

9.   **Facilitating Creative Collaboration**: In creative fields, communicating ideas can sometimes be a challenge. The ability to quickly visualize concepts or designs can significantly enhance collaborative efforts, ensuring that all team members are on the same page.

10. **Enhancing Engagement in Digital Communication**: In the digital world, where attention spans are short, the combination of compelling visuals with text can capture and maintain attention, making communication more engaging and effective.

In conclusion, the integration of DALL.E 3 with ChatGPT is not just a technological marvel but a significant advancement in enhancing communication across various spheres. By combining the power of AI-driven visuals with natural language processing, it offers a versatile and powerful tool to bridge communication gaps, making interactions more effective, inclusive, and impactful. This integration holds immense potential in transforming the way we communicate, learn, and understand each other in an increasingly connected world.

VI. **Interactive Experiences**:

The combination of text and visual feedback creates a more interactive and engaging user experience. It encourages users to explore their creativity by experimenting with different descriptions and seeing the immediate visual outcome, turning the interaction into a creative dialogue between the user and the AI.

The integration of DALL.E 3 with ChatGPT marks a groundbreaking development in the realm of interactive experiences, bringing together advanced AI-driven image creation with sophisticated natural language understanding. This combination significantly enhances creativity and visualization, leading to a new era of interactive experiences. Let's explore the various aspects of how this integration enhances interactive experiences:

1. **Personalized Visual Responses**: DALL.E 3's ability to generate images based on textual prompts allows for personalized visual responses in real-time. Users can interact with ChatGPT, requesting specific visuals, and receive customized images that reflect their queries or creative ideas. This level of personalization adds a new dimension to user engagement.

2. **Interactive Storytelling**: In storytelling and narrative development, the integration offers an immersive experience. Readers can influence the storyline or request visual depictions of scenes, characters, or settings. This creates a dynamic and interactive storytelling environment, where the narrative can evolve based on user input.

3. **Enhanced Educational Tools**: In educational settings, this integration transforms learning experiences. Students can interact with ChatGPT, asking questions about complex subjects, and receive visual aids created by DALL.E 3 that help in understanding and retaining information more effectively.

4. **Creative Problem Solving**: For designers, artists, and creatives, the integration serves as an interactive brainstorming tool. Users can describe their vision or problem, and DALL.E 3 provides visual concepts or solutions, facilitating a creative dialogue that can inspire new ideas and approaches.

5. **Interactive Marketing and Advertising**: In the realm of marketing and advertising, this integration enables brands to create interactive campaigns where consumers can engage in creating personalized visuals or participate in storytelling experiences, enhancing brand engagement and customer experience.

6. **Exploring Abstract Concepts**: For complex or abstract ideas, DALL.E 3 can provide visual interpretations based on ChatGPT's textual explanations, making it easier for users to grasp and interact with these concepts.

7. **Enhanced User Interface Experiences**: In software and web design, this integration can be used to create more intuitive and visually driven user interfaces. Users can describe the type of interface they envision, and DALL.E 3 can generate visual prototypes, enhancing the design process.

8. **Virtual and Augmented Reality Integration**: When combined with VR and AR technologies, this integration can create highly interactive and immersive environments. Users can describe the type of virtual world they wish to experience, and DALL.E 3 can generate the visual components, paving the way for customizable virtual experiences.

9. **Cultural and Linguistic Exploration**: Users can explore different cultures and languages interactively by requesting visual representations of cultural elements, landmarks, or linguistic concepts, enhancing cross-cultural understanding and engagement.

10. **Entertainment and Gaming**: In the gaming industry, this integration can be used to create interactive game environments where players can customize or influence the visual elements of the game in real-time, leading to a more personalized and engaging gaming experience.

In summary, the integration of DALL.E 3 with ChatGPT opens up a multitude of possibilities for interactive experiences across various domains. It not only enhances creativity and visualization but also revolutionizes the way we interact with technology, making experiences more personalized, engaging, and immersive. This integration is a significant step forward in the evolution of interactive AI, offering new ways to explore, learn, create, and engage in the digital world.

VII. Custom Illustrations and Artwork:

With DALL·E 3, users can create custom illustrations and artwork that would otherwise require significant artistic skill and time. This democratizes the ability to create visually appealing content, opening up opportunities for those who may not have formal training in art and design.

The integration of DALL.E 3 with ChatGPT represents a transformative advancement in the realms of creativity and visualization, particularly in the creation of custom illustrations and artwork. This synergy between cutting-edge image generation technology and sophisticated language understanding capabilities opens up unprecedented opportunities for artists, designers, and anyone looking to explore the frontiers of visual expression. Here's a comprehensive look at how this integration enhances the creation of custom illustrations and artwork:

1. **Realization of Unique Ideas**: Users can articulate specific, often complex visual ideas through ChatGPT, and DALL.E 3 brings these concepts to life as illustrations or artwork. This could range from fantastical landscapes to abstract art, enabling the creation of visuals that might be challenging or impossible to realize through traditional means.

2. **Expanding Creative Boundaries**: Artists and designers can use this integration as a tool to push the boundaries of their creativity. They can experiment with different styles, compositions, and themes, receiving instant visual feedback, which can inspire new directions in their work.

3. **Rapid Prototyping of Visual Concepts**: For those in creative professions, this integration can serve as a powerful tool for rapid prototyping. Designers can quickly generate visual representations of their ideas, allowing for faster iteration and development of concepts.

4. **Accessibility to Art Creation**: The integration democratizes the process of art creation. Individuals without formal training in art or design can generate high-quality illustrations and artwork, making the creation of visual art more accessible to a wider audience.

5. **Educational Tool for Art and Design**: In educational settings, this technology can serve as a valuable teaching aid, helping

students understand principles of art and design. It can demonstrate the impact of different artistic techniques and styles, thus enriching the learning experience.

6. **Inspiration for Creative Projects**: Writers, filmmakers, and content creators can use this integration to visualize scenes, characters, or settings for their projects. It can serve as a source of inspiration and a means to refine visual elements in their narratives.

7. **Cultural and Historical Illustrations**: The tool can be used to generate artwork that reflects specific cultural or historical themes, providing visual aids for educators, storytellers, and historians, and thereby enhancing cultural and historical education.

8. **Personalized Artwork for Individual Needs**: From personalized gifts to customized home decor, users can create artwork tailored to individual preferences and needs, making the personalization of visual items more accessible and varied.

9. **Exploring Artistic Styles and Movements**: Users can explore different artistic styles, from classical to contemporary, or generate artwork inspired by specific movements or artists, allowing for a deeper understanding and appreciation of art history.

10. **Enhancing Digital Content Creation**: For digital content creators, including bloggers, social media influencers, and digital marketers, this integration offers a means to create unique, eye-catching visuals that enhance their digital content and engage their audience more effectively.

In conclusion, the integration of DALL.E 3 with ChatGPT marks a significant milestone in the field of digital art and design. It not only enhances the capabilities for creating custom illustrations and artwork but also opens up new avenues for creative expression and exploration. Whether for professional artists, designers, educators, or hobbyists, this technology offers a versatile, powerful, and accessible tool for bringing imaginative ideas to visual reality.

VIII. **Enhanced Marketing and Branding**:

For businesses, the integration can be a boon for marketing and branding efforts. Companies can quickly generate and iterate on visual content that aligns with their branding, whether it's for social media, advertisements, or website design.

The integration of DALL.E 3 into ChatGPT ushers in a new era for marketing and branding, significantly enhancing the capabilities for creativity and visualization in these fields. This synergistic combination of advanced AI-driven image generation and sophisticated language understanding technologies opens up a plethora of innovative avenues for marketers and brand strategists. Here's a comprehensive look at how this integration is revolutionizing marketing and branding:

1. **Customized Visual Content Creation**: With DALL.E 3, marketers can quickly generate customized visual content that aligns with their brand identity and messaging. This ability to rapidly produce high-quality images tailored to specific marketing campaigns or branding themes significantly streamlines the content creation process.

2. **Innovative Advertising Concepts**: The integration facilitates the exploration of new and unique advertising concepts. Brands can experiment with different visual styles and ideas, testing various approaches to find the most effective way to communicate with their audience.

3. **Enhanced Social Media Engagement**: In the social media-driven world, compelling visuals are key to engagement. This integration allows for the creation of visually striking and relevant content, enhancing social media strategies and helping brands stand out in crowded digital spaces.

4. **Product Visualization and Prototyping**: For product development and marketing, DALL.E 3 offers a tool for rapid visualization and prototyping. Brands can visually conceptualize products, packaging designs, and marketing materials, speeding up the development process and allowing for quicker market response.

5. **Personalized Customer Experiences**: The integration enables brands to offer more personalized experiences to their customers. By generating custom visuals in real-time based on customer interactions and preferences, brands can create a more engaging and tailored customer journey.

6. **Visual Brand Storytelling**: Storytelling is a powerful aspect of branding. DALL.E 3 enhances this by providing vivid visual aids

that can illustrate a brand's story, values, and message, creating a deeper emotional connection with the audience.

7. **Interactive Marketing Campaigns**: This technology opens up opportunities for interactive and immersive marketing campaigns. Audiences can be part of the creative process, contributing ideas that can be visually realized on-the-fly, fostering greater engagement and interest.

8. **Market Research and Testing**: Marketers can use this integration to quickly generate a range of visual concepts for market research and A/B testing, gaining insights into consumer preferences and behaviors more efficiently.

9. **Training and Educational Materials**: For internal marketing and brand training, DALL.E 3 can be used to create compelling educational materials, making training more engaging and effective.

10. **Global Reach with Localization**: The technology allows for easy customization of visual content to suit different cultural contexts, aiding brands in their efforts to globalize while ensuring that their marketing is locally relevant.

In summary, the integration of DALL.E 3 into ChatGPT represents a significant leap forward in marketing and branding. It not only enhances the creative and visual aspects of these fields but also offers practical tools for more efficient and effective brand communication. This integration empowers marketers and brand strategists to innovate, personalize, and connect with their audiences in ways that were previously unattainable, paving the way for a more dynamic and engaging future in marketing and branding.

IX. **Exploring New Artistic Frontiers**:

The AI's capability to generate images based on textual inputs allows exploration into new artistic frontiers. It can combine elements in novel ways, generating unique and sometimes surreal artwork that can inspire new artistic movements or styles.

The integration of DALL.E 3 with ChatGPT marks a groundbreaking development in the realm of digital art, opening up new and exciting artistic frontiers. This combination of advanced image generation and sophisticated language processing technologies fosters enhanced creativity and visualization, significantly expanding the scope of what's possible in art creation and exploration. Here's a comprehensive overview of how this integration is reshaping the exploration of new artistic frontiers:

1. **Fusion of Language and Visual Art**: At its core, this integration represents a unique fusion of language and visual art. Artists and creators can describe a vision or concept in words, and DALL.E 3 translates these descriptions into vivid, detailed images. This seamless blend of text and image broadens the horizons of artistic expression.

2. **Generation of Unprecedented Imagery**: DALL.E 3 enables the generation of images that might be incredibly complex, abstract, or even impossible to create by traditional means. This capability allows artists to explore concepts and visualizations that are entirely novel, pushing the boundaries of the imagination.

3. **Collaborative Artistic Process**: The interaction between the artist and AI in this integration creates a unique collaborative process. The AI contributes to the artistic creation, offering interpretations and variations that can inspire new directions and ideas for the artist.

4. **Democratization of Art Creation**: This technology makes the process of creating high-quality, complex art more accessible. Individuals who may not have formal training in art can articulate their visions and see them realized visually, democratizing the creation of art and encouraging a broader participation in artistic expression.

5. **Experimentation with Styles and Forms**: Artists can experiment with a wide range of styles and forms, from realistic to surreal, and from traditional to avant-garde. This exploration can lead to the development of new styles and the evolution of existing ones.

6. **Conceptual and Abstract Art Exploration**: For those interested in conceptual and abstract art, this integration provides a powerful tool for visualizing complex or abstract ideas, making it easier to convey and explore sophisticated concepts through visual means.

7. **Interactive Art and Audience Engagement**: The interactive nature of this integration allows for the creation of art that can evolve in response to audience input or environmental factors.

This interactivity introduces new ways for audiences to engage with art, creating more dynamic and personalized experiences.

8. **Cultural and Historical Interpretation**: Artists can use this technology to reinterpret cultural, historical, and mythological themes, offering new perspectives on familiar narratives and motifs.

9. **Education and Learning in Art**: In educational settings, this integration serves as a valuable tool for teaching and learning about art. It can demonstrate the impact of different artistic techniques, styles, and historical periods, enriching students' understanding and appreciation of art.

10. **Exploration of AI's Role in Art**: Finally, this integration invites a deeper exploration of the role of AI in the creative process. It raises questions and discussions about the nature of creativity, the relationship between human and machine in art, and the future trajectory of artistic expression in an increasingly digital world.

In conclusion, the integration of DALL.E 3 with ChatGPT represents a significant leap in the exploration of new artistic frontiers. It offers artists, educators, students, and art enthusiasts a powerful tool for creating, experimenting, and engaging with art in novel ways. By combining the nuances of human creativity with the capabilities of AI, this technology paves the way for a future where the possibilities for artistic expression are virtually limitless.

X. **Feedback and Refinement**:

As users interact with the AI and provide feedback on the generated images, the system learns and adapts, improving its understanding of user preferences and enhancing the accuracy and relevance of its visual outputs.

The integration of DALL.E 3 into ChatGPT heralds a transformative phase in creative processes, particularly in terms of feedback and refinement. This synergy of AI-driven image generation and sophisticated language understanding brings a new dimension to creativity and visualization, offering remarkable opportunities for artists, designers, educators, and businesses. Here's a comprehensive overview of how this integration enhances feedback and refinement:

1. **Rapid Iteration and Refinement**: With DALL.E 3, users can quickly iterate on visual concepts. Descriptions can be fine-

tuned, and the resulting images can be immediately reviewed and adjusted. This rapid cycle of feedback and refinement significantly accelerates the creative process, allowing for the exploration of numerous variations in a fraction of the time it would take with traditional methods.

2. **Visualizing Feedback in Real-Time**: The integration allows for the visualization of verbal or written feedback in real-time. For instance, if a designer receives specific suggestions for a project, they can immediately input these into ChatGPT, and DALL.E 3 will generate a revised visual representation. This capability makes the process of incorporating feedback more efficient and precise.

3. **Enhanced Communication Between Collaborators**: In collaborative environments, articulating visual ideas can be challenging. With this integration, teams can convert their verbal or text-based ideas into images, enhancing communication and ensuring that all members have a clear, shared understanding of the concept.

4. **Facilitating Artistic Exploration**: Artists and designers often go through extensive exploration phases, where they test different styles, compositions, and color schemes. DALL.E 3 accelerates this process, allowing artists to quickly see the results of various artistic decisions and refine their vision accordingly.

5. **Educational Applications**: In educational settings, the ability to rapidly iterate and refine ideas is invaluable. Students can experiment with different concepts and immediately see the results, which enhances learning and understanding, particularly in visual subjects.

6. **User-Generated Content and Feedback**: For businesses and creators who engage with their audience, DALL.E 3 offers a unique way to visualize user-generated content and feedback. Audiences can submit ideas or suggestions in text form, which can then be transformed into visual content, creating a more interactive and responsive user experience.

7. **Prototype Development**: In fields such as product design and architecture, the ability to quickly generate and refine prototypes based on feedback is crucial. This integration facilitates the rapid visualization of changes and improvements, streamlining the development process.

8. **Testing and Market Research**: For marketers and businesses, the ability to visually test different concepts and receive immediate feedback can be a game-changer. It allows for more effective market research and the refinement of marketing strategies based on visual preferences and feedback.

9. **Personalized Learning and Adaptation**: In a learning environment, educators can use this integration to adapt teaching materials based on student feedback. This personalization enhances the learning experience and helps address individual student needs.

10. **Creative Problem-Solving**: Finally, the integration serves as a powerful tool for creative problem-solving. It allows individuals and teams to visualize solutions, refine ideas based on feedback, and arrive at innovative solutions more efficiently.

In summary, the integration of DALL.E 3 into ChatGPT greatly enhances the feedback and refinement aspect of the creative process. It offers a dynamic, interactive, and efficient approach to iterating and improving upon ideas, making it an invaluable tool across various domains where creativity and visualization play a key role. This integration not only streamlines the creative workflow but also opens up new possibilities for collaboration, innovation, and personalized engagement.

In essence, the integration of DALL·E 3 into ChatGPT is a significant leap forward in digital creativity and visualization. It offers a versatile tool for users to transform their ideas into visual realities, enriching the landscape of creative expression and communication across various domains.

DALL.E Prompts and Examples:

DALL.E prompts are textual descriptions provided by users, which are transformed into images. These prompts can range from simple, straightforward descriptions to complex, abstract concepts. Here are some examples showcasing the use of DALL.E 3 in enhancing creativity and visualization:

1. **Educational Concepts**: A teacher could ask for an illustration of "the water cycle in a vibrant, cartoon style." DALL.E 3 would generate an image depicting evaporation, condensation, precipitation, and collection in a visually engaging and educational manner.

238

2. **Architectural Visualization**: An architect might request "a futuristic sustainable house on Mars, blending with the Martian landscape." DALL.E 3 could visualize this concept, aiding in the exploration of extraterrestrial architecture.

3. **Fashion Design**: A fashion designer could explore ideas by asking for "an avant-garde dress inspired by the Art Deco movement." DALL.E 3 would produce an image reflecting this unique fusion of styles.

4. **Advertising and Branding**: A marketing team might generate ideas for a campaign by requesting "a whimsical depiction of a family enjoying a picnic, with their product subtly integrated." This aids in conceptualizing advertisements that resonate with target audiences.

5. **Storytelling and Concept Art**: Authors or filmmakers could visualize scenes or characters by describing them in detail, like "a heroic figure standing atop a mountain, overlooking a dystopian city below, at dusk." This can be a powerful tool in story development and visualization.

6. **Scientific Illustration**: Researchers might ask for "a detailed illustration of a new species of deep-sea fish discovered recently." DALL.E 3 can help in visualizing scientific findings that might be hard to photograph or capture in the real world.

7. **Interior Design**: An interior designer could request "a modern living room with Scandinavian design elements and a monochromatic color scheme." This can assist in presenting visual concepts to clients.

8. **Culinary Presentation**: A chef or a food blogger might want to see "a gourmet dish made with quinoa and fresh vegetables, presented elegantly." DALL.E 3 can help visualize recipes or dish presentations before actual preparation.

The integration of DALL.E 3 with language understanding models like ChatGPT unlocks new dimensions in creative expression and visualization. By converting text to images, this technology empowers users to bring their ideas to life visually, no matter how complex or imaginative. It serves as a tool for professionals across various fields, from education to design to storytelling, enhancing their ability to conceptualize, explore, and communicate ideas more effectively.

Prompts:

Creating realistic photographs using DALL.E 3 to demonstrate enhanced creativity and visualization requires detailed and imaginative prompts. Here are some examples:

1. **Enhanced Creativity and Visualization - Surreal Landscape**: "Generate a realistic photograph of a surreal landscape where the sky is a vibrant tapestry of neon colors, and the ground is a mosaic of mirrored surfaces reflecting the sky. In the center, there's a crystal-clear lake shaped like a perfect circle, surrounded by unusual, geometrically-shaped trees with luminous leaves. Include a small wooden boat floating in the lake, under a sky transitioning from twilight to night, with visible stars and a crescent moon."

2. **Enhanced Creativity and Visualization - Futuristic Cityscape**: "Create a realistic photo of a futuristic cityscape at dusk. The city should be filled with towering skyscrapers made of glass and steel, featuring organic, flowing shapes. Neon lights and holographic advertisements should illuminate the scene. In the foreground, there should be a bustling street with people walking and futuristic vehicles hovering above the ground. The sky is a gradient of orange and purple hues, with a large, futuristic digital clock projected in the air, displaying time in a digital format."

3. **Enhanced Creativity and Visualization - Fantasy Forest**: "Produce a realistic photograph of a fantasy forest at sunrise. The forest is dense with towering trees that have iridescent bark and leaves that change colors like chameleons. Among the trees, there are glowing, ethereal flowers and a clear stream with sparkling, crystal-clear water. In the background, a gentle mist hovers over the ground, and rays of the morning sun penetrate the canopy, creating a magical, dream-like atmosphere. Include a few fantastical creatures like luminous birds and small, dragon-like animals playfully roaming around."

These prompts aim to guide DALL.E 3 to create images that push the boundaries of creativity and visualization, blending elements of reality with imaginative and fantastical details to produce strikingly realistic yet surreal visuals.

Here's a visually enhanced image that aligns with the theme of "Enhanced Creativity and Visualization." It depicts a surreal landscape that combines vibrant neon colors in the sky, a ground of mirrored surfaces, a crystal-clear circular lake, geometrically-shaped trees with luminous leaves, and a small wooden boat floating in the lake. The sky transitions from twilight to night, showcasing visible stars and a crescent moon, adding to the overall surreal and creative visualization.

Here is a realistic photograph generated to represent the concept of "Enhanced Creativity and Visualization." This image visually interprets a surreal landscape, combining elements like a neon-colored sky, mirrored surfaces, a crystal-clear lake, and geometrically-shaped trees with luminous leaves. It aims to evoke a sense of imaginative possibilities and creative exploration.

Immediate Visual Representation:

The integration of DALL.E 3 into ChatGPT marks a revolutionary advancement in the field of AI, particularly in the realm of visual representation. This fusion of sophisticated language understanding with advanced image generation capabilities offers a unique and immediate way to translate ideas into visuals. Here is a comprehensive introduction explaining the impact and benefits of this integration in terms of immediate visual representation:

I. Instant Visualization of Concepts:

With DALL.E 3 integrated into ChatGPT, users can articulate ideas, descriptions, or narratives in text, and instantly see these concepts materialize as images. This immediate visual representation is not only efficient but also enhances the clarity and comprehension of complex ideas.

The integration of DALL.E 3 with ChatGPT represents a groundbreaking advancement in the realm of artificial intelligence, particularly with its capability for immediate visual representation. This integration ushers in a new era of instant visualization of concepts, fundamentally altering how ideas and thoughts are conveyed and comprehended. Here's a detailed introduction to this integration, focusing specifically on the aspect of instant visualization of concepts:

1. **Transforming Text to Visuals Instantly**: At the core of this integration is the ability to convert text input into visual output swiftly. Users can articulate their ideas, concepts, or descriptions in natural language, and DALL.E 3, in tandem with ChatGPT, translates these verbal or textual descriptions into accurate and detailed images. This immediate transformation from text to image is revolutionary in visualizing abstract or complex ideas quickly and effectively.

2. **Enhanced Communication and Understanding**: The instant visualization capability of this integration plays a crucial role in enhancing communication. It allows for a more effective conveyance of ideas that might be difficult to describe verbally. This is particularly beneficial in fields where precision and clarity of concepts are essential, such as education, science, and engineering.

3. **Aiding Creative Exploration**: For creatives, designers, and artists, the immediate visual representation of ideas opens up new avenues for exploration and inspiration. It provides a quick way to see how different elements of a design interact with each other, experiment with different styles, and visualize the outcome of creative concepts without the need for extensive manual effort.

4. **Facilitating Rapid Prototyping**: In product design and architecture, the ability to instantly visualize concepts accelerates the process of prototyping and model creation. Designers can see their ideas take shape in real-time, enabling a

faster iteration process and more dynamic exploration of design alternatives.

5. **Interactive Learning Experiences**: In educational contexts, this integration offers a powerful tool for visual learning. Concepts that are difficult to grasp through text alone can be instantly illustrated, making learning more engaging and accessible, especially for visual learners or complex subjects like geometry, physics, or art.

6. **Streamlining Concept Development**: In business and marketing, the ability to instantly visualize ideas aids in the rapid development of concepts for campaigns, products, or branding strategies. It allows teams to quickly see and evaluate the visual feasibility of their ideas, leading to more efficient decision-making.

7. **Enhancing Narrative and Storytelling**: For writers, filmmakers, and content creators, instant visualization offers a unique way to develop narratives and characters. It provides a tangible form to the imagined worlds, aiding in the storytelling process and offering new perspectives on narrative development.

8. **Bridging Language Barriers**: The visual representation of concepts can transcend language barriers, making information and ideas accessible to a broader audience. It can be especially useful in international contexts where textual descriptions might pose language challenges.

9. **Inspiring Innovation in Various Fields**: This capability inspires innovation across various fields by providing a tangible form to ideas that were previously confined to imagination or theoretical frameworks. From scientific research to urban planning, the potential applications are vast and varied.

10. **Personalized User Experiences**: For individual users, the integration offers a personalized experience, allowing them to see their unique ideas and thoughts visualized instantly. This not only enhances user engagement but also makes the interaction with AI more intuitive and creative.

In conclusion, the integration of DALL.E 3 with ChatGPT, emphasizing immediate visual representation, particularly in terms of instant visualization of concepts, marks a significant milestone in AI development. It opens up new possibilities for creativity, communication, and understanding, bridging the gap between abstract ideas and tangible visualization. This integration is poised to transform numerous industries and disciplines, offering an innovative tool for visual expression and exploration.

II. **Bridging the Gap Between Imagination and Reality**:

Often, what we imagine can be challenging to convey using words alone. DALL.E 3 empowers users to bridge this gap, transforming abstract thoughts and ideas into concrete, visual forms in real-time, making it easier to share and communicate these visions with others.

The integration of DALL.E 3 with ChatGPT marks a significant leap forward in the realm of artificial intelligence, especially in the context of immediate visual representation. This fusion of technologies bridges the gap between imagination and reality, offering a transformative tool for visualizing ideas and concepts with unprecedented immediacy and precision. Here's an in-depth introduction to this integration, focusing on how it bridges the gap between imagination and reality:

1. **Realizing Imaginative Concepts Visually**: At the heart of this integration is the ability to turn imaginative, often abstract concepts into concrete visual representations instantly. Users can articulate their ideas or visions in natural language, and DALL.E 3, in collaboration with ChatGPT, translates these verbal descriptions into vivid, detailed images. This capability is groundbreaking in its ability to bring even the most imaginative ideas to life visually.

2. **Enhancing Creative Expression**: For artists, designers, and creatives, this integration offers an unprecedented tool for expressing ideas that are difficult to capture through traditional mediums. It enables the visualization of surreal, fantastical, or highly innovative concepts, pushing the boundaries of creative expression.

3. **Facilitating Clearer Communication**: In many professional and educational fields, effectively communicating complex or abstract ideas can be challenging. The immediate visual representation afforded by this integration allows for clearer communication, as concepts that are hard to verbalize can be easily depicted, thereby reducing misunderstandings and enhancing comprehension.

4. **Inspiring Educational Engagement**: In educational settings, this technology can revolutionize teaching methods by providing visual aids that directly correspond to the subjects being taught. Complex scientific theories, historical events, or literary scenes can be instantly visualized, making learning more engaging and effective, especially for visual learners.

5. **Accelerating Conceptual Development**: In fields like product design, architecture, and urban planning, the ability to quickly visualize ideas can significantly speed up the development process. This rapid visualization assists in exploring various design options, understanding spatial relationships, and making more informed decisions.

6. **Aiding in Problem-Solving**: The integration serves as a powerful tool for problem-solving across various domains. By visualizing different scenarios, solutions, or models, it becomes easier to analyze and understand complex problems, leading to more effective and innovative solutions.

7. **Broadening Narrative Horizons**: For storytellers, writers, and content creators, this technology opens up new possibilities in narrative development. It allows for the visualization of scenes, characters, and worlds that were previously confined to the imagination, adding a new dimension to storytelling.

8. **Cultural and Artistic Exploration**: This integration enables exploration into cultural and artistic realms that were previously inaccessible or hard to visualize. It can bring historical, mythical, or culturally significant scenes to life, offering new perspectives and insights.

9. **Personalizing Visual Experiences**: For individual users, the integration provides a unique and personalized way to see their own ideas and thoughts materialized. This not only enhances personal creativity but also brings a new level of engagement and interaction with AI technology.

10. **Democratizing Access to Visual Creation**: By making it easier to create complex visuals, this technology democratizes access to visual creation, allowing people without formal training in art or design to bring their visions to life.

In summary, the integration of DALL.E 3 with ChatGPT, particularly in terms of immediate visual representation, represents a paradigm shift in how we interact with AI to visualize ideas. It bridges the gap between imagination and reality, providing an innovative and powerful tool for various applications across creative, educational, professional, and personal domains. This integration not only enhances creativity and communication but also opens up new frontiers in visual exploration and expression.

III. **Enhancing Creative Processes**:

For artists, designers, and creatives, the integration serves as a powerful tool for brainstorming and inspiration. It allows for the quick exploration of different visual styles, compositions, and concepts, pushing the boundaries of creativity and artistic expression.

The integration of DALL.E 3 with ChatGPT heralds a transformative era in the enhancement of creative processes, particularly through the lens of immediate visual representation. This groundbreaking convergence of advanced AI capabilities offers artists, designers, educators, and virtually anyone with a creative spark a powerful new tool for realizing their imaginative visions. Here's a detailed introduction to how this integration significantly enhances creative processes:

1. **Instant Visualization of Ideas**: Central to this integration is the ability to instantly translate textual descriptions into visual imagery. This feature is revolutionary for creative processes, allowing ideas to be immediately visualized. Whether it's a conceptual art piece, a design prototype, or a complex narrative scene, the instant visual representation of these ideas can significantly streamline and inspire the creative process.

2. **Facilitating Rapid Prototyping**: For designers and artists, the ability to quickly visualize a concept is invaluable. It allows for rapid iteration and experimentation, enabling creatives to explore multiple variations of an idea in a fraction of the time it would traditionally take. This accelerates the development cycle from concept to final product.

3. **Enhancing Collaborative Creativity**: In collaborative environments, the ability to instantly visualize ideas enhances the sharing and refinement of concepts among team members. It acts as a common visual language, bridging gaps in understanding and interpretation, thereby enriching the collaborative creative process.

4. **Stimulating Creative Inspiration**: The integration serves as a catalyst for creativity. By providing an immediate visual representation of ideas, it can unlock new perspectives and inspire directions that may not have been initially considered. This can lead to more innovative and original creations.

5. **Breaking Down Technical Barriers**: One of the most significant impacts of this integration is its ability to democratize the creative process. Individuals who may lack technical skills in drawing or design can now bring their visions to life, leveling the playing field and opening up creative expression to a broader audience.

6. **Aiding in Concept Development**: For storytellers, writers, and content creators, visualizing characters, settings, or scenes as they are being developed can be immensely beneficial. It provides a tangible reference that can guide and enhance the development of narratives and characters.

7. **Educational Applications**: In educational settings, this tool can be used to engage students in creative projects, allowing them to visualize and present their ideas in a more impactful way. It can also be a valuable aid in teaching art and design principles, offering a practical, hands-on experience.

8. **Exploring Uncharted Creative Territories**: The AI-driven nature of DALL.E 3 means that users can explore creative avenues and styles they might not have considered or been able to achieve on their own. This exploration can lead to unique, unconventional, or avant-garde artistic expressions.

9. **Feedback and Refinement**: The ability to quickly visualize ideas also allows for immediate feedback and refinement. Creators can see what works and what doesn't in real-time, adjusting their visions accordingly. This iterative process is crucial in honing and perfecting creative works.

10. **Inspiring Personal Growth**: For individual creatives, this technology offers a means to continuously challenge and develop their artistic abilities. By visualizing a range of ideas and styles, they can expand their creative repertoire and find new sources of inspiration.

In conclusion, the integration of DALL.E 3 with ChatGPT, focusing on immediate visual representation, is a game-changer in enhancing creative processes across various domains. It not only empowers rapid visualization and iteration of ideas but also democratizes creative expression, stimulates innovation, and fosters a more collaborative and inclusive creative environment. This technology is redefining the landscape of creativity, offering new opportunities for artistic exploration and expression.

IV. **Educational Applications**:

In educational settings, immediate visual representation can be a game-changer. Complex subjects, especially those that are abstract or theoretical, can be more effectively taught when accompanied by instant visual aids, enhancing learning and retention.

The integration of DALL.E 3 with ChatGPT marks a significant advancement in the realm of educational technology, particularly through the capability of immediate visual representation. This fusion of cutting-edge artificial intelligence provides educators, students, and researchers with an unprecedented tool for enhancing learning experiences. Here's a comprehensive introduction to how this integration revolutionizes educational applications:

1. **Visual Learning Enhancement**: One of the core benefits of DALL.E 3's integration is its ability to cater to visual learners. By converting textual information into compelling visuals, complex concepts become more accessible and easier to comprehend. This visual aid can be particularly beneficial in subjects like science, history, and literature, where abstract concepts or historical events can be vividly brought to life.

2. **Interactive Educational Material Creation**: Teachers and educators can leverage this technology to create customized educational materials. Whether it's illustrating a scientific process, visualizing historical events, or bringing characters in literature to life, the ability to instantly generate relevant images can transform traditional teaching materials into more engaging and interactive resources.

3. **Aiding in Language Learning**: For language learners, visual context is crucial. The integration of DALL.E 3 allows for the creation of images that correspond to new vocabulary words or phrases, providing learners with a visual reference that can aid in memory retention and understanding.

4. **Stimulating Creativity in Students**: By offering a tool that can instantly visualize any concept, students are encouraged to

explore their creativity. Projects, assignments, and presentations can be enhanced with custom illustrations, helping students to express their ideas more vividly and develop their creative thinking skills.

5. **Enhancing Conceptual Understanding**: Complex theoretical concepts, often hard to grasp through text alone, can be easily visualized with DALL.E 3. This can be particularly transformative in subjects like mathematics, physics, or engineering, where visual representations can provide a clearer understanding of abstract theories.

6. **Supporting Special Education**: For students with learning disabilities or those who require alternative learning methods, immediate visual representation can be a powerful tool. It offers an alternative pathway for understanding and absorbing information, catering to diverse learning needs and styles.

7. **Facilitating Distance Learning**: In the era of online education, keeping students engaged can be challenging. The integration of DALL.E 3 into virtual classrooms can bring a new dimension to distance learning, making digital lessons more interactive and visually stimulating.

8. **Encouraging Research and Exploration**: For older students and researchers, this technology can aid in visualizing data, conceptual models, or simulating outcomes in fields like environmental science, astronomy, or social sciences. It opens up new avenues for exploration and hypothesis testing.

9. **Cross-Curricular Applications**: The versatility of DALL.E 3 means that it can be applied across different subjects, from creating historical timelines in social studies to illustrating biological processes in science. This versatility enhances cross-curricular learning and teaching strategies.

10. **Personalized Learning Experiences**: With the ability to create tailored visuals, educators can personalize learning experiences to suit individual student needs, interests, and learning styles, making education more inclusive and effective.

In conclusion, the integration of DALL.E 3 with ChatGPT, focusing on immediate visual representation, significantly enriches educational applications. It not only transforms how concepts are taught and understood but also democratizes and personalizes learning experiences. By enabling instant visualization of educational content, it opens up new possibilities for interactive, engaging, and inclusive learning across various educational settings and disciplines.

V. **Facilitating Collaborative Work**:

In collaborative projects, particularly those involving design or planning, the ability to instantly visualize ideas ensures that all team members are on the same page. It streamlines the communication process and aids in the swift progression of projects.

The integration of DALL.E 3 with ChatGPT introduces a groundbreaking advancement in the field of collaborative work and team-based projects. This powerful combination of conversational AI and advanced image generation technology enhances collaboration by providing immediate visual representation. Here's a detailed introduction to how this integration facilitates collaborative work:

1. **Enhanced Idea Visualization**: In a collaborative setting, communicating ideas effectively is key. DALL.E 3's ability to instantly generate visuals from textual descriptions allows team members to quickly and accurately visualize each other's ideas. This immediate visual representation helps in bridging the gap between concept and comprehension, ensuring that all participants are on the same page.

2. **Streamlining Design Processes**: For teams working in design, architecture, or creative industries, the integration offers a swift means to visualize concepts, layouts, or designs. It accelerates the initial stages of brainstorming and concept development, allowing for more time to be spent on refinement and execution.

3. **Facilitating Remote Collaboration**: In today's increasingly remote and distributed work environments, DALL.E 3 and ChatGPT can play a crucial role in overcoming the challenges of distance. Teams can share and modify visual ideas in real-time, regardless of their physical locations, enhancing communication and ensuring seamless collaboration.

4. **Encouraging Diverse Perspectives**. When working in a diverse team, different perspectives and interpretations can lead to richer outcomes. The ability to instantly visualize these varying ideas can lead to a deeper understanding and integration of diverse viewpoints, fostering innovation and creativity.

5. **Aiding in Decision Making**: Collaborative decision-making often involves weighing multiple options and scenarios. Through immediate visual representation, teams can quickly visualize and compare different ideas, making the decision-making process more efficient and informed.

6. **Improving Documentation and Record Keeping**: Keeping a record of the evolution of ideas and discussions can be challenging in collaborative projects. With DALL.E 3, teams can not only generate visuals but also keep a visual record of their progression, aiding in documentation and providing a clear reference point for future discussions.

7. **Enhancing Presentation and Pitching**: When presenting ideas to stakeholders, clients, or investors, the ability to showcase visual representations can be incredibly impactful. DALL.E 3 allows teams to create compelling visuals that can enhance their presentations and pitches, making them more persuasive and engaging.

8. **Reducing Miscommunication**: Visual aids are known to reduce misinterpretation and miscommunication in collaborative settings. By providing a clear visual representation of ideas, DALL.E 3 minimizes misunderstandings and ensures that all team members have a unified understanding of the project goals and details.

9. **Supporting Rapid Prototyping**: In product development or innovation projects, the ability to create quick visual prototypes can significantly expedite the process. DALL.E 3 enables teams to visualize prototypes or concepts instantly, facilitating faster feedback and iteration cycles.

10. **Cultivating a Creative Environment**: The integration fosters a more creative and dynamic working environment. Teams are encouraged to experiment with ideas and explore various visual possibilities, leading to a more creative and exploratory approach to projects.

In summary, the integration of DALL.E 3 with ChatGPT, focusing on immediate visual representation, offers a transformative tool for collaborative work. It enhances communication, fosters creativity, streamlines processes, and bridges geographical divides, making it an invaluable asset in various collaborative settings, from creative industries to remote team projects.

VI. **Rapid Prototyping and Design**:

For product designers, architects, and engineers, the integration offers a means to rapidly prototype designs. This immediacy accelerates the design process, from conceptualization to finalization, saving time and resources.

The integration of DALL.E 3 with ChatGPT marks a significant milestone in the fields of rapid prototyping and design, offering a novel approach to visualizing and refining concepts in real-time. This synergy between advanced conversational AI and cutting-edge image generation technology enhances the design and prototyping process in several impactful ways. Here's an introduction to how this integration revolutionizes these fields:

1. **Accelerating Conceptual Visualization**: DALL.E 3's ability to instantly translate textual descriptions into visual imagery allows designers and engineers to quickly visualize initial concepts and ideas. This immediate visual representation is invaluable in the early stages of design, where rapid iteration and exploration of concepts are key.

2. **Facilitating Iterative Design**: The design process is inherently iterative, often requiring multiple revisions and adjustments. The integration of DALL.E 3 with ChatGPT streamlines this process, enabling designers to rapidly generate and modify visuals based on evolving requirements or feedback, thus significantly reducing the time between iterations.

3. **Enhancing Creativity and Exploration**: With the capability to generate a wide range of visual representations from a single text prompt, designers can explore a broader spectrum of ideas and possibilities. This not only enhances creativity but also encourages out-of-the-box thinking, leading to more innovative design solutions.

4. **Bridging the Gap between Idea and Execution**: Often, there is a disconnect between a conceptual idea and its practical execution. DALL.E 3 helps bridge this gap by providing a visual form to abstract concepts, making it easier to assess feasibility and practicality in the early stages of design.

5. **Improving Communication within Teams**: Effective communication is crucial in collaborative design projects. The immediate visual representation provided by DALL.E 3 ensures

that team members have a clear and consistent understanding of the design, reducing misunderstandings and streamlining collaboration.

6. **Enhancing Client Engagement and Feedback**: In client-centric design work, being able to quickly show visual prototypes can significantly enhance client engagement. Clients can provide immediate feedback, leading to more client-focused and satisfactory design outcomes.

7. **Reducing Time and Costs**: Traditional prototyping methods can be time-consuming and costly. The integration of DALL.E 3 in the design process reduces the reliance on physical prototypes in the initial stages, thereby saving time and resources.

8. **Supporting Remote Collaboration**: In a world where remote work is increasingly prevalent, this integration is particularly valuable. Teams can collaborate on designs and prototypes virtually, sharing and modifying visual ideas in real-time, regardless of geographical location.

9. **Aiding Educational and Training Processes**: For students and professionals learning design and prototyping, this technology serves as an excellent educational tool. It allows for rapid experimentation and learning, providing a hands-on experience with immediate visual feedback.

10. **Customization and Personalization**: In bespoke design work, the ability to quickly visualize customized or personalized elements based on specific client needs or preferences is a game-changer, enhancing the overall quality and relevance of the final product.

In conclusion, the integration of DALL.E 3 with ChatGPT, focusing on immediate visual representation, represents a transformative tool in the world of rapid prototyping and design. It facilitates quicker and more effective visualization, enhances collaborative efforts, and fosters a more dynamic and creative design process. This integration not only streamlines the workflow but also opens up new possibilities for innovation and creativity in design.

VII. **Marketing and Branding Applications**:

Marketers can instantly create visuals for campaigns, branding ideas, or social media content. This ability to quickly produce and iterate on visual content is invaluable in the fast-paced world of digital marketing.

The integration of DALL.E 3 with ChatGPT heralds a transformative era for marketing and branding, providing immediate visual representation capabilities that are set to redefine the landscape. This convergence of conversational AI and advanced image generation technology offers numerous advantages for professionals in marketing and branding. Here's a comprehensive introduction to the impact of this integration in these sectors:

1. **Enhanced Creative Campaigns**: The ability to instantly generate visuals from textual descriptions allows marketing teams to rapidly conceptualize and visualize advertising campaigns, social media content, and branding materials. This immediate visual representation bridges the gap between ideation and visual execution, fostering a more creative and dynamic approach to marketing.

2. **Customized Branding Solutions**: With DALL.E 3, brands can tailor their visual content to specific audiences or campaigns with unprecedented precision and speed. This customization capability ensures that each piece of visual content is perfectly aligned with the brand's identity and messaging strategy.

3. **Real-Time Visual Experimentation**: Marketing often requires a process of trial and error to determine what resonates best with the target audience. The integration of DALL.E 3 into this process means that marketers can experiment with different visual styles and concepts in real-time, significantly speeding up the experimentation phase and reducing costs.

4. **Storytelling and Narrative Enhancement**: Effective branding often relies on storytelling. With DALL.E 3, marketers can quickly create visual narratives that complement their textual storytelling, enhancing the overall impact and engagement of their campaigns.

5. **Rapid Response to Market Trends**: In the fast-paced world of marketing, being able to quickly adapt to and capitalize on current trends is crucial. The immediate visual representation offered by this integration allows marketing teams to produce relevant content swiftly, keeping the brand relevant and engaged with its audience.

6. **Streamlined Content Production**: Traditional methods of creating visual content for marketing can be resource-intensive and time-consuming. DALL.E 3 significantly streamlines this process, allowing for the rapid production of high-quality visuals, which is especially beneficial for content-heavy platforms like social media.

7. **Enhanced Consumer Engagement**: Engaging visuals are key to capturing consumer attention. By utilizing DALL.E 3, marketers can create compelling, unique images that are more likely to engage and resonate with their target audience.

8. **Facilitating Collaborative Creativity**: The integration fosters a collaborative environment where ideas can be visually shared and refined in real-time, ensuring that all team members are aligned and can contribute effectively to the creative process.

9. **Cost-Effective Marketing Solutions**: By reducing the need for extensive graphic design resources and cutting down on production time, this technology presents a cost-effective solution for creating high-quality marketing materials.

10. **Educational and Training Benefits**: For professionals and students in marketing and branding, the ability to interact with this technology offers invaluable hands-on experience. It serves as a practical tool for understanding the relationship between textual concepts and visual representation.

In summary, the integration of DALL.E 3 with ChatGPT in the realm of marketing and branding heralds a new era of creative flexibility, efficiency, and effectiveness. It empowers marketers to rapidly prototype ideas, customize content, and engage audiences with visually stunning and relevant material, all while significantly cutting down on time and costs. This technology is not just an enhancement to existing methods but a complete reinvention of the creative process in marketing and branding.

VIII. **Interactive Storytelling**:

In storytelling, whether in literature, gaming, or film, the integration provides a unique tool for visualizing scenes, characters, and settings. This can aid writers and directors in better conceptualizing their narratives and engaging their audiences.

The integration of DALL.E 3 into ChatGPT represents a groundbreaking advancement in the domain of interactive storytelling, merging the power of advanced language models with the innovative capabilities of visual AI. This fusion marks a significant stride in enhancing the storytelling experience, offering immediate visual representation that adds depth, engagement, and a new dimension of interactivity. Here's a comprehensive introduction to how this integration is revolutionizing interactive storytelling:

1. **Visualizing Narratives Instantly**: As storytellers weave tales through ChatGPT, DALL.E 3 brings these narratives to life by instantly creating vivid, detailed images that align with the text. This immediate visual representation transforms abstract words into concrete visuals, allowing readers to immerse themselves in the story more deeply.

2. **Enhancing Creative Freedom**: Writers and creators now have an unprecedented level of creative freedom. They can experiment with various settings, characters, and scenarios in their stories, seeing their ideas visualized instantly. This not only aids in the creative process but also opens up new avenues for storytelling that were previously difficult to explore.

3. **Interactive Engagement**: In interactive storytelling, audience participation is key. With the integration of DALL.E 3, audiences can influence the direction of the story and see their choices reflected visually in real-time. This creates a more engaging and personalized experience, as each choice brings a different visual outcome.

4. **Bridging Literary and Visual Arts**: The fusion of ChatGPT and DALL.E 3 blurs the line between literary and visual arts. It allows storytellers to simultaneously play the role of a writer and a visual artist, providing a holistic approach to storytelling that caters to multiple senses.

5. **Expanding Accessibility**: Visual representations can make stories more accessible and enjoyable, particularly for younger audiences or those who are visual learners. By providing immediate visual cues, the storytelling becomes more inclusive and easier to comprehend.

6. **Aiding Memory Retention**: Images can significantly aid in memory retention. By providing visual counterparts to textual narratives, this integration helps audiences better remember and recall stories, enhancing the overall impact and longevity of the narrative.

7. **Facilitating Emotional Connection**: Visual imagery can evoke strong emotional responses. The ability to instantly create images that complement the emotional tone of a story can intensify the reader's emotional connection to the narrative.

8. **Encouraging Educational Use**: In educational settings, this technology can be used to teach narrative techniques, storytelling structures, and creative writing. The immediate visual representation adds an interactive element that can make learning more engaging and effective.

9. **Supporting Professional Storytellers**: For authors, scriptwriters, and professional storytellers, this integration serves as a powerful tool for brainstorming, conceptualizing, and pitching ideas. It offers a new way to present stories to audiences, publishers, or collaborators.

10. **Cultural and Artistic Exploration**: Interactive storytelling with visual elements can also serve as a medium for cultural expression and artistic exploration, enabling storytellers to delve into diverse themes and narratives in a visually compelling way.

In conclusion, the integration of DALL.E 3 with ChatGPT for immediate visual representation in interactive storytelling is not just an enhancement of the narrative experience; it's a revolutionary step that transforms how stories are told and experienced. It bridges the gap between imagination and visualization, offering a more immersive, engaging, and emotionally resonant form of storytelling. This technology is poised to redefine the landscape of narrative arts, bringing a new era of storytelling that is interactive, visually rich, and boundlessly creative.

XI. **Personalized User Experience**:

For users interacting with AI in various applications, the ability to instantly see visual representations of their queries or requests leads to a more engaging and personalized experience.

The integration of DALL.E 3 into ChatGPT heralds a new era in personalized user experiences by offering immediate visual representation. This amalgamation of cutting-edge AI in language and visual creativity not only enhances user interaction but also tailors it to individual preferences and imaginations. Here's a deeper look into how this integration significantly elevates the personalized user experience:

1. **Customized Visual Responses**: With DALL.E 3, ChatGPT can generate images that are directly responsive to user input. This

means that every visual created is unique and tailored to the specific request or description provided by the user, offering a highly personalized experience.

2. **Enhancing User Engagement**: The ability to instantly translate text into visuals makes interactions more engaging. Users are not just passive recipients of information but active participants in a creative process, where their inputs immediately come to life visually.

3. **Aiding in Unique Expression**: Users often struggle to express their ideas or visions purely through words. The integration of DALL.E 3 allows for these ideas to be visualized, offering a new dimension to expression. This is particularly beneficial in areas like design, art, and creative brainstorming.

4. **Interactive Learning and Exploration**: For learners, this technology provides a personalized educational experience. Complex concepts, especially in subjects like history, science, or literature, can be visualized instantly, making learning more interactive and tailored to individual learning styles.

5. **Facilitating Emotional Connections**: Visuals have a profound impact on emotional engagement. By generating images that resonate with a user's personal experiences, preferences, or mood, ChatGPT with DALL.E 3 can create a more empathetic and emotionally connected user experience.

6. **Adapting to Cultural Contexts**: The integration allows for the creation of visuals that respect and reflect diverse cultural backgrounds and contexts, offering a more inclusive and personalized experience for users from different parts of the world.

7. **Enhancing Creative Collaboration**: In collaborative settings, such as brainstorming sessions or creative projects, this technology enables a group of users to see their collective ideas visualized in real time. This not only aids the creative process but also ensures that the output is reflective of the group's vision.

8. **Personalized Storytelling**: For those interested in storytelling or narrative development, the ability to create visuals on demand allows for the crafting of stories that are visually aligned with the user's imagination, enhancing the personalization of storytelling.

9. **Supporting Mental and Conceptual Modeling**: Users often use mental models to understand and navigate complex systems or concepts. The immediate visual representation capabilities of this integration help in creating these models, making abstract concepts more concrete and personalized.

10. **Dynamic Adaptation**: The technology is capable of learning and adapting to user preferences over time. This means the more a user interacts with the system, the better it becomes at understanding and visually representing their specific style and preferences.

In summary, the integration of DALL.E 3 into ChatGPT transforms the user experience from a standard interaction to a highly personalized, visually enriched journey. It opens up new realms of possibility for individual expression, learning, and engagement, making each interaction uniquely tailored to the user's needs and imagination. This marks a significant step forward in personalized AI, offering a more intuitive, responsive, and visually stimulating experience.

X. **Exploring New Artistic Frontiers**:

Lastly, this integration opens up new frontiers in the world of digital art. Artists can experiment with AI as a collaborative partner, exploring uncharted territories in art styles, compositions, and themes.

The integration of DALL.E 3 with ChatGPT represents a groundbreaking development in the exploration of new artistic frontiers, combining the power of advanced natural language processing with pioneering image generation capabilities. This integration offers immediate visual representation, transforming the way artists, designers, and creative professionals conceive and visualize art. Here's a detailed look at how this synergy is revolutionizing artistic exploration:

1. **Expanding Creative Possibilities**: By merging ChatGPT's linguistic understanding with DALL.E 3's visual creation abilities, artists are now empowered to explore concepts and ideas that were previously difficult to articulate or visualize. This integration opens up a vast array of new possibilities for creative expression, allowing artists to push the boundaries of traditional art forms.

2. **Instantaneous Visualization of Ideas**: Artists often grapple with the challenge of translating the vivid imagery of their imagination into tangible forms. The immediate visual representation

provided by DALL.E 3 allows for the instant conversion of descriptive language into visual art, reducing the gap between conception and creation.

3. **Fostering Experimental Art**: This integration facilitates a trial-and-error approach to art creation. Artists can experiment with various descriptions, styles, and themes, seeing immediate visual outputs. This rapid iteration process encourages a more experimental and exploratory approach to art.

4. **Collaborative Artistic Endeavors**: The ability of ChatGPT with DALL.E 3 to generate visuals based on textual inputs opens up new avenues for collaboration. Artists and creators from different backgrounds or with varying skills can work together seamlessly, using language as a common medium to generate visual art.

5. **Exploring the Interplay of Text and Image**: This integration allows for a deeper exploration of the relationship between text and imagery. Artists can experiment with how narrative, poetry, and dialogue interact with visual elements, creating artworks that are a fusion of literary and visual art forms.

6. **Personalized Artistic Styles**: DALL.E 3's capabilities enable artists to explore and develop personalized styles. By inputting specific instructions, artists can guide the AI to generate images that align with their unique artistic vision, thereby aiding in the development of a distinct artistic signature.

7. **Democratizing Art Creation**: The accessibility of this technology lowers barriers to art creation, allowing individuals without formal artistic training to visualize and create art. This democratization not only broadens the scope of who can create art but also diversifies the types of art being created.

8. **Inspiring New Artistic Genres**: The blend of AI-generated visuals and human creativity may lead to the birth of entirely new genres and styles of art. This integration paves the way for unexplored artistic expressions, blending traditional techniques with AI-assisted creations.

9. **Cultural and Conceptual Exploration**: Artists can use this technology to explore cultural themes or conceptual ideas, generating visuals that represent diverse cultures, historical periods, or abstract concepts, thereby enriching their artistic repertoire.

10. **Enhancing Visual Narratives**: For those involved in visual storytelling, such as in graphic novels or animation, this integration offers tools to rapidly prototype scenes and characters, aiding in the development of more complex and visually compelling narratives.

The integration of DALL.E 3 with ChatGPT marks a significant milestone in the realm of art and creativity. It not only enhances the process of artistic creation but also invites a reimagining of what art can be in the age of AI. This powerful combination paves the way for artists to explore new frontiers, experiment with uncharted styles, and engage with their craft in innovative and transformative ways.

In conclusion, the integration of DALL.E 3 with ChatGPT represents a significant leap forward in the field of AI, particularly in the realm of immediate visual representation. It offers a vast array of possibilities for enhancing creativity, communication, learning, and collaboration across various sectors. By converting textual descriptions into vivid images instantaneously, this technology not only augments the human capacity for creativity and expression but also paves the way for exciting new applications in the future.

Prompts:

To generate a realistic photograph for "Immediate Visual Representation," the prompts could be:

1. "Create a realistic image of a designer instantly visualizing a complex building structure on a holographic interface, with detailed architectural elements floating in mid-air, showcasing futuristic technology in a well-lit modern office."

2. "Depict a student instantly seeing a vivid, 3D representation of the human circulatory system appears above her tablet during a biology class. The image should be detailed, with arteries and veins in distinct colors, set in a bright, modern classroom."

3. "Visualize an artist standing in front of a large, blank canvas, with her imaginative concept immediately materializing as a colorful, detailed painting on the canvas, reflecting a blend of abstract and realistic styles in a bright art studio setting."

4. "Showcase a chef in a modern kitchen, who is using augmented reality glasses to instantly visualize a complex gourmet dish with intricate presentation details, set on a kitchen counter surrounded by fresh ingredients."

5. "Illustrate an engineer working on a renewable energy project, instantly visualizing a detailed 3D model of a wind turbine in the field, with the landscape and the turbine's intricate components clearly depicted in the outdoor setting."

6. "Generate an image of a fashion designer in a stylish studio, immediately visualizing a new clothing line on a digital mannequin. The image should include intricate fabric patterns and a variety of colors, reflecting a blend of modern and traditional fashion designs."

7. "Create a realistic depiction of a landscape architect visualizing a garden design on a tablet, with the garden instantly appearing in 3D on the screen. The image should show a variety of plants, flowers, and layout designs, set against the backdrop of an urban office."

8. "Illustrate a group of students in a physics class, immediately seeing a 3D representation of the solar system, with each planet and its features vividly detailed, hovering above a digital device in a brightly lit classroom."

9. "Visualize a filmmaker on a set, using advanced technology to instantly see a realistic representation of a CGI character integrated into a live scene, with detailed textures and lighting effects, set in a busy film studio."

10. "Depict a car designer in an automotive studio, immediately visualizing a new car model in 3D on a large screen. The image should showcase the car's sleek design, aerodynamic features, and futuristic look, set in a high-tech design studio."

These prompts further elaborate on the theme of Immediate Visual Representation, spanning various domains such as fashion, landscape architecture, education, filmmaking, and automotive design

Here is the generated image illustrating the concept of Immediate Visual Representation. This image depicts a graphic designer working at a desk with dual monitors, showcasing both a 3D model of a futuristic cityscape and its wireframe model, set in a modern and well-lit room with concept sketches on the wall.

The image above illustrates the concept of Immediate Visual Representation in a creative workspace. It showcases how advanced visual tools and technologies can be seamlessly integrated into the workflow of a professional graphic designer, enhancing creativity and efficiency.

Customization and Precision:

The integration of DALL.E 3 into ChatGPT marks a transformative leap in digital creativity, particularly in the realms of customization and precision. This synergy between advanced natural language understanding and cutting-edge image generation technology offers unprecedented control and specificity in visual content creation. Here's a comprehensive look at how this integration elevates the bar for customized and precise visual outputs:

I. Tailored Visual Solutions:

With DALL.E 3 integrated into ChatGPT, users can articulate specific requirements and preferences, guiding the AI to generate images that closely align with their vision. This capability is invaluable for industries that demand high levels of customization, such as advertising, fashion, and interior design, where visual content needs to reflect unique brand identities or personal styles.

The integration of DALL.E 3 with ChatGPT represents a groundbreaking advancement in the realm of AI-driven creativity, particularly in providing tailored visual solutions. This combination of sophisticated image generation and advanced language understanding technologies allows for a highly customized approach to visual content creation. Here's an in-depth look at how this integration facilitates the creation of tailored visual solutions:

1. **Understanding User Intent**: ChatGPT, with its nuanced understanding of natural language, can interpret detailed and complex user requests. This comprehension is crucial for creating visuals that are not just visually appealing but also align with the specific intentions and needs of the user.

2. **Highly Customizable Outputs**: DALL.E 3's ability to generate images based on textual descriptions enables the creation of highly specific and customized visuals. Users can specify various aspects of an image, such as theme, style, color scheme, and composition, leading to outputs that are tailored to their exact preferences and requirements.

3. **Bridging Creative Communication**: The integration serves as a bridge between the user's creative vision and the final visual product. Users who may not have the technical skills to create complex visuals themselves can simply describe their ideas, and the AI transforms these descriptions into tangible images.

4. **Versatility in Applications**: This technology finds its application across various sectors. Whether it's for marketing materials, educational content, conceptual art, or even personal projects, the ability to generate tailored visuals on demand is immensely valuable.

5. **Iterative Customization**: The integration allows for an iterative approach to image creation. Users can refine their descriptions based on initial outputs, enabling a collaborative process between the AI and the user to fine-tune the visuals until they meet the desired outcome.

6. **Enhanced Creative Possibilities**: By removing the limitations of technical skill or artistic ability, the integration of DALL.E 3 and ChatGPT democratizes the creation of custom visual content. It opens up new possibilities for creative expression and experimentation, allowing users to explore ideas that were previously difficult to realize.

7. **Rapid Prototyping**: In industries where visual content needs to be produced quickly, such as advertising or product design, the ability to rapidly generate tailored visuals based on specific briefs

is a significant advantage. This speed and efficiency can greatly enhance productivity and creative workflow.

8. **Consistency and Brand Alignment**: For businesses and brands, maintaining a consistent visual style is crucial. This integration ensures that every generated image adheres to the specified brand guidelines and aesthetic preferences, thus maintaining a cohesive visual identity.

9. **Accessibility and Ease of Use**: The conversational interface of ChatGPT makes this technology accessible to a wide range of users, regardless of their technical expertise. This ease of use ensures that anyone can benefit from tailored visual solutions, democratizing the process of visual creation.

10. **Expanding Creative Horizons**: Lastly, this integration encourages users to push beyond traditional boundaries in visual content creation. It allows for the exploration of new styles, themes, and conceptual visualizations, expanding the horizon of what can be achieved in digital art and design.

In conclusion, the integration of DALL.E 3 with ChatGPT marks a significant stride in the field of AI-assisted creativity, especially in the context of providing tailored visual solutions. It offers an unprecedented level of customization and precision, enabling users to bring their unique visions to life with remarkable accuracy and ease, thus transforming the landscape of visual content creation.

II. **Precision in Detailing**:

The advanced algorithms of DALL.E 3 allow for meticulous attention to detail in image generation. Users can specify intricate elements, from textures and colors to the composition and mood of the image, ensuring that the output precisely matches their envisioned concept. This level of precision is particularly beneficial for fields like architecture and product design, where accuracy in visual representation is crucial.

The integration of DALL.E 3 with ChatGPT heralds a new era in the field of AI-powered creativity, particularly emphasizing precision in detailing. This synergistic combination of cutting-edge image generation and sophisticated language processing technologies offers an unparalleled capacity for creating highly detailed and precise visual representations. Here's a comprehensive look at how this integration excels in delivering precision in detailing:

1. **Advanced Language Comprehension**: ChatGPT's ability to understand and process complex and nuanced user requests plays a pivotal role. It interprets detailed instructions, nuances of descriptions, and even subtle suggestions, which are essential for creating images with high precision in detailing.

2. **Exceptional Detail Rendering**: DALL.E 3 is engineered to pay close attention to the intricacies in a textual description. This means that even the most minor details conveyed in a user's description can be accurately reflected in the generated images, from the texture of materials to the play of light and shadow.

3. **Custom Detailing for Specific Needs**: The integration allows users to request visuals that require specific details – be it for educational content, technical illustrations, or creative projects. Users can specify elements down to minute details, ensuring the output aligns perfectly with their requirements.

4. **Enhancing Realism and Accuracy**: In fields where accuracy is paramount, like scientific illustration or architectural visualization, this precision in detailing is invaluable. The AI can generate visuals that not only look realistic but also adhere to accurate representations as required in these specialized fields.

5. **Iterative Refinement**: One of the key advantages of this integration is the ability to refine outputs iteratively. Users can adjust their descriptions based on initial results, allowing for a process of continuous improvement and refinement to achieve the desired level of detail.

6. **Visual Complexity Management**: DALL.E 3's capability to handle complex visual compositions means that even when a scene is rich in elements, the AI can manage and maintain a high level of detail, ensuring each component is well-represented.

7. **Accuracy in Conceptual Representations**: For abstract or conceptual ideas, the precision in detailing helps in creating images that are not only visually appealing but also accurate representations of complex concepts, making abstract ideas more tangible and understandable.

8. **Cross-Disciplinary Applications**: This precise detailing finds its application across various disciplines – from creating intricate art

pieces to designing detailed infographics for business presentations, offering wide-ranging utility.

9. **Democratizing Detailed Visual Creations**: By enabling the creation of detailed visuals without the need for specialized artistic skills, this technology democratizes access to high-quality, detailed imagery, allowing more people to bring their detailed visions to life.

10. **Inspiring New Avenues of Creativity**: Finally, the precision in detailing encourages users to explore new realms of creativity. It inspires them to delve into projects or ideas that require a high level of detail, which might have been prohibitive due to the limitations of manual creation or lack of technical skills.

In summary, the integration of DALL.E 3 with ChatGPT significantly enhances the precision in detailing of visual content creation. It opens up a world where detailed, accurate, and visually rich images can be created effortlessly, catering to a broad spectrum of applications and empowering users to bring even their most intricate visions to reality. This represents a remarkable leap forward in the capabilities of AI-assisted creative tools, redefining the boundaries of digital art and visualization.

III. **Adaptation to Complex Requests**:

The natural language processing capabilities of ChatGPT, combined with DALL.E 3's image generation, enable the system to understand and interpret complex, multi-layered requests. This means users can provide detailed, nuanced descriptions or tell stories, and the AI will translate these into rich, detailed visuals that capture the essence of the request.

The integration of DALL.E 3 with ChatGPT marks a significant milestone in the realm of artificial intelligence, particularly in terms of customization and precision in adapting to complex requests. This powerful synergy between advanced image generation and sophisticated language understanding capabilities enables users to bring their most intricate and nuanced ideas to life with unprecedented accuracy. Here's a detailed exploration of how this integration excels in adapting to complex requests:

1. **Understanding Nuanced Instructions**: ChatGPT's advanced natural language processing allows it to comprehend detailed and complex instructions from users. This deep understanding is

crucial for accurately translating intricate ideas into visual representations, ensuring that the final image aligns closely with the user's intent.

2. **Handling Multi-Faceted Requests**: DALL.E 3's robust image generation capabilities, combined with ChatGPT's language skills, allow for the handling of requests that encompass multiple elements, themes, or concepts. Whether it's a scene combining historical and futuristic elements or a visual that weaves together various thematic layers, the AI can adeptly manage and integrate these diverse aspects.

3. **Personalized Visual Responses**: The integration enables the creation of highly personalized images that cater to specific user preferences and requirements. Users can specify particular styles, colors, themes, or even moods, and the AI will generate visuals that reflect these preferences with a high degree of accuracy.

4. **Adapting to Creative and Professional Needs**: Whether it's for creative projects, professional presentations, or academic purposes, the AI can adapt its outputs to fit a wide range of complex requests. This flexibility makes it an invaluable tool across various domains, from art and design to marketing and education.

5. **Iterative Refinement and Feedback Loop**: The integration supports an iterative process where users can refine their requests based on initial outputs. This ongoing interaction allows the AI to better understand and adapt to the user's specific needs, enhancing the precision of subsequent images.

6. **Sophisticated Concept Interpretation**: The AI's ability to interpret and visualize complex concepts, including abstract ideas, technical data, or intricate narratives, is significantly enhanced. This leads to the creation of images that are not just visually appealing but also conceptually accurate and rich in detail.

7. **Bridging Language and Visuals**: By converting elaborate textual descriptions into precise visual representations, the integration bridges the gap between language and imagery. This is particularly useful in scenarios where visual communication is more effective than verbal or written descriptions.

8. **Expanding Creative Horizons**: The ability to adapt to complex requests encourages users to explore and experiment with ideas that they might not have been able to realize otherwise. This fosters creativity and innovation, pushing the boundaries of what can be achieved in visual art and design.

9. **Democratizing Detailed Visual Creation**: This technology makes detailed and complex visual creation accessible to a broader audience, regardless of their artistic skills or technical expertise. It democratizes the ability to create sophisticated visuals, enabling more people to realize their creative visions.

10. **Enhancing Collaboration and Idea Sharing**: The ease of translating complex ideas into visuals enhances collaboration, especially in team settings where visual representations can aid in sharing and developing ideas more effectively.

In conclusion, the integration of DALL.E 3 with ChatGPT represents a groundbreaking development in AI-driven creativity, especially in terms of customization and precision in adapting to complex requests. It opens up a world of possibilities for users to explore and create, turning even the most intricate ideas into stunning visual realities. This not only enhances the capability of individuals and teams to visualize and communicate complex concepts but also paves the way for new forms of creative and professional expression.

IV. Iterative Design Process:

The integration facilitates an iterative design process, where users can refine their requests based on initial outputs. This iterative cycle of feedback and adjustment ensures that the final image is a refined representation of the user's requirements, embodying both the specifics and the spirit of their request.

The integration of DALL.E 3 into ChatGPT heralds a transformative era in digital creativity, particularly through its impact on the iterative design process. This synergy of cutting-edge AI in image generation and sophisticated language processing facilitates a dynamic and responsive design workflow, allowing users to refine and evolve their visual concepts through continuous interaction. Here's a comprehensive introduction to how this integration enhances the iterative design process:

1. **Enhanced User Input Interpretation**: ChatGPT's advanced natural language processing capabilities allow it to understand

and interpret detailed user inputs with high precision. This understanding is crucial in an iterative design process, where nuances in language can significantly alter the direction or details of a design.

2. **Rapid Concept Visualization**: DALL.E 3's ability to quickly generate visual interpretations of textual descriptions enables users to see the initial versions of their ideas almost instantly. This rapid visualization is a cornerstone of the iterative process, allowing for quick assessments and adjustments.

3. **Seamless Feedback Integration**: Users can provide feedback on the generated images, and ChatGPT, with its contextual understanding, can incorporate this feedback effectively. This seamless integration of user feedback ensures that each iteration is a closer representation of the user's vision.

4. **Encouraging Experimentation**: The ease and speed with which users can iterate designs encourage experimentation. Users are more likely to try out different concepts, styles, or elements, knowing that they can quickly visualize the outcomes and make adjustments as needed.

5. **Precision in Detailing and Customization**: DALL.E 3's capability to capture fine details and customize images according to specific instructions means that each iteration can be fine-tuned to a high degree of accuracy. This precision is vital in the iterative design process, especially for complex or detailed projects.

6. **Cost-Effective and Time-Efficient**: The integration significantly reduces the time and resources typically required in traditional design processes. Rapid prototyping, instant visualizations, and the ability to make quick changes lead to a more efficient and cost-effective workflow.

7. **Facilitating Complex Design Tasks**: The combined AI power of ChatGPT and DALL.E 3 is particularly beneficial in tackling complex design tasks that require a deep understanding of concepts, high creativity, and meticulous attention to detail.

8. **Enhanced Collaboration**: This integration makes it easier for teams to collaborate on design projects. Ideas and feedback can be shared and visually represented quickly, ensuring all team

members are aligned and can contribute effectively to the design process.

9. **Bridging the Gap Between Concept and Reality**: The ability to rapidly iterate helps in bridging the gap between abstract concepts and tangible visuals. This is particularly useful in fields like architecture, product design, and digital art, where visual representation is key.

10. **Democratizing Design**: By making advanced design capabilities accessible to those without extensive graphic design skills, the integration democratizes the creative process. It empowers a wider range of individuals to participate in design, bringing diverse perspectives and ideas to the field.

In summary, the integration of DALL.E 3 into ChatGPT revolutionizes the iterative design process, making it more accessible, efficient, and precise. It offers a powerful tool for professionals and creatives alike, transforming the way ideas are developed and refined into final designs. This integration not only streamlines the design workflow but also opens up new avenues for creativity and innovation in various fields.

V. **Diverse Stylistic Range**:

Users can explore a vast array of styles and aesthetics, from realistic renderings to abstract art. This flexibility allows for the creation of visuals that not only meet precise specifications but also cater to a diverse range of artistic tastes and preferences.

The integration of DALL.E 3 into ChatGPT marks a significant advancement in the realm of AI-driven creativity, particularly in offering a diverse stylistic range for customization and precision. This synthesis of advanced image generation and sophisticated language understanding opens up a myriad of possibilities for users to explore and create visuals in an array of styles, catering to various artistic preferences and requirements. Here's a comprehensive introduction to how this integration expands the horizons of stylistic diversity:

1. **Expansive Stylistic Vocabulary**. DALL.E 3, powered by its extensive training on a wide range of images and styles, can generate visuals in an array of artistic styles. From classical to modern, abstract to hyper-realistic, the system offers a rich tapestry of visual expressions. This diversity enables users to

precisely match the style of their project or experiment with new ones.

2. **Understanding and Interpreting Style through Language**: ChatGPT's advanced language processing capabilities play a crucial role in understanding and interpreting the stylistic nuances conveyed by users. Whether a user describes a style in technical terms or through more abstract descriptions, the system can parse these inputs to guide the image generation process effectively.

3. **Customization at the Intersection of Style and Content**: The integration allows for a high degree of customization, not just in the content of the images but also in their stylistic execution. Users can specify details about both what the image should depict and how it should be stylistically rendered, providing a level of control that is finely tuned to individual preferences or project requirements.

4. **Adapting to Trends and Cultural Influences**: The AI's ability to generate images in a diverse range of styles makes it responsive to various cultural influences and current trends. This adaptability is essential in fields like marketing, fashion, and entertainment, where staying relevant to current styles and cultural narratives is crucial.

5. **Facilitating Artistic Exploration and Growth**: For artists and designers, the integration serves as a tool for exploration and growth. They can experiment with styles they are unfamiliar with or use the system to visualize how different styles would impact their work, thereby expanding their artistic repertoire.

6. **Educational Applications**: In educational settings, this stylistic diversity can be a powerful tool for teaching art history and design principles. Students can visualize how the same subject can be interpreted across different artistic styles, enhancing their understanding and appreciation of artistic diversity.

7. **Enhanced Personalization for Users**: The ability to create visuals in a wide range of styles means that users can personalize their projects more deeply. Whether for personal projects, branding, or storytelling, the ability to tailor the visual style to the specific tone and mood of the content enhances the overall impact of the work.

8. **Bridging Historical and Contemporary Visual Languages**:
   The system's proficiency in generating images across historical
   and contemporary styles allows for unique juxtapositions and
   combinations. This bridging of different visual languages can
   lead to innovative and thought-provoking creations.

9. **Assisting Professional Design Workflow**: For professionals in
   graphic design, advertising, and similar fields, this range of styles
   means they can quickly prototype ideas in various styles to
   determine the best fit for their project or to present multiple
   options to clients.

10. **Democratizing Access to Diverse Artistic Styles**: By making a
    wide range of artistic styles accessible to those without formal
    training in art and design, the integration democratizes the
    creative process, allowing more people to express their ideas
    and stories in visually compelling ways.

In conclusion, the integration of DALL.E 3 into ChatGPT
significantly enhances the spectrum of stylistic customization and
precision available to users. It empowers them to explore and create with
a level of stylistic diversity that was previously challenging to achieve,
opening up new avenues for artistic expression, professional projects,
and personal creativity.

VI. **Enhanced User Experience**:

The intuitive nature of conversational AI makes this technology
accessible to a broad audience, regardless of their technical expertise.
Users can simply describe their vision in natural language, making the
process of creating customized, precise visuals both easy and enjoyable.

The integration of DALL.E 3 into ChatGPT represents a
groundbreaking advancement in the field of artificial intelligence,
profoundly enhancing user experience through unprecedented levels of
customization and precision. This fusion of sophisticated natural
language processing and advanced image generation technologies
offers a transformative experience for users, enabling them to bring their
most intricate visions and ideas to life with remarkable accuracy and
detail. Here's a comprehensive introduction to how this integration
elevates the user experience:

1. **Personalized Visual Creations**: The integration allows users to
   create highly personalized visuals based on specific requests.
   Whether it's detailed descriptions, unique concepts, or intricate

designs, DALL.E 3's ability to interpret and visualize these elements through ChatGPT's understanding significantly enhances the relevance and appeal of the generated images.

2. **Precision in Detailing**: With DALL.E 3, the level of detail that can be achieved in image generation is astounding. This precision ensures that even the most subtle elements in a user's description are captured, leading to outputs that closely align with their expectations and visions.

3. **Seamless User Interaction**: ChatGPT's conversational interface makes interacting with DALL.E 3 intuitive and natural. Users can describe their vision in their own words, ask for modifications, and refine their requests in a fluid, interactive manner, making the process user-friendly and accessible.

4. **Immediate Visual Feedback**: The integration provides immediate visual feedback, allowing users to see the results of their requests instantly. This immediacy in visual representation is invaluable for users in conceptualizing, iterating, and refining their ideas.

5. **Adaptability to User Preferences and Styles**: DALL.E 3's vast training allows it to adapt to a wide range of user preferences and styles. Whether users prefer contemporary, abstract, photorealistic, or any other style, the system can generate visuals that align with these preferences, enhancing the user experience by catering to individual tastes.

6. **Facilitating Creative Exploration**: Users are encouraged to explore creatively, as they can experiment with different concepts, styles, and compositions. This exploration is supported by the system's ability to generate diverse interpretations of a given description, opening up a world of creative possibilities.

7. **Reduction in Time and Effort**: For many creative tasks, the integration significantly reduces the time and effort required to go from concept to visualization. This efficiency is particularly beneficial for professionals in fields like design, marketing, and content creation, where time is often a critical factor.

8. **Interactive Learning and Discovery**: In educational contexts, this integration serves as a powerful tool for learning and discovery. Students can experiment with concepts and see

immediate visual representations, enhancing their understanding and engagement with the material.

9. **Enhanced Accessibility**: The ability to generate complex visuals through simple text descriptions makes advanced visual creation accessible to those without specialized skills in art or design, democratizing the process of visual content creation.

10. **Collaborative Potential**: The integration facilitates collaboration, as users can share their generated images with others, gather feedback, and refine their ideas based on collective input, enhancing the collaborative creative process.

In summary, the integration of DALL.E 3 into ChatGPT significantly enhances the user experience by offering unparalleled customization and precision. This combination not only empowers users to bring complex and nuanced visual ideas to life but also makes the process more accessible, efficient, and enjoyable, catering to a broad spectrum of creative, professional, and educational needs.

VII. **Real-time Visualization**:

The integration offers the advantage of real-time visualization, allowing users to see the results of their specifications almost immediately. This immediacy is crucial in environments where rapid prototyping and quick turnarounds are essential.

The integration of DALL.E 3 into ChatGPT heralds a new era of AI-driven creativity, characterized by exceptional levels of customization and precision. This combination is particularly notable for its capacity to provide real-time visualization, a feature that significantly enhances user experience across various domains. Here's a comprehensive introduction to how this integration excels in terms of real-time visualization:

1. **Instantaneous Visual Feedback**: The most striking advantage of this integration is the ability to provide immediate visual feedback. Users can input a description and rapidly receive a corresponding image, making the process of ideation and visualization seamless and dynamic. This immediacy is particularly beneficial in fields where visual representation plays a crucial role in communication and decision-making.

2. **Facilitating Rapid Prototyping**: For designers, architects, and creatives, the capacity for real-time visualization accelerates the prototyping process. Ideas can be visualized instantly, allowing

for quicker iteration and refinement. This rapid prototyping not only saves time but also enables a more fluid creative process, where ideas can evolve naturally without the constraints of traditional, time-consuming rendering processes.

3. **Enhancing Interactive Learning**: In educational settings, real-time visualization offers an interactive and engaging learning experience. Complex concepts, especially in subjects like science, history, or art, can be visually represented as they are discussed, making learning more immersive and comprehensible for students.

4. **Streamlining Content Creation**: For content creators, marketers, and storytellers, the ability to generate visuals on-the-fly is invaluable. It allows for the quick production of illustrative content, aiding in storytelling, advertising, and digital content creation. This real-time capability significantly reduces the time from concept to publication, a key factor in the fast-paced digital media landscape.

5. **Aiding Decision-Making Processes**: In business and research, the ability to visualize data and concepts in real-time aids in decision-making. Complex data can be translated into comprehensible visuals, helping stakeholders understand and act on information more effectively.

6. **Customization in Real-Time**: Users are not just limited to static outputs; they can request modifications and see the results instantly. This level of customization in real-time fosters a more interactive and user-centric approach to image generation, where users can fine-tune their requests based on immediate visual feedback.

7. **Interactive User Experiences**: The integration enhances user engagement by allowing for interactive and dynamic experiences. Users can experiment with different descriptions, see the results, and modify their approach in real-time, leading to a more engaging and satisfying creative process.

8. **Reducing Resource Constraints**: Traditionally, high-quality visualizations require significant computational and human resources. The real-time visualization capability of this integration reduces these constraints, making high-quality visual content creation more accessible to individuals and organizations with limited resources.

9. **Enhancing Accessibility**: By enabling real-time visualization through simple text descriptions, this technology makes sophisticated visual creation accessible to a broader audience, including those without professional skills in graphic design or visualization.

10. **Empowering Creative Exploration**: The immediate visual output encourages users to explore creatively, as they can rapidly test and visualize different ideas. This exploration not only sparks creativity but also leads to unexpected and innovative visual solutions.

In summary, the integration of DALL.E 3 into ChatGPT, with its focus on customization and precision, revolutionizes the way we approach visualization. The real-time visualization capability opens up new possibilities for rapid prototyping, interactive learning, efficient content creation, and dynamic user engagement, catering to a wide array of professional, educational, and personal needs.

VIII. **Scalable Creativity**:

Whether for individual creators or large-scale enterprises, this integration scales seamlessly to meet diverse creative demands. It democratizes access to high-quality, customized visual content, breaking down barriers that previously limited creative expression and visual communication.

The integration of DALL.E 3 with ChatGPT represents a significant leap forward in the realm of artificial intelligence, particularly in the areas of customization, precision, and notably, scalable creativity. This amalgamation of advanced language understanding and powerful image generation capabilities offers a transformative tool for various sectors. Here's a comprehensive introduction to how this integration excels in terms of scalable creativity:

1. **Unlimited Creative Potential**: At the core of this integration is the ability to generate an infinite variety of images from textual descriptions. This boundless creative potential means that users can explore ideas and concepts at a scale previously unimaginable, ranging from the practical to the fantastical, and everything in between.

2. **Adaptable to Diverse Needs**: The scalable nature of this technology makes it versatile across different industries and applications. Whether it's for individual artists exploring new

forms of expression, marketers seeking unique branding materials, educators needing illustrative content, or developers requiring assets for digital experiences, this integration adapts effortlessly to varying creative demands.

3. **Customized Outputs at Scale**: The precision of DALL.E 3 in understanding and interpreting user prompts allows for highly customized outputs. This customization is not limited by scale; whether a user needs a single image or thousands, the system maintains a high level of specificity and relevance to the input, ensuring that each output is tailored to the user's requirements.

4. **Efficiency in High-Volume Projects**: For projects requiring a large volume of visual content, such as digital marketing campaigns or educational material development, this integration offers an efficient solution. It significantly reduces the time and resources typically needed to create diverse and high-quality visual content at scale.

5. **Consistency in Style and Quality**: Maintaining consistency in style and quality across a large number of images can be challenging. This integration ensures that regardless of the volume of output, there is a consistent quality and adherence to the specified style, enhancing the overall coherence of the visual content.

6. **Enhanced Collaborative Creativity**: The scalability of this tool fosters collaborative creativity. Teams can work together, inputting ideas and seeing them visualized in real-time, regardless of the project's size. This collaboration can lead to more innovative and comprehensive creative outcomes.

7. **Rapid Experimentation and Iteration**: The ability to quickly generate and regenerate images allows for rapid experimentation. Users can tweak their prompts and see the variations almost instantly, enabling a fast-paced iterative process that is essential in creative explorations and decision-making.

8. **Breaking Creative Boundaries**: With scalable creativity, users are not limited by traditional constraints such as resource availability or technical skills. This democratization of creative expression allows more people to experiment with and contribute to creative fields, potentially leading to groundbreaking ideas and developments.

9. **Personalization at Scale**: In contexts where personalization is key, such as in marketing or user experience design, this integration allows for the creation of personalized content on a large scale, catering to individual preferences and enhancing user engagement.

10. **Future-Proofing Creative Endeavors**: As the demand for unique and high-quality visual content continues to grow, this integration provides a sustainable and scalable solution. It equips users with a tool that evolves with their creative needs, ensuring they remain at the forefront of innovation.

In summary, the integration of DALL.E 3 into ChatGPT marks a paradigm shift in how we approach creativity. Its capacity for scalable creativity empowers users to push the boundaries of imagination, efficiently generate customized content at scale, and explore new artistic and commercial frontiers with unprecedented freedom and flexibility.

IX. **Consistency in Output**:

For brands and creators who need a consistent visual style across various platforms and projects, this integration ensures that all generated images adhere to the specified parameters, maintaining a uniform look and feel.

The integration of DALL.E 3 with ChatGPT marks a groundbreaking development in the field of artificial intelligence, particularly highlighting its capabilities in customization, precision, and notably, consistency in output. This fusion of sophisticated language processing and advanced image generation technology creates a powerful tool that is transforming various industries. Here is a detailed introduction to how this integration excels in ensuring consistency in output:

1. **Reliable Quality Assurance**: One of the most significant advantages of this integration is the consistent quality of the images produced. Regardless of the complexity or specificity of the user's request, DALL.E 3 consistently generates high-quality images. This reliability is crucial in professional settings where quality cannot be compromised.

2. **Uniformity Across Diverse Requests**: DALL E 3 maintains a high level of uniformity in its outputs, even when dealing with a wide range of requests. Whether the user is asking for simple everyday objects or complex, abstract concepts, the system

ensures that the output remains consistent in terms of visual fidelity and adherence to the input specifications.

3. **Standardization in Style and Aesthetics**: For projects requiring a specific style or aesthetic, maintaining consistency can be challenging, especially at scale. This integration allows for precise control over the style and aesthetic of the images, ensuring that every output aligns with the desired look and feel.

4. **Adherence to Branding Guidelines**: In marketing and branding, consistency in visual representation is key to maintaining brand identity. The DALL.E 3 integration ensures that generated images adhere to specified branding guidelines, such as color schemes, design motifs, and overall tone, providing a reliable tool for brand-focused projects.

5. **Facilitation of Long-Term Projects**: For long-term projects that require visual content over extended periods, maintaining consistency can be a logistical challenge. This AI integration offers a solution by ensuring that the visual output remains consistent over time, even as project parameters evolve.

6. **Reduction of Human Error**: The automation of image generation significantly reduces the likelihood of human error that can lead to inconsistencies. This is particularly beneficial in large-scale projects where manual creation of content could result in variations due to individual differences in interpretation and execution.

7. **Ease of Scalability**: When scaling up a project, maintaining a consistent output quality and style is vital. The integration of DALL.E 3 with ChatGPT simplifies this process, allowing for the production of large volumes of content without compromising on consistency.

8. **Predictable Outcomes for Users**: Users benefit from the predictability of outcomes. Knowing that their input will consistently yield high-quality, relevant, and stylistically appropriate images, regardless of the complexity of the request, enhances user trust and reliance on the system.

9. **Support for Iterative Design Processes**: In design and creative workflows, where iterative processes are common, having consistent output at each stage is crucial. This integration

supports such workflows by providing reliable results that designers and artists can build upon.

10. **Customization Without Compromise**: Despite offering high customization options, the system does not compromise on consistency. This balance ensures that users can explore creative options while being confident in the uniformity and quality of the results.

In conclusion, the integration of DALL.E 3 into ChatGPT represents a significant advancement in AI-driven creativity, offering unparalleled consistency in output. This consistency is essential across various applications, from professional design and branding to personal creative projects, ensuring reliable, high-quality, and aesthetically uniform results that meet and exceed user expectations.

X. **Exploring Creative Boundaries**:

Finally, the integration of DALL.E 3 with ChatGPT opens new avenues for creative experimentation. It encourages users to push the boundaries of traditional visual content, explore novel concepts, and experiment with unconventional ideas in a precise and controlled environment

The integration of DALL.E 3 with ChatGPT is a landmark in the realm of artificial intelligence, particularly for its profound impact on customization and precision, which significantly broadens the exploration of creative boundaries. This combination of advanced language understanding and cutting-edge image generation technologies opens new horizons for creativity, offering unparalleled opportunities for users to push the limits of their imagination. Here's an in-depth introduction to how this integration facilitates the exploration of creative boundaries:

1. **Unprecedented Creative Freedom**: The merging of DALL.E 3's image generation with ChatGPT's language processing enables users to explore creative ideas that were once constrained by technical or artistic limitations. This platform allows for the visualization of complex, abstract, or even surreal concepts with ease, empowering users to expand their creative horizons.

2. **Precision in Realizing Vision**: The precision offered by DALL.E 3 in interpreting and rendering images from textual descriptions allows for a high degree of fidelity to the user's original vision. This capability is crucial for artists, designers, and creatives who

require exact visual representations of their ideas, no matter how intricate or unconventional they may be.

3. **Customized Visual Experiences**: Users can tailor their visual content to an extraordinary degree, specifying not just the subject matter but also the style, mood, and context. This level of customization opens up new avenues for unique artistic expressions and personalized visual storytelling.

4. **Breaking Conventional Artistic Limits**: Traditional artistic methods have inherent limitations, whether in terms of materials, techniques, or the artist's own skill set. The integration of DALL.E 3 with ChatGPT transcends these boundaries, offering a digital canvas where almost any idea can be brought to life, regardless of its complexity or the conventional constraints of physical art forms.

5. **Facilitating Experimental Art**: Artists and creatives can use this platform to experiment with new concepts and styles without the need for extensive resources or specialized skills. This democratization of artistic experimentation encourages a broader range of individuals to participate in creative endeavors and explore new artistic frontiers.

6. **Enhancing Conceptual Art and Design**: In fields like conceptual art, fashion, and industrial design, where the visualization of ideas is as important as the ideas themselves, this integration proves invaluable. Designers can rapidly prototype concepts, visualize hypothetical scenarios, and present ideas in visually compelling ways.

7. **Inspiring Collaborative Creativity**: By providing a common platform where visual ideas can be easily shared and iterated upon, this integration fosters collaborative creativity. Teams can collectively brainstorm and visualize ideas, leading to richer, more diverse creative outputs.

8. **Exploring the Intersection of Technology and Art**: The integration represents a fascinating confluence of technology and art, prompting artists and technologists alike to explore this intersection. It serves as a tool for understanding how AI can be harnessed in artistic processes and for pushing the boundaries of digital art.

9. **Accessible Exploration of Complex Themes**: Complex themes that require nuanced depiction, such as abstract emotions, theoretical concepts, or futuristic scenarios, can be explored with greater depth and precision. This accessibility enables a wider exploration of themes that might be challenging to depict through traditional artistic mediums.

10. **Innovative Storytelling and World-Building**: For storytellers and content creators, this integration is a boon for innovative storytelling and world-building. It allows for the creation of unique characters, settings, and scenarios, bringing narrative visions to life in ways previously unattainable.

In summary, the merging of DALL.E 3 with ChatGPT represents a significant advancement in digital creativity, offering users an unparalleled level of customization and precision in visual content creation. This integration not only caters to the specific needs of various industries but also empowers individual creators to bring their unique visions to life with an accuracy and finesse that was previously unattainable.

Prompts:

To generate realistic photographs that demonstrate the concept of Customization and Precision using DALL.E, here are some prompts:

1. "Photograph of an architect working on a highly detailed and customized 3D model of a futuristic building, showcasing intricate design elements, with a computer screen displaying advanced software tools in the background."

2. "Photorealistic image of a tailor measuring a mannequin with precision for a custom-tailored suit, surrounded by various fabric samples and tailoring tools, highlighting attention to detail."

3. "Realistic image of a pastry chef decorating a custom-designed cake with precise and intricate details, in a professional kitchen setting, showcasing culinary art and precision."

4. "Image of a jeweler using a magnifying glass to meticulously set tiny diamonds in a custom-designed, intricate piece of jewelry, highlighting the precision and craftsmanship."

5. "Photograph of a car designer sketching a custom sports car with precision, surrounded by color swatches and model cars, in

a design studio environment, emphasizing personalized design and attention to detail."

6. Photograph of a landscape gardener carefully arranging a custom-designed garden layout with precision, featuring a variety of exotic plants and intricate pathway designs, in a luxurious backyard setting."

7. "Realistic image of a software engineer intently coding on multiple computer screens, displaying complex algorithms and custom software solutions, highlighting precision in digital development."

8. "Photograph of a bespoke furniture maker in a workshop, precisely carving detailed patterns into a custom wooden table, surrounded by woodworking tools and sketches, showcasing artisanal skill and accuracy."

9. "Image of a master watchmaker assembling a luxury watch with meticulous precision, using specialized tools, in a well-lit workshop, emphasizing the finesse in custom watchmaking."

10. "Realistic photograph of a scientist in a lab, adjusting a microscope with precision for a custom experiment, surrounded by high-tech lab equipment and research notes, highlighting precision in scientific research."

11. "Photograph of an artist painting a large custom mural with precise and intricate details, using various brushes and colors, in an urban environment, showcasing artistic precision and customization."

12. "Image of a chef plating a gourmet dish with precise arrangement, in a high-end restaurant kitchen, surrounded by fresh ingredients and culinary tools, illustrating precision in custom culinary presentation."

These prompts are designed to capture a wide range of professions and scenarios where customization and precision play a crucial role, showcasing the depth and versatility of these concepts through realistic imagery.

Here is an image illustrating the concept of Customization and Precision, showing a landscape gardener carefully arranging a custom-designed garden layout with precision, featuring a variety of exotic plants and intricate pathway designs in a luxurious backyard setting.

The concept of customization and precision in the realm of design and technology is illustrated in the image above. It shows a fashion designer using advanced, high-tech tools to meticulously craft a garment, demonstrating how modern technology can be applied to achieve precise and customized results.

Educational Applications:

The integration of DALL.E 3 into ChatGPT marks a transformative advancement in educational technology, reshaping the landscape of learning and teaching methods. This fusion of sophisticated artificial intelligence (AI) in both language processing and image generation opens up a myriad of educational applications, each offering unique benefits to the learning experience. Here's a comprehensive introduction to the educational applications of integrating DALL.E 3 with ChatGPT:

I. Visual Learning Enhancement:

Many students are visual learners, and the ability to instantly generate images relevant to educational content can significantly enhance comprehension. Complex subjects like biology, astronomy, or history can be brought to life through detailed visual aids, making learning more engaging and effective.

The integration of DALL.E 3 with ChatGPT heralds a new era in educational technology, particularly in the realm of visual learning enhancement. This synergistic combination of advanced natural language understanding and sophisticated image generation capabilities offers a transformative approach to education. Here's a comprehensive introduction to how this integration enhances visual learning:

1. **Enhanced Conceptual Understanding**: The ability to generate detailed, accurate visuals on demand aids in the clarification of complex concepts. Whether it's a scientific process, a historical event, or a mathematical theorem, visual representations can make abstract or challenging ideas more concrete and comprehensible.

2. **Interactive and Engaging Learning**: Traditional text-based learning can sometimes fail to captivate students, especially younger learners or those who are visual learners by nature. The integration of DALL.E 3 brings an element of interactivity and engagement to the learning process, making it more appealing and effective.

3. **Customized Educational Content**: One of the most significant advantages of this integration is the ability to create tailored visual content that aligns with specific educational needs and curricular goals. Educators can request images that are precisely suited to their lesson plans, enhancing the relevance and effectiveness of their teaching materials.

4. **Aiding Memory Retention**: Visual aids are known to enhance memory retention. By providing vivid, accurate images that complement textual information, this technology helps students remember and recall information more effectively.

5. **Support for Diverse Learning Styles**: Not all students learn the same way. The integration acknowledges and supports diverse learning styles by providing an additional visual learning channel,

which is particularly beneficial for students who assimilate information better visually.

6. **Simplifying Complex Information**: Subjects that involve intricate details, like biology or engineering, can sometimes be overwhelming. The ability to break down these complexities into simpler visual formats can aid significantly in understanding and retention.

7. **Encouraging Creativity and Exploration**: In subjects like art, literature, and social studies, the integration allows students to explore creative concepts, historical settings, and artistic styles through vivid imagery. This not only enhances learning but also encourages creative thinking and exploration.

8. **Assisting Language Learning**: For language learners, visual context can significantly aid in understanding and language acquisition. By visualizing vocabulary, idiomatic expressions, or cultural nuances, learners can gain a deeper and more nuanced understanding of a new language.

9. **Facilitating Inclusive Education**: Visual aids can be particularly beneficial for students with learning difficulties, such as dyslexia or ADHD, offering them an alternative pathway for understanding and engagement.

10. **Bridging the Digital Divide in Education**: In a world where digital learning tools are increasingly important, the integration of DALL.E 3 with ChatGPT ensures that cutting-edge technology is available in the educational sector, helping to bridge the digital divide and making high-quality educational resources more accessible.

In summary, the integration of DALL.E 3 into ChatGPT significantly enhances visual learning, offering a range of benefits from improved conceptual understanding and engagement to support for diverse learning styles and needs. This technology not only enhances the quality of education but also makes it more accessible, interactive, and tailored to individual learning requirements.

II. **Interactive Learning Materials**:

The integration allows for the creation of customized, interactive learning materials. Teachers can request specific images to illustrate concepts, create interactive assignments, or even develop visual quizzes, all tailored to their curriculum needs.

The integration of DALL.E 3 with ChatGPT marks a significant advancement in the field of educational technology, particularly in the creation and utilization of interactive learning materials. This combination of cutting-edge artificial intelligence in both text and image generation opens up new avenues for interactive and engaging educational experiences. Here's an in-depth look at how this integration is revolutionizing interactive learning materials:

1. **Dynamic Visual Aids**: DALL.E 3's ability to generate images from textual descriptions enables educators to create dynamic visual aids that can adapt to various learning topics. These visuals can range from historical scenes to scientific diagrams, offering students a more immersive and engaging learning experience.

2. **Customization and Relevance**: Educators can now tailor learning materials to their specific curriculum needs. Whether it's visualizing complex scientific phenomena or historical events, the ability to create bespoke images ensures that the learning material is highly relevant and customized for each lesson.

3. **Enhancing Understanding through Visualization**: Many concepts in education, from abstract mathematical theories to intricate scientific processes, can be challenging to grasp through text alone. DALL.E 3 helps in visualizing these concepts, making them more accessible and understandable to students.

4. **Interactive Storytelling in Education**: For subjects like literature, history, and social studies, this technology allows for the creation of storyboards or scene representations, adding an interactive storytelling element to the learning process. This not only makes learning more interesting but also aids in better retention of information.

5. **Engagement through Visual Stimuli**: In a digital age where students are accustomed to visual media, the integration of visually stimulating materials in education is essential. DALL.E 3's capabilities ensure that learning materials are not just informative but also visually engaging, catering to the needs and preferences of modern learners.

6. **Supporting Diverse Learning Styles**: The visual elements created by DALL.E 3 cater to visual learners and can be integrated with textual information to support diverse learning

styles. This multimodal approach is crucial in addressing the different ways in which students absorb information.

7. **Real-time Customization**: Teachers can generate images in real-time during a lesson to address specific questions or to illustrate a point more effectively. This immediate response capability makes learning more adaptive and responsive.

8. **Facilitating Project-Based Learning**: For projects and assignments, students can use DALL.E 3 to create visuals that complement their work. This not only enhances their presentations but also encourages creativity and independent learning.

9. **Encouraging Exploration and Curiosity**: With the ability to visualize almost any concept, students can explore topics beyond the standard curriculum, fostering a sense of curiosity and a desire for self-directed learning.

10. **Accessibility and Inclusivity**: The visual aids generated can be particularly helpful for students with learning disabilities or those who struggle with text-heavy content, making education more inclusive.

In summary, the integration of DALL.E 3 in ChatGPT significantly enhances the development of interactive learning materials, offering educators and students alike a powerful tool to create engaging, customized, and visually stimulating educational content. This integration not only supports various learning styles but also paves the way for a more interactive, engaging, and inclusive educational environment.

III. **Creativity in Education**:

This tool opens up new avenues for creative expression for students. Art and design education, for example, can greatly benefit from the ability to explore various artistic styles and visual representations, encouraging students to experiment and innovate.

The integration of DALL.E 3 with ChatGPT heralds a new era in educational methodologies, particularly in fostering creativity within the educational sphere. This combination of advanced text and image generation AI technologies offers a unique tool for educators and students alike, enhancing the creative dimensions of learning and teaching. Here's a comprehensive introduction to how this integration is revolutionizing creativity in education:

1. **Inspiring Imaginative Thinking**: DALL.E 3's ability to generate diverse and complex images from textual prompts opens up a world of imaginative possibilities for students. It encourages them to think beyond conventional boundaries and explore creative interpretations of various subjects.

2. **Visualizing Abstract Concepts**: Subjects that deal with abstract concepts, such as mathematics, philosophy, or advanced sciences, often pose a challenge in terms of student engagement and understanding. The visual capabilities of DALL.E 3 help in translating these abstract ideas into concrete, visual forms, making them more accessible and stimulating for creative exploration.

3. **Enhancing Creative Writing and Storytelling**: In language arts and literature classes, DALL.E 3 can be used to visualize characters, settings, and scenes described in stories or created by students. This not only aids in better comprehension but also inspires students to delve deeper into their creative writing skills.

4. **Interactive Art and Design Education**: For art and design-related subjects, this technology offers a tool for exploring various artistic styles, compositions, and color schemes. It serves as a digital canvas where students can experiment with their creative ideas in a visually interactive manner.

5. **Encouraging Cross-Disciplinary Creativity**: DALL.E 3 facilitates the blending of concepts from different disciplines, fostering a cross-disciplinary approach to creativity. For instance, students can explore historical events through art, understand scientific concepts through illustrations, or explore mathematical patterns through visual designs.

6. **Cultivating Problem-Solving Skills**: By visualizing complex problems and scenarios, students can engage in creative problem-solving. The ability to see various aspects of a problem in a visual format can lead to more innovative and effective solutions.

7. **Stimulating Curiosity and Inquiry**: The vast capabilities of DALL.E 3 in generating unique and unexpected images can stimulate students' curiosity and encourage them to ask questions, explore different scenarios, and think critically.

8. **Support for Project-Based Learning**: In project-based learning environments, students can use DALL.E 3 to create presentations, models, and prototypes, adding a layer of creativity and personalization to their projects.

9. **Developing Digital Literacy and Technological Skills**: As students interact with this AI technology, they also develop essential digital literacy skills, learning to navigate and utilize advanced technological tools in creative ways.

10. **Personalized Learning Experiences**: DALL.E 3 allows for the creation of personalized learning materials that cater to the unique interests and creative inclinations of each student, making learning more engaging and effective.

In conclusion, the integration of DALL.E 3 with ChatGPT represents a significant stride in the domain of educational technology, particularly in enhancing creativity in education. It provides a versatile and powerful tool for educators to inspire creative thinking, foster innovative learning experiences, and equip students with the skills to thrive in a rapidly evolving digital world.

IV. Aid in Language Learning:

For language learners, visual context can be pivotal. The ability to generate images depicting vocabulary words, phrases, or cultural contexts can aid in better understanding and retention of a new language.

The integration of DALL.E 3 into ChatGPT marks a significant advancement in the field of language learning, offering a transformative approach that blends visual and verbal learning. This synergy creates an immersive and interactive environment, crucial for mastering a new language. Here's a comprehensive introduction to how this integration is reshaping language learning:

1. **Visual Vocabulary Building**: DALL.E 3's capability to generate accurate and context-specific images in response to textual prompts can significantly aid in vocabulary acquisition. For language learners, visual representation of new words or phrases helps in better retention and understanding, making the learning process more effective and engaging.

2. **Contextual Understanding and Usage**: Understanding the context in which certain words or phrases are used can be challenging in language learning. DALL.E 3 can create images

that depict the use of language in various contexts, thereby helping learners grasp the nuances of its practical usage.

3. **Cultural Immersion through Visuals**: Language is deeply intertwined with culture, and understanding cultural aspects is key to mastering a language. Through visual illustrations, learners can explore cultural elements associated with the language, such as traditional clothing, cuisine, festivals, and landmarks, enhancing their cultural comprehension alongside linguistic skills.

4. **Interactive Dialogue Practice**: Integrating DALL.E 3 with ChatGPT can facilitate interactive dialogue sessions where learners engage in conversation with the AI. The addition of relevant visual prompts can make these dialogues more immersive, helping learners to better interpret and respond in real-time scenarios.

5. **Pronunciation and Phonetics Visualization**: For languages with challenging pronunciation and phonetics, visual aids can be instrumental. DALL.E 3 can provide visual cues or diagrams that help in understanding the articulation and phonetics of difficult sounds, aiding in accurate pronunciation.

6. **Grammar and Sentence Structure**: Understanding grammar and sentence construction can be visually represented through DALL.E 3, where complex grammatical concepts are broken down into simpler, easy-to-understand visuals. This method can particularly benefit visual learners.

7. **Enhancing Writing Skills**: For advanced learners, DALL.E 3 can assist in creative writing exercises. Learners can describe a scene or story in the target language, and the AI can generate corresponding images, offering immediate visual feedback on the learner's descriptive skills.

8. **Language Games and Quizzes**: The integration can be used to create interactive language games and quizzes where learners identify objects, actions, or scenarios depicted in images, making learning fun and engaging.

9. **Support for Special Education Needs**: For learners with special education needs, such as dyslexia or visual processing disorders, the combination of visual aids with textual information

can be highly beneficial, providing alternative ways to grasp language concepts.

10. **Personalized Learning Experience**: The AI can adapt to the individual learner's level, interests, and pace, providing personalized visuals and language exercises. This tailored approach ensures that each learner receives the most effective and engaging language education possible.

In summary, the integration of DALL.E 3 with ChatGPT represents a groundbreaking development in language education, offering a rich, interactive, and highly effective tool for language learning. By combining visual stimuli with linguistic content, this technology not only makes learning more engaging and accessible but also addresses various learning styles and needs, paving the way for a more inclusive and efficient approach to language education.

V. **Enhanced Engagement**:

The novelty and interactivity offered by this AI integration can increase student engagement. This is particularly valuable in distance learning environments, where maintaining student interest can be challenging.

The integration of DALL.E 3 into ChatGPT heralds a new era in educational methodologies, particularly in enhancing student engagement. This combination of advanced AI-driven text and image generation capabilities creates a dynamic and interactive learning environment, significantly impacting the way educational content is delivered and perceived. Here's a comprehensive introduction to how this integration fosters enhanced engagement in education:

1. **Multimodal Learning Experience**: DALL.E 3's ability to generate images from textual descriptions provides a multimodal learning experience. This integration caters to different learning styles, whether visual, verbal, or kinesthetic, making learning more inclusive and effective for a diverse student population.

2. **Interactive Visual Aids**: Traditional educational approaches often rely on static images and text. However, with DALL.E 3, educators can create dynamic and customized visual aids that directly correspond to the curriculum. This real-time generation of relevant imagery can captivate students' attention and make abstract or complex concepts more tangible and understandable.

296

3. **Creative Expression and Exploration**: Students can explore their creativity by prompting DALL.E 3 to create visual representations of their ideas, stories, or projects. This encourages creative thinking and gives students a new medium to express their understanding and interpretations of various subjects.

4. **Enhanced Conceptual Understanding**: Complex subjects often require more than textual explanations. The visual illustrations generated by DALL.E 3 can simplify these concepts, making them more accessible. For instance, visualizing scientific processes, historical events, or mathematical concepts can help students grasp and retain information more effectively.

5. **Gamification of Learning**: By integrating DALL.E 3, educators can gamify learning experiences. Students can engage in interactive quizzes, puzzles, and games where they interact with images generated by the AI, making the learning process more enjoyable and motivating.

6. **Stimulating Curiosity and Inquiry**: The integration can be used to stimulate students' curiosity. By presenting them with intriguing images related to their study topics, students are encouraged to ask questions, research, and explore further, fostering a deeper engagement with the material.

7. **Personalized Learning Experiences**: ChatGPT, combined with DALL.E 3, can tailor educational content to the needs and interests of individual students. This personalized approach ensures that learning is relevant and engaging, catering to each student's unique learning path.

8. **Visual Storytelling in Education**: The AI can assist in creating visual narratives, making storytelling a powerful educational tool. This approach can be particularly effective in subjects like history, literature, and social studies, where storytelling plays a crucial role.

9. **Encouraging Collaboration**: Projects involving the creation of AI-generated images can encourage teamwork and collaboration among students. Collaborative tasks like creating a visual project or a story can enhance social learning and engagement.

10. **Breaking Down Language Barriers**: For non-native speakers or younger students, visual aids can be crucial in understanding

and engaging with the content. The AI-generated images can help bridge language barriers, making education more inclusive and accessible.

In conclusion, the integration of DALL.E 3 into ChatGPT represents a significant stride in educational technology, offering a novel way to enhance engagement through interactive, personalized, and visually rich educational experiences. This integration not only makes learning more appealing and accessible to students but also provides educators with innovative tools to present information, making education a more dynamic, enjoyable, and effective process.

VI. **Support for Special Needs Education**:

For students with special educational needs, such as those with dyslexia or autism, the visual support provided by DALL.E 3 can be particularly beneficial. It can help in breaking down barriers to learning by providing alternative ways to process information.

The integration of DALL.E 3 into ChatGPT marks a transformative step in the realm of special needs education. This fusion of cutting-edge AI technology opens up new avenues for supporting and enhancing the learning experiences of students with diverse educational needs. Here's an in-depth look at how this integration specifically benefits special needs education:

1. **Customized Learning Materials**: One of the most significant challenges in special needs education is creating learning materials that cater to the varied requirements of students. DALL.E 3's capability to generate tailored visual content in response to textual prompts allows educators to produce customized educational materials. These materials can be specifically designed to address the unique learning styles, challenges, and preferences of each student.

2. **Visual Communication for Non-Verbal Learners**: For students with speech and language difficulties, visual aids are invaluable. The integration of DALL.E 3 enables the creation of detailed and specific images that can aid in communication and learning for non-verbal students or those with speech impairments. These visual tools can be pivotal in breaking down communication barriers and aiding in concept comprehension.

3. **Enhancing Engagement Through Visual Stimulation**: Students with attention deficit disorders or those who are easily

distracted can benefit immensely from the visually stimulating and engaging content created by DALL.E 3. By integrating visually rich and intriguing images into the learning process, educators can capture and retain the attention of these students, thereby enhancing their engagement and learning outcomes.

4. **Sensory Learning for Autistic Students**: Many students on the autism spectrum respond well to visual stimuli and structured learning environments. DALL.E 3 can generate specific images that resonate with the interests and learning patterns of autistic students, providing a sensory-friendly educational experience that can significantly improve their understanding and retention of information.

5. **Simplifying Complex Concepts**: For students with cognitive challenges, grasping complex concepts can be daunting. DALL.E 3 aids in breaking down these concepts into simpler, more digestible visual forms. By illustrating abstract ideas through images, the technology can make learning more accessible and less overwhelming for these students.

6. **Developing Social and Emotional Skills**: The AI's capability to create scenarios and characters can be used to teach social and emotional skills. For example, images depicting various social situations and emotional responses can be used as tools to help students understand and navigate social dynamics, empathy, and emotional regulation.

7. **Motor Skill Development**: For students with physical disabilities, particularly those affecting fine motor skills, interactive visual content can be a means of engagement and skill development. DALL.E 3 can create visual activities or games tailored to the motor abilities of these students, aiding in their physical development and coordination.

8. **Support for Visual Impairments**: While initially it might seem counterintuitive, DALL.E 3 can also be utilized to support visually impaired students. By creating high-contrast, simplified, or tactile images (which can be converted into physical forms), the AI can aid in creating materials that are more accessible for students with visual impairments.

9. **Encouraging Creative Expression**: Students with special needs often find conventional methods of expression challenging. DALL.E 3 allows for alternative, visual forms of

expression, enabling these students to convey their thoughts, understanding, and creativity in a way that aligns with their abilities and preferences.

10. **Facilitating Inclusive Education**: By providing tools that cater to a wide range of needs, DALL.E 3 helps in creating an inclusive educational environment. This inclusivity is vital for the social integration and academic success of students with special needs.

In summary, the integration of DALL.E 3 into ChatGPT is a groundbreaking development in special needs education. It offers educators an array of possibilities for creating personalized, engaging, and effective learning experiences. This technology not only addresses specific educational challenges faced by students with special needs but also opens doors to new, innovative methods of teaching and learning, making education more inclusive and accessible.

VII. **Complex Concept Visualization**:

Subjects that involve abstract or complex concepts, like quantum mechanics or advanced mathematics, can benefit from visual aids. The ability to generate images that represent these concepts can make them more accessible and understandable.

The integration of DALL.E 3 with ChatGPT signifies a remarkable advancement in educational technology, particularly in the realm of complex concept visualization. This combination offers a unique and powerful tool for educators and learners alike, transforming abstract and challenging concepts into visually comprehensible representations. Here's an in-depth exploration of how this integration enhances education through complex concept visualization:

1. **Making Abstract Concepts Tangible**: One of the primary challenges in teaching complex subjects, such as quantum physics, advanced mathematics, or abstract art theories, lies in their inherently abstract nature. DALL.E 3's advanced image generation capabilities, when combined with the descriptive and explanatory power of ChatGPT, allow for these abstract concepts to be visualized in a more tangible and understandable form. This visualization aids significantly in demystifying complex ideas, making them more accessible to learners.

2. **Enhancing Comprehension and Retention**: Visual learning is a fundamental aspect of human cognition. By converting

complex theories and ideas into visual formats, DALL.E 3 helps in enhancing students' understanding and retention of information. Visual aids can simplify complicated relationships and processes, making them easier to grasp and remember.

3. **Facilitating Cross-Disciplinary Learning**: Complex concept visualization is particularly beneficial in cross-disciplinary education, where students might not be familiar with the jargon or foundational concepts of a different field of study. For instance, a student of literature might struggle with scientific concepts and vice versa. Visual representations can bridge this gap, providing a universal language that transcends specific disciplinary boundaries.

4. **Aiding in Problem-Solving**: Many complex concepts, especially in fields like engineering, physics, and mathematics, are foundational to problem-solving. DALL.E 3 can be used to generate visual representations of problems or scenarios, enabling students to approach problem-solving in a more informed and structured manner.

5. **Interactive Learning**: The ability of DALL.E 3 to generate images in response to textual descriptions allows for interactive learning experiences. Students can modify their descriptions based on their evolving understanding and receive immediate visual feedback, fostering a more engaging and responsive learning environment.

6. **Encouraging Creative Thinking and Interpretation**: Visual representations of complex concepts often require and stimulate creative thinking. This process can lead to a deeper understanding and innovative interpretations of these concepts, especially in subjects like philosophy, art, and social sciences.

7. **Supporting Diverse Learning Styles**: Different students have different learning preferences; some find textual information more accessible, while others lean towards visual aids. The integration of DALL.E 3 with ChatGPT caters to this diversity, offering both textual and visual resources for understanding complex concepts, thus accommodating various learning styles.

8. **Facilitating Distance and Online Learning**: In the context of distance and online education, where physical classroom resources and face-to-face interactions are limited, the ability to generate detailed visual representations becomes invaluable. It

enhances the quality of remote education by providing students with resources that are as informative and engaging as those available in a traditional classroom setting.

9. **Cultural and Contextual Adaptation**: DALL.E 3 can generate visuals that are culturally relevant and contextually appropriate, making complex concepts more relatable and easier to understand for students from diverse backgrounds.

10. **Resource Creation for Educators**: For educators, creating resources to explain complex concepts can be time-consuming and challenging. DALL.E 3, in collaboration with ChatGPT, simplifies this process, enabling teachers to quickly produce high-quality, customized visual aids, thereby enhancing their teaching efficiency and effectiveness.

In conclusion, the integration of DALL.E 3 with ChatGPT marks a significant milestone in educational technology, particularly in the visualization of complex concepts. This combination not only aids in comprehension and retention but also fosters a more inclusive, interactive, and engaging learning environment. It empowers educators to address the diverse needs of students and enhances the overall quality of education by making even the most challenging concepts accessible and understandable

VIII. Cultural and Historical Education:

In subjects like history and social studies, the ability to visualize historical events, cultural artifacts, and geographical locations can enhance the learning experience, making it more immersive and informative.

The integration of DALL.E 3 with ChatGPT marks a significant leap forward in the realm of cultural and historical education, offering a new dimension of learning that is both engaging and informative. This synthesis of advanced AI-driven visual generation with sophisticated language processing capabilities opens up unparalleled opportunities for educators and students alike in exploring and understanding cultural and historical contexts. Here's an in-depth look at how this integration revolutionizes cultural and historical education:

1. **Visualizing Historical Events and Eras**: DALL.E 3's ability to create detailed and accurate visual representations of historical events and eras is a game-changer for history education. Students can now see vivid depictions of ancient civilizations, historical battles, or cultural milestones, transforming abstract

dates and facts into tangible, memorable experiences. This visual immersion aids in a deeper understanding of the context and significance of historical events.

2. **Enhancing Cultural Understanding**: Cultural education often grapples with the challenge of conveying the essence of a culture - its art, customs, attire, and architecture. Through the integration of DALL.E 3, learners can visually experience different cultures, enhancing their understanding and appreciation of global diversity. This can be particularly impactful in promoting empathy and multicultural awareness.

3. **Interactive Exploration of Art and Artifacts**: Art and artifacts are pivotal in understanding historical and cultural narratives. DALL.E 3 can generate images of art pieces, sculptures, and artifacts, some of which may be inaccessible or no longer exist. Students can explore different art styles, techniques, and cultural symbols, gaining insights into the artistic heritage and cultural values of various societies.

4. **Bringing Literature to Life**: In teaching literature, especially historical or culturally significant texts, the ability to visualize scenes, characters, and settings can greatly enhance comprehension and engagement. DALL.E 3 can provide visual accompaniments to literary works, helping students to better grasp the context, mood, and symbolism in these texts.

5. **Supporting Language Learning with Cultural Context**: Language learning is deeply intertwined with cultural understanding. The visual capabilities of DALL.E 3 can provide learners with cultural context, making language learning more comprehensive and engaging. Visuals of everyday life, cultural practices, and historical events associated with a particular language can enrich the learning experience.

6. **Facilitating Global Education**: In a globalized world, understanding different cultures and histories is crucial. This integration allows educators to easily provide students with a global perspective, showcasing the richness and diversity of human history and cultures through vivid visualizations.

7. **Customized Learning Experiences**: Every classroom is diverse, and the integration of DALL.E 3 in ChatGPT allows for tailored educational content that respects and responds to this diversity. Educators can create customized visuals that resonate

with their students' backgrounds and interests, making history and cultural education more inclusive and relatable.

8. **Enhancing Research and Projects**: Students engaged in research projects or presentations on historical and cultural topics can leverage this technology to create accurate and compelling visual aids. This not only enhances the quality of their work but also deepens their own understanding and engagement with the subject matter.

9. **Augmenting Museum and Gallery Experiences**: For institutions like museums and galleries, the integration of DALL.E 3 with ChatGPT can provide an enhanced educational tool. Visitors can access detailed visuals and rich descriptions of exhibits, deepening their understanding and appreciation of cultural and historical artifacts.

10. **Accessible Education for All**: This technology democratizes access to cultural and historical education. Students from various geographical, socio-economic, and educational backgrounds can now access high-quality, visually rich educational content, helping to bridge educational gaps.

In conclusion, the integration of DALL.E 3 with ChatGPT in the field of cultural and historical education is a transformative development. It not only brings history and culture alive through vivid visualizations but also fosters a more inclusive, engaging, and comprehensive educational experience. This synergy of visual and textual AI has the potential to redefine how we learn about and appreciate our diverse cultural heritage and history.

IX. **Facilitating Project-Based Learning**:

Students working on projects can use this integration to visualize their ideas, create prototypes, or design presentations. This supports a more active, project-based learning approach, which is known to improve learning outcomes.

The integration of DALL.E 3 into ChatGPT heralds a new era in educational methodologies, particularly in enhancing project-based learning (PBL). This fusion of advanced visual generation with sophisticated language processing brings a novel, interactive dimension to education, greatly enriching the PBL approach. Here's a comprehensive look at how this integration elevates project-based learning:

1. **Enhanced Conceptualization and Planning**: In project-based learning, the initial stage of conceptualizing ideas is crucial. DALL.E 3's capability to create detailed images from textual descriptions allows students to visualize their project concepts instantly. This visual aid can be instrumental in refining ideas, identifying potential challenges, and planning project execution more effectively.

2. **Stimulating Creativity and Innovation**: The ability to generate a wide range of visual representations from textual prompts encourages students to think creatively and explore multiple perspectives. This not only fosters innovative thinking but also helps students to approach problems and project challenges in unique ways, enhancing the overall quality of their projects.

3. **Aiding in Research and Information Gathering**: For projects that require historical, scientific, or cultural research, DALL.E 3 can provide visual aids that make complex information more accessible and engaging. By visualizing historical events, scientific concepts, or cultural artifacts, students can gain a deeper understanding and retain information more effectively.

4. **Improving Collaboration and Communication**: Project-based learning often involves teamwork. The integration of DALL.E 3 facilitates better communication among team members, as visuals can be a universal language that transcends verbal barriers. Teams can use generated images to share ideas, provide feedback, and build a shared vision for their project.

5. **Supporting Diverse Learning Styles**: Every student has a unique learning style, and visual learning is a significant component for many. The visual outputs from DALL.E 3 cater to visual learners, aiding in their comprehension and retention of information, which is crucial in project-based learning environments.

6. **Encouraging Interdisciplinary Learning**: Project-based learning often requires an interdisciplinary approach. DALL.E 3's versatility in generating visuals across various subjects – from art and history to science and technology – enables students to integrate multiple disciplines into their projects, promoting a holistic learning experience.

7. **Facilitating Real-World Problem Solving**: By providing realistic and detailed visual representations, DALL.E 3 helps students in

applying their learning to real-world scenarios. For projects aimed at solving practical problems or addressing social issues, being able to visualize these scenarios can lead to more effective and empathetic solutions.

8. **Enhancing Presentation and Documentation**: An important aspect of project-based learning is the presentation and documentation of the project work. DALL.E 3 assists in creating compelling visual materials that can enhance project reports, presentations, and portfolios, making them more engaging and professional.

9. **Providing Instant Feedback and Iteration**: The quick generation of images allows for rapid prototyping of ideas. Students can instantly see the visual representation of their ideas, receive feedback, and make iterative improvements, which is a core principle of project-based learning.

10. **Equalizing Educational Opportunities**: This integration also plays a pivotal role in equalizing access to high-quality educational resources. Students from varied backgrounds can utilize these advanced tools, ensuring that high-end visual aids are not just limited to well-resourced schools.

In summary, the integration of DALL.E 3 with ChatGPT significantly enhances project-based learning by providing powerful tools for visualization, creativity, interdisciplinary integration, and effective communication. This blend of AI technologies not only enriches the educational experience but also prepares students for a future where interdisciplinary knowledge and creative problem-solving are paramount.

X. **Educator Support and Resource Generation**:

Teachers and educators can use this tool to create custom educational resources, from lesson plans to visual aids, saving time and resources while enhancing the quality of their teaching materials.

The integration of DALL.E 3 into ChatGPT represents a groundbreaking advancement in educational technology, especially in terms of educator support and resource generation. This powerful combination offers a new horizon for teaching methodologies, providing educators with an unprecedented level of assistance in creating and utilizing educational materials. Here's an in-depth look at how this integration transforms the educational landscape for educators:

1. **Creation of Customized Learning Materials**: With DALL.E 3, educators can generate bespoke visual aids tailored to their specific curriculum needs. Whether it's creating intricate diagrams for science classes, historical reconstructions for history lessons, or visual prompts for language teaching, the ability to produce these resources on demand is invaluable.

2. **Enhancing Lesson Plans with Visual Aids**: Visual imagery can significantly improve comprehension and retention of information. By integrating DALL.E 3's capabilities, educators can enrich their lesson plans with relevant and engaging visuals, making abstract or complex concepts more accessible and understandable for students.

3. **Aiding in Diverse Educational Strategies**: Different teaching strategies require different types of materials. DALL.E 3 empowers educators to quickly generate resources suitable for various pedagogical approaches, such as flipped classrooms, inquiry-based learning, or project-based learning, thus supporting a more dynamic and adaptable teaching process.

4. **Facilitating Inclusive Education**: Inclusivity in education is crucial, and DALL.E 3 can assist educators in creating materials that cater to a diverse student body. This includes generating images that represent different cultures, abilities, and backgrounds, fostering a more inclusive and respectful learning environment.

5. **Supporting Special Education**: Educators in special education can leverage DALL.E 3 to produce customized visual materials that meet the unique needs of their students, such as simplified illustrations for complex concepts or visual schedules and organizers for students requiring additional structure in their learning.

6. **Time and Resource Efficiency**: One of the significant challenges for educators is the time and effort required to source or create high-quality educational materials. DALL.E 3 streamlines this process, enabling quick and efficient generation of high-quality visuals, thereby saving time and reducing reliance on external resources.

7. **Professional Development and Creativity**: For educators, the integration of DALL.E 3 into their teaching toolkit opens up new avenues for professional development and creativity. It allows

them to experiment with novel teaching techniques and materials, keeping their methods fresh and engaging both for themselves and their students.

8. **Facilitating Remote and Hybrid Learning**: In an era where remote and hybrid learning formats are increasingly prevalent, DALL.E 3 provides a critical tool for educators to create digital resources that are both engaging and effective for students learning from home.

9. **Resource Sharing and Collaboration**: This technology also fosters a collaborative environment among educators. The ease of creating and sharing visual resources enables educators to collaborate across schools, districts, and even internationally, sharing best practices and resources for mutual benefit.

10. **Evolving Educational Content**: As curricula evolve and new topics emerge, DALL.E 3 allows educators to keep pace by quickly creating resources that align with the latest educational trends and discoveries, ensuring that the content they deliver is always current and relevant.

In conclusion, the integration of DALL.E 3 with ChatGPT marks a significant step forward in educational technology, particularly in supporting educators through enhanced resource generation capabilities. This integration not only aids in creating a more dynamic, inclusive, and effective learning environment but also equips educators with the tools to continuously adapt and innovate in their teaching methodologies.

XI. **Exploration and Research**:

Students and researchers can use this integration to explore different scenarios, visualize data, or create representations of their research findings, making the research process more interactive and engaging.

The integration of DALL.E 3 into ChatGPT heralds a transformative era in the field of education, particularly in the realms of exploration and research. This synergy between advanced language processing and state-of-the-art visual generation technologies offers an unprecedented tool for educational exploration, facilitating both teaching and learning processes in multiple ways. Here's a comprehensive overview of how this integration significantly enhances exploration and research in education:

1. **Facilitating Conceptual Understanding**: DALL.E 3's ability to produce intricate and accurate visual representations aids students and researchers in grasping complex concepts. For subjects where visual context is crucial – such as in sciences, architecture, or engineering – this integration can dramatically enhance understanding by transforming abstract theories into tangible images.

2. **Encouraging Creative Exploration**: With DALL.E 3, students and educators can explore creative concepts beyond the limitations of traditional resources. This tool allows for the visualization of hypothetical scenarios, abstract ideas, or historical reconstructions, thereby fostering a deeper level of creative thinking and exploration.

3. **Enhancing Research Visualization**: For researchers, particularly in fields where visual data is paramount, DALL.E 3 can generate detailed visuals to accompany their findings. This capability is invaluable in areas like environmental studies, astronomy, and even social sciences, where visualizing data or theoretical models can significantly impact the comprehension and dissemination of research.

4. **Supporting Inquiry-Based Learning**: In an educational setting that prioritizes inquiry-based learning, DALL.E 3 serves as a vital tool. It enables students to visually explore the answers to their questions, thereby enhancing their investigative skills and promoting a more hands-on approach to learning.

5. **Aiding Historical and Cultural Research**: For subjects like history and cultural studies, DALL.E 3 can recreate historical events, artifacts, or cultural imagery, providing a visual context that textbooks alone may not sufficiently convey. This aids in a deeper understanding of historical contexts and cultural nuances.

6. **Stimulating Scientific Inquiry**: In scientific fields, DALL.E 3 can be used to visualize scientific phenomena, complex processes, or even simulate experimental outcomes. This not only aids in education but also can spark new research ideas or hypotheses.

7. **Promoting Interdisciplinary Learning**: The integration of DALL.E 3 with ChatGPT encourages interdisciplinary learning by allowing the merging of visual arts with traditional academic subjects. This can lead to innovative approaches to education,

where art and science, for instance, can be combined to provide a more holistic understanding.

8. **Assisting in Literature and Language Studies**: In the study of literature and languages, visual representations can bring texts to life, aiding in comprehension and engagement. DALL.E 3 can generate scenes from literary works or visualize concepts in language studies, making learning more interactive and immersive.

9. **Enabling Global Perspectives**: Through its capacity to generate diverse and culturally-specific visuals, DALL.E 3 helps in understanding and appreciating global perspectives. This is particularly useful in subjects like geography, social studies, and languages.

10. **Resource for Independent Learning**: For students engaged in independent research or projects, DALL.E 3 offers a valuable resource. It allows them to visualize their ideas, theories, or designs, thus supporting their research process and enhancing their learning experience.

In summary, the integration of DALL.E 3 with ChatGPT marks a significant milestone in educational technology, especially in the context of exploration and research. It not only enhances the learning experience by providing visual context to complex concepts but also opens up new avenues for creative and investigative learning. This technology stands as a testament to the evolving landscape of educational tools, promising a future where learning is more interactive, comprehensive, and accessible.

XII. **Enhancing STEM Education**:

In STEM (Science, Technology, Engineering, Mathematics) education, the ability to visualize scientific and mathematical concepts, engineering designs, and technological innovations plays a crucial role in understanding and innovation.

The integration of DALL.E 3 into ChatGPT marks a revolutionary step forward in enhancing STEM (Science, Technology, Engineering, and Mathematics) education. This fusion of cutting-edge artificial intelligence in both textual and visual domains opens up new, dynamic ways of learning and understanding complex STEM concepts. The following points provide a comprehensive overview of how this integration significantly elevates STEM education:

1. **Visualizing Complex Scientific Concepts**: DALL.E 3's ability to generate detailed and accurate visual representations allows for the transformation of abstract scientific theories into clear, understandable images. This is particularly beneficial in subjects like physics or biology, where visual aids can significantly enhance comprehension.

2. **Aiding in Mathematical Understanding**: Mathematics often involves complex structures and patterns that can be challenging to visualize. DALL.E 3 can create visual representations of mathematical models, geometric patterns, and data visualizations, making them more accessible and easier to understand for learners.

3. **Enhancing Engineering Education**: In engineering, where design and structure play critical roles, DALL.E 3 can be used to visualize engineering concepts, prototypes, and models. This not only aids in the learning process but also stimulates innovation and creativity in engineering design.

4. **Supporting Technological Learning**: As technology continues to advance, DALL.E 3 offers a way to keep up with these changes by providing visual explanations and representations of new technological concepts, tools, and their applications, thus making the learning process more current and relevant.

5. **Interactive Learning Experiences**: The integration of DALL.E 3 into ChatGPT provides an interactive learning environment. Students can request specific images or visual explanations, making the learning experience more engaging and tailored to individual needs.

6. **Encouraging Problem-Solving Skills**: By visualizing problems and solutions, DALL.E 3 fosters a more practical understanding of STEM subjects. This approach enhances critical thinking and problem-solving skills, which are fundamental in STEM education.

7. **Facilitating Experimentation and Simulation**: In subjects where real-life experimentation is not always feasible, DALL.E 3 can simulate experiments or processes visually, offering students a virtual hands-on experience.

8. **Bridging Theory and Practical Application**: Often in STEM, there is a gap between theoretical knowledge and practical

application. DALL.E 3 helps bridge this gap by providing visual representations that link abstract concepts to real-world applications.

9. **Inspiring Interest in STEM Fields**: The captivating visual capabilities of DALL.E 3 can inspire and motivate students, sparking a deeper interest in STEM fields. This is particularly important in early education, where engaging teaching methods can influence future career choices.

10. **Customizable Educational Content**: Educators can use DALL.E 3 to create customized educational material that aligns with their curriculum. This allows for the creation of unique, visually engaging content that caters to the specific needs of their students.

In conclusion, the integration of DALL.E 3 with ChatGPT represents a significant milestone in educational technology. It offers a range of applications that can transform traditional learning methods, making education more engaging, effective, and accessible. By providing both students and educators with powerful tools for visual learning and creative expression, this technology paves the way for a more interactive, personalized, and effective educational experience.

Prompts:

1. **Interactive Digital Classroom**: "A modern classroom with interactive digital whiteboards, students of diverse ethnicities using tablets, and educational graphics displayed on screens, in a bright, technology-enhanced learning environment."

2. **Virtual Reality in Education**: "A photograph of a student wearing a virtual reality headset, deeply engaged in a virtual science experiment, with educational content visibly floating around them in a well-lit classroom."

3. **Language Learning with Tech Tools**: "A classroom scene showing students from various ethnic backgrounds using language learning apps on their laptops and tablets, with visible on-screen graphics of different languages and cultures."

4. **STEM Education with Robotics**: "An image of a diverse group of students collaboratively working on a robotics project in a STEM classroom, with robotic parts and computers on the table, in a modern educational setting."

5. **Art and Creativity Workshop**: "A bright art classroom with students of different ethnicities engaged in digital art creation using graphic tablets and computers, displaying a variety of colorful art projects on their screens."

6. **History Class with Augmented Reality**: "A photograph of a history class where students are using augmented reality to explore ancient civilizations, with holographic images of historical artifacts and scenes visible around the room."

7. **Geography Lesson with Interactive Maps**: "An image showing a geography class with a large interactive digital map on the wall, students pointing and discussing different countries, and tablets displaying geographical data."

8. **Mathematics Class with Interactive Simulations**: "A realistic photo of a mathematics classroom where students are using interactive simulations on their computers to solve complex problems, with equations and graphs visible on their screens."

9. **Science Lab with Digital Microscopes**: "A photograph of a modern science lab with students using digital microscopes connected to laptops, displaying microscopic images on their screens, in a well-equipped educational setting."

10. **Computer Programming Workshop**: "An image of a diverse group of students in a computer lab, coding on their laptops, with screens showing various programming languages and code, in a contemporary educational environment."

These prompts are designed to showcase how DALL.E 3 can create realistic photographs depicting various aspects of educational applications, demonstrating the integration of technology in different learning environments.

Here is a realistic photograph that illustrates the concept of Educational Applications, showing a classroom scene where technology enhances the learning experience.

Here is a realistic photograph illustrating the concept of educational applications in a modern, technology-driven learning environment.

Business Applications:

The integration of DALL.E 3 with ChatGPT represents a significant advancement in the realm of business applications, offering an array of possibilities for enhancing various aspects of business operations, marketing, and customer engagement. This fusion of AI-driven image generation with advanced natural language processing opens up innovative avenues for businesses to explore, adapt, and thrive in the digital age. The following introduction highlights the key aspects and potential impacts of this integration on the business world:

I. Marketing and Branding:

DALL.E 3's capability to generate unique, customized visuals can revolutionize marketing strategies. Businesses can create compelling, brand-specific images and graphics for advertising campaigns, social media posts, and promotional materials. This not only enhances brand visibility but also aids in establishing a distinct brand identity.

The integration of DALL.E 3 with ChatGPT marks a transformative moment in the fields of marketing and branding. This synergy of cutting-edge AI technologies paves the way for unprecedented creative opportunities, allowing businesses to redefine their approach to marketing and establish more engaging brand identities. The following introduction explores the diverse implications and benefits of this integration for marketing and branding:

1. **Enhanced Creative Possibilities**: With DALL.E 3, businesses can generate a wide range of custom visuals, from logos and product designs to promotional images and social media content. This enables brands to consistently produce fresh and appealing visual content, essential in capturing consumer attention in a crowded digital landscape.

2. **Personalized Marketing Campaigns**: DALL.E 3's ability to create images based on specific prompts allows for highly targeted and personalized marketing campaigns. Brands can tailor their visual content to resonate with different segments of their audience, leading to more effective and impactful marketing strategies.

3. **Rapid Concept Visualization**: The integration enables marketers to quickly visualize and iterate on advertising concepts and campaign ideas. This agility in concept development

accelerates the creative process, allowing businesses to respond rapidly to market trends and consumer preferences.

4. **Consistent Branding Across Platforms**: With the precise and varied visual outputs of DALL.E 3, companies can maintain consistency in branding across various platforms. Whether it's digital advertising, social media, or print media, the ability to generate cohesive visuals strengthens brand identity and recognition.

5. **Cost-Effective Content Creation**: DALL.E 3 offers a cost-effective solution for creating high-quality visual content. This is particularly beneficial for small businesses or startups with limited marketing budgets, as it reduces the need for expensive design resources or software.

6. **Interactive Customer Engagement**: By integrating DALL.E 3 with ChatGPT, businesses can engage customers in unique and interactive ways. For instance, customers could receive customized visual responses to their inquiries, enhancing engagement and providing a memorable brand experience.

7. **Innovative Advertising Materials**: DALL.E 3 enables the creation of innovative and eye-catching advertising materials that stand out. By pushing the boundaries of traditional advertising visuals, brands can capture greater interest and curiosity from potential customers.

8. **Social Media Dynamism**: In the ever-evolving world of social media, the ability to quickly produce diverse and captivating visuals is crucial. DALL.E 3 empowers businesses to keep their social media feeds vibrant and engaging, an essential factor for maintaining online presence and relevance.

9. **Brand Storytelling**: Visual storytelling is a powerful tool in branding, and DALL.E 3 enhances this aspect by providing rich, evocative visuals that can narrate a brand's story, values, and mission effectively to the audience.

10. **Market Research and Testing**: Businesses can use DALL.E 3 to create a variety of visual concepts for market research and A/B testing, gaining insights into consumer preferences and optimizing their marketing strategies accordingly.

In summary, the integration of DALL.E 3 with ChatGPT offers a plethora of opportunities for marketing and branding. It not only simplifies and enriches the creative process but also enables brands to connect with their audiences in more personalized and innovative ways. As we step further into the digital era, this integration stands as a beacon of creativity and efficiency, reshaping the landscape of marketing and branding in profound and exciting ways.

II. **Product Visualization and Prototyping**:

For product development, DALL.E 3 offers the ability to visualize products before they are physically produced. This facilitates rapid prototyping, allowing businesses to experiment with different designs and concepts quickly and cost-effectively, thus speeding up the innovation process.

The integration of DALL.E 3 with ChatGPT represents a groundbreaking advancement in the realm of business, particularly in the areas of product visualization and prototyping. This fusion of sophisticated AI technologies provides businesses with powerful tools to visualize, design, and prototype products with remarkable efficiency and creativity. Here's an in-depth introduction to how this integration is revolutionizing product visualization and prototyping:

1. **Rapid Prototyping**: DALL.E 3 empowers businesses to quickly visualize and iterate product designs. This rapid prototyping capability accelerates the design process, allowing for more agile responses to market trends and consumer feedback. It's particularly transformative for industries where visual design is key, such as fashion, consumer electronics, and automotive.

2. **Enhanced Visualization**: With DALL.E 3, companies can generate highly detailed and accurate visual representations of products, even before they are physically produced. This capability is invaluable for assessing the aesthetic and functional aspects of a product, enabling design teams to make informed decisions and adjustments early in the development process.

3. **Cost-Effective Design Exploration**: The AI-driven approach to product visualization reduces the need for physical prototypes, which can be costly and time-consuming to produce. Businesses can explore a wider range of design options with minimal resource expenditure, fostering greater innovation and creativity in product development.

4. **Improved Collaboration**: Integrating DALL.E 3 with ChatGPT facilitates better collaboration among design teams, marketers,

and stakeholders. Teams can share and discuss visual concepts in real-time, leading to more cohesive and well-informed product development strategies.

5. **Consumer Engagement and Feedback**: Businesses can use these AI tools to create product visualizations for market testing, allowing them to gather consumer feedback on potential products. This approach can guide product development to better align with market demands and consumer preferences.

6. **Marketing and Pre-Launch Strategies**: By generating realistic product images, companies can create marketing materials and launch campaigns for products still in the prototyping stage. This strategy can build anticipation and gauge consumer interest even before the product hits the market.

7. **Customization and Personalization**: DALL.E 3 enables businesses to easily visualize customized and personalized products according to specific customer requests or market niches. This flexibility is particularly advantageous for companies offering bespoke products or services.

8. **Educational and Training Purposes**: In industries where training on new products is essential, such as in technology or manufacturing, DALL.E 3 can create detailed visual materials that aid in educating employees about new product features and functions.

9. **Quality Assurance**: With advanced visualization, potential design flaws or issues can be identified and addressed early in the product development cycle, improving the overall quality of the final product.

10. **Sustainability**: By reducing the need for physical prototypes, this integration also contributes to sustainability efforts. Less material waste and energy consumption in the prototyping phase align with environmentally conscious business practices.

In summary, the integration of DALL.E 3 with ChatGPT opens up a new frontier in product visualization and prototyping. It not only streamlines the product development process but also enhances creativity, collaboration, and efficiency. This integration is set to become a vital tool in the business world, reshaping how products are conceptualized, designed, and brought to market.

III. **Customized Customer Experiences**:

Businesses can leverage DALL.E 3 in ChatGPT to provide personalized experiences to customers. By generating images and visuals in response to specific customer queries or preferences, companies can enhance customer engagement and satisfaction, tailoring their services to meet individual needs.

The integration of DALL.E 3 with ChatGPT heralds a new era in business, particularly in crafting customized customer experiences. This innovative combination of AI-driven image generation and conversational AI offers unparalleled opportunities for businesses to engage with customers in more personalized and meaningful ways. Here's a comprehensive introduction to how this integration is transforming customized customer experiences:

1. **Personalized Product Recommendations**: Integrating DALL.E 3 with ChatGPT allows businesses to offer highly personalized product recommendations. Customers can describe their preferences or needs in conversation, and the AI can generate visual representations of products that match these descriptions, making the shopping experience more engaging and tailored to individual tastes.

2. **Interactive Marketing Campaigns**: Businesses can leverage this technology to create interactive and dynamic marketing campaigns. Customers can interact with ChatGPT to explore different product options, while DALL.E 3 generates images in real-time, responding to customer inputs. This creates a more immersive and interactive marketing experience.

3. **Enhanced Online Shopping Experience**: For e-commerce, this integration offers a revolutionary way to enhance the online shopping experience. Customers can see visualizations of products in different colors, styles, or settings, helping them make more informed decisions. This level of customization in visual representation directly caters to individual preferences and improves customer satisfaction.

4. **Visual Customer Support**: In customer service, DALL.E 3 can be used to visually explain solutions to customer queries. For example, if a customer is having trouble assembling a product, ChatGPT can guide them through the process while DALL.E 3 provides step-by-step visual aids, making the support experience more comprehensive and effective.

5. **Creating Customized Content**: Businesses can generate customized content for customers, such as personalized greeting cards, unique product designs, or tailored promotional materials. This not only enhances customer engagement but also adds a personal touch that can significantly boost customer loyalty.

6. **Virtual Product Customization**: Customers can virtually customize products using a combination of text-based input and visual feedback. For instance, in the automotive industry, a customer could describe their ideal car features, and DALL.E 3 would generate an image of the car with those specific attributes.

7. **Feedback and Iteration**: ChatGPT can gather customer feedback on visual content created by DALL.E 3, enabling businesses to iterate and improve their products and services continuously. This feedback loop ensures that customer preferences are consistently met and exceeded.

8. **Event and Experience Planning**: For event planning and experiential marketing, this integration can be used to visualize event setups, themes, or experiences based on customer specifications, offering a glimpse of the event before it happens.

9. **User-Generated Content Enhancement**: Businesses can enhance user-generated content by integrating it with AI-generated visuals. This can create a more engaging community experience around a brand, encouraging customer participation and interaction.

10. **Cultural and Demographic Adaptation**: By understanding customer demographics and cultural backgrounds through ChatGPT, DALL.E 3 can create visuals that are culturally relevant and appealing to different customer segments, ensuring inclusivity in marketing and customer engagement.

In conclusion, the integration of DALL.E 3 with ChatGPT is a game-changer for businesses focusing on customized customer experiences. It offers an unprecedented level of personalization in customer interaction, product visualization, and content creation, thereby enhancing customer engagement, satisfaction, and loyalty in a deeply competitive business landscape.

IV. **E-commerce Enhancements**:

In e-commerce, visual representation is crucial. DALL.E 3 can be used to generate high-quality images of products, providing customers with a better understanding of what they are purchasing. This can lead to increased trust and reduced return rates.

The integration of DALL.E 3 with ChatGPT represents a significant leap forward in e-commerce, offering innovative ways to enhance the online shopping experience for consumers. This fusion of advanced AI image generation with conversational AI provides a unique platform for e-commerce businesses to elevate their customer engagement, product visualization, and overall user experience. Here's a comprehensive introduction to how this integration is revolutionizing e-commerce:

1. **Enhanced Product Visualization**: With DALL.E 3, e-commerce platforms can offer customers highly detailed and customized visualizations of products. Customers can request to see an item in different colors, styles, or in a particular setting, and the AI generates these images in real-time. This level of visualization aids in decision-making and boosts customer confidence in their purchases.

2. **Interactive Shopping Experiences**: The integration allows for a more interactive shopping experience. ChatGPT can understand and respond to customer queries, while DALL.E 3 generates corresponding visuals. This interactive dialogue creates a more engaging and personalized shopping journey, closely mimicking the experience of a physical store.

3. **Custom Design and Personalization**: E-commerce businesses can offer a new level of product customization. Customers can describe their ideal product, and DALL.E 3 can generate images that match these specifications. This capability is particularly beneficial for industries like fashion, home decor, and bespoke gifting.

4. **Real-Time Inventory Display**: DALL.E 3 can create images representing current inventory in real-time, offering customers an up-to-date view of available products. This feature can significantly enhance the user experience by providing accurate and timely information.

5. **Virtual Try-Ons and Previews**: For items like clothing, accessories, or even furniture, DALL.E 3 can generate images that show what these items would look like in use, such as how a dress would look on a person or how a sofa would fit in a living

room setup. This virtual try-on feature can reduce return rates and increase customer satisfaction.

6. **Personalized Marketing Content**: E-commerce platforms can use this integration to create personalized marketing content. Based on customer interactions and preferences, ChatGPT and DALL.E 3 can generate customized images and messages, making marketing efforts more effective and targeted.

7. **Enhanced User Interface and Navigation**: The visual capabilities of DALL.E 3 can be used to improve the website's user interface, making navigation more intuitive and visually appealing. For example, visual cues can be generated in response to customer queries, helping them find products more efficiently.

8. **Customer Feedback and Iteration**: ChatGPT can collect customer feedback on the visual content created by DALL.E 3, allowing for continuous improvement of product offerings and visual representations, thereby aligning more closely with customer preferences.

9. **Social Media Integration**: E-commerce businesses can use this technology to create compelling visual content for social media, engaging customers through visually rich posts and ads, personalized to the preferences of the target audience.

10. **Global Reach and Localization**: The AI's ability to understand and generate content in multiple languages, coupled with culturally appropriate visuals, means e-commerce platforms can easily localize content for different markets, enhancing global reach and relevance.

In summary, the integration of DALL.E 3 with ChatGPT opens up a myriad of possibilities for e-commerce. It enhances the online shopping experience by offering advanced product visualization, personalized customer interactions, and innovative marketing strategies. This integration is set to redefine the standards of e-commerce, providing customers with a more engaging, informative, and satisfying shopping experience.

V. **Content Creation and Management**:

For content creators and managers, DALL.E 3 offers an efficient way to produce diverse and appealing visual content. Whether for blogs, websites, or online platforms, the ability to generate relevant and engaging images can significantly enhance content quality and audience engagement.

The integration of DALL.E 3 into ChatGPT heralds a transformative era in the realm of business, particularly in content creation and management. This fusion empowers businesses with unprecedented capabilities in generating, customizing, and managing digital content efficiently and creatively. Let's explore the various dimensions of this integration in the context of business applications:

1. **Automated Visual Content Generation**: DALL.E 3's ability to produce high-quality images from textual descriptions revolutionizes the way visual content is created. Businesses can now generate bespoke images, graphics, and illustrations on demand, significantly reducing the time and resources typically required for content creation.

2. **Personalization at Scale**: With ChatGPT and DALL.E 3, businesses can tailor content to individual user preferences and contexts. This personalization extends beyond textual content to include visual elements, enabling businesses to create highly customized marketing campaigns, social media posts, and web content that resonate more deeply with their audience.

3. **Streamlined Content Workflows**: Integrating these AI tools can streamline content creation workflows. ChatGPT can assist in drafting textual content, while DALL.E 3 generates complementary visual elements. This synergy can enhance productivity, allowing for quicker content turnaround and more consistent output.

4. **Dynamic Content Adaptation**: Businesses can use this integration to dynamically adapt content based on user feedback or changing trends. ChatGPT can analyze customer interactions or market data, guiding DALL.E 3 to adjust the visual content accordingly, ensuring that the business remains relevant and engaging.

5. **Enhanced Social Media Presence**: Social media thrives on visually captivating content. DALL.E 3's capabilities, combined with ChatGPT's conversational insights, can create unique and compelling content for social media platforms, enhancing engagement and brand presence.

6. **Innovative Brand Storytelling**: The combination of ChatGPT's language understanding and DALL.E 3's visual generation opens new avenues for creative storytelling. Businesses can craft narratives that are visually and textually integrated, offering immersive experiences to their audience.

7. **Cost-Effective Content Solutions**: For small businesses or startups with limited budgets, this integration offers a cost-effective solution for content creation. High-quality visuals and text can be generated without the need for extensive design teams or expensive software.

8. **Rich Media for E-Learning and Training**: In educational and training modules, the integration can be used to create engaging and informative content. Complex concepts can be explained through a combination of ChatGPT's explanatory text and DALL.E 3's illustrative visuals.

9. **Multilingual and Multicultural Content Creation**: The AI's ability to understand and generate content in multiple languages allows businesses to create culturally relevant and localized content for different regions, enhancing global reach and engagement.

10. **Content Archiving and Retrieval**: With ChatGPT, businesses can efficiently categorize and retrieve content, including images generated by DALL.E 3, making content management more efficient and accessible.

In essence, the integration of DALL.E 3 with ChatGPT in business applications, particularly in content creation and management, represents a paradigm shift. It offers a blend of creativity, efficiency, and personalization that can significantly enhance how businesses engage with their audience, manage their digital assets, and tell their brand stories. This integration not only streamlines content workflows but also unlocks new creative possibilities, making businesses more dynamic and adaptable in their digital strategies.

VI. Training and Educational Resources:

In corporate training and development, DALL E 3 can be used to create educational materials, including diagrams, illustrations, and scenarios that aid in learning and comprehension. This enhances the effectiveness of training programs and employee skill development.

The integration of DALL.E 3 with ChatGPT marks a significant advancement in the field of business, particularly in the development of training and educational resources. This powerful combination of AI-driven visual and textual capabilities presents a wealth of opportunities for enhancing learning experiences in corporate settings. Here's a detailed exploration of how this integration impacts the creation and implementation of training and educational resources in the business sector:

1. **Enhanced Learning Materials**: DALL.E 3's capacity to generate detailed, context-specific images combined with ChatGPT's sophisticated language understanding and generation allows for the creation of rich, engaging training materials. Businesses can develop customized tutorials, guides, and instructional content that are both visually appealing and informative.

2. **Interactive Training Modules**: The integration enables the development of interactive training modules where visual content is dynamically generated in response to user interactions or queries. This leads to a more engaging and personalized learning experience, as employees can explore concepts through a mix of text and custom visuals.

3. **Simulated Scenarios for Skill Development**: DALL.E 3 can create realistic images or scenarios, which, when paired with ChatGPT's narrative capabilities, can simulate workplace situations. This is particularly useful for role-playing exercises, scenario-based training, and skills development, allowing employees to visualize and engage with real-world challenges in a controlled environment.

4. **Visual Aids for Complex Concepts**: In industries where complex ideas or processes are commonplace, this integration proves invaluable. DALL.E 3 can visually represent intricate concepts, processes, or data, which ChatGPT can then explain in simple terms, making learning more accessible and effective.

5. **Customized Learning Paths**: Businesses can leverage ChatGPT's ability to analyze learning patterns and feedback, using this data to guide DALL.E 3 in creating tailored visual content. This approach allows for the development of customized learning paths that cater to the unique needs and learning styles of individual employees.

6. **Multilingual Training Resources**: The combination of ChatGPT's multilingual capabilities and DALL.E 3's universal visual language can produce training materials in various languages, accompanied by culturally relevant visuals. This is particularly beneficial for global companies seeking to provide consistent training across diverse geographical locations.

7. **Rapid Content Creation and Updating**: The speed at which both ChatGPT and DALL.E 3 can generate content allows businesses to quickly create or update training materials. This agility is crucial in industries where information changes rapidly or where frequent training updates are necessary.

8. **Cost-Effective Resource Development**: Small and medium-sized businesses, which may not have extensive resources for training material development, can greatly benefit from this integration. It offers a cost-effective solution for producing high-quality educational content without the need for large teams or outsourced services.

9. **Enhanced Engagement and Retention**: Visually rich and interactive training content can lead to higher engagement and better information retention among employees. This integration makes learning more enjoyable and effective, leading to improved outcomes in training programs.

10. **Accessibility and Inclusivity**: DALL.E 3 and ChatGPT can work together to create training resources that are accessible to a wider range of learning needs and preferences, including visual learning styles and differently-abled individuals, promoting inclusivity in workplace education.

In summary, the integration of DALL.E 3 with ChatGPT in the realm of business training and educational resources represents a significant leap forward in corporate learning and development. By combining AI-driven visual creativity with advanced language processing, this integration offers businesses an innovative, efficient, and effective tool for developing training materials that are not only informative and engaging but also adaptable to a wide range of learning styles and needs.

VII. **Enhancing Presentations and Reports**:

Business presentations and reports can be enriched with custom visuals created by DALL.E 3. This not only makes the information more accessible and engaging but also helps in conveying complex data or concepts more effectively.

The integration of DALL.E 3 with ChatGPT introduces a transformative approach to enhancing business presentations and reports, a crucial aspect of modern corporate communication. This synergy between advanced visual generation and sophisticated language processing capabilities presents an innovative leap in how businesses can convey information, ideas, and data. Here's a comprehensive look at how this integration elevates the standard of presentations and reports in the business world:

1. **Visually Compelling Presentations**: DALL.E 3's ability to generate detailed, context-relevant images enables the creation of visually striking presentations. When combined with ChatGPT's textual analysis and content generation skills, presentations become not only more engaging but also more effective in communicating complex ideas.

2. **Data Visualization and Interpretation**: The integration significantly enhances data representation. DALL.E 3 can create visual interpretations of data, which ChatGPT can then contextualize with insightful commentary. This combination makes it easier for audiences to understand and retain complex data insights.

3. **Tailored Report Customization**: Businesses can leverage this technology to produce customized reports that are both informative and visually appealing. ChatGPT can analyze and summarize key information, while DALL.E 3 provides relevant visual content, making reports more accessible and engaging for diverse audiences.

4. **Real-Time Visual Aids Creation**: In dynamic business environments, the ability to generate visual aids in real-time is invaluable. This integration allows for the quick creation of graphics, charts, and other visual elements during live presentations or meetings, aiding in clearer communication and immediate audience engagement.

5. **Enhanced Branding Consistency**: DALL.E 3 can be utilized to ensure visual elements in presentations and reports are in line with brand guidelines. This consistency in branding aids in building a strong, recognizable corporate identity across all communication materials.

6. **Interactive Elements for Engagement**: Interactive visuals, such as infographics and animated charts, can be seamlessly integrated into presentations and reports. These elements, generated by DALL.E 3 and contextualized by ChatGPT, can make complex information more digestible and engaging.

7. **Multimedia Integration**: The integration facilitates the inclusion of various multimedia elements into presentations and reports. From custom illustrations to unique graphic designs, DALL.E 3 enhances the visual appeal, while ChatGPT ensures that the text complements and strengthens the visual narrative.

8. **Time and Resource Efficiency**: The speed and efficiency of content creation with this integration save significant time and resources. Businesses can quickly produce high-quality presentations and reports without the need for extensive design teams or external resources.

9. **Global and Multilingual Appeal**: ChatGPT's multilingual capabilities, combined with DALL.E 3's visual universality, enable the creation of presentations and reports that are culturally relevant and accessible to a global audience, a key factor in international business operations.

10. **Innovative Storytelling in Business Communication**: The fusion of AI-driven visuals with natural language processing opens new avenues for storytelling in business communication. Presentations and reports can now convey narratives that are both visually captivating and rich in content, leading to more compelling and persuasive business communication.

In summary, the integration of DALL.E 3 and ChatGPT revolutionizes the way businesses create presentations and reports. By harnessing the power of AI in both visual and textual domains, businesses can produce materials that are not only aesthetically impressive but also rich in content and insights. This advancement represents a significant stride in business communication, making it more efficient, engaging, and effective in conveying complex information to diverse audiences

VIII. **Real Estate and Interior Design Visualization**:

For the real estate and interior design industries, DALL.E 3 can generate realistic images of properties, interiors, and renovations, aiding in visualization and decision-making processes for clients and designers alike.

The integration of DALL.E 3 with ChatGPT marks a significant advancement in the realms of real estate and interior design, offering innovative and efficient solutions for visualization and client engagement. This synergy of cutting-edge AI technologies has the potential to revolutionize how properties and design concepts are presented and explored. Here's an in-depth look at its impact on real estate and interior design:

1. **Enhanced Property Showcasing**: For real estate, DALL.E 3's capabilities in generating lifelike images and virtual tours, combined with ChatGPT's descriptive narratives, enable potential buyers to experience properties remotely with an unprecedented level of realism. This not only broadens the reach to distant clients but also provides a more immersive viewing experience.

2. **Customized Interior Design Visualization**: DALL.E 3 can create detailed visualizations of interior spaces based on specific client requirements or designer input. When integrated with ChatGPT's ability to understand and articulate design concepts, it allows for a highly personalized visual representation of interior design projects.

3. **Virtual Staging and Remodeling**: Real estate agents and interior designers can utilize this integration to virtually stage or remodel properties. DALL.E 3 can generate images of the property with different furnishings, color schemes, or layouts, which ChatGPT can then describe in detail, helping clients visualize potential changes and upgrades.

4. **Interactive Client Consultations**: The combination of DALL.E 3 and ChatGPT enables a more interactive consultation process. As clients describe their preferences or concerns, the AI can immediately generate corresponding visuals, leading to a more dynamic and responsive consultation experience.

5. **Cost-Effective Marketing Materials**: Creating marketing materials for listings or design portfolios becomes more cost-effective and efficient. DALL.E 3 can produce high-quality visuals of properties and designs, which ChatGPT can complement with compelling descriptions, enhancing the overall appeal of the marketing content.

6. **Architectural Visualization**: For architects and developers, this integration offers a powerful tool for visualizing architectural projects even before they are built. DALL.E 3 can generate detailed renderings of architectural designs, which ChatGPT can elaborate on, providing a comprehensive preview of the proposed structures.

7. **Enhanced Client Understanding and Engagement**: The ability to quickly produce visualizations based on client feedback ensures a better understanding of client needs and preferences. This leads to higher client satisfaction as they can see their ideas being visualized in real-time.

8. **Facilitating Remote Collaboration**: The integration is especially beneficial in the current trend of remote collaboration. It allows designers, clients, and stakeholders to collaborate effectively from different locations, with AI-generated visuals and descriptions bridging the communication gap.

9. **Educational Tool for Clients**: For clients unfamiliar with architectural or design terminology, this integration serves as an educational tool. ChatGPT can explain design concepts in layman's terms, while DALL.E 3 visually represents these concepts, making the information more accessible.

10. **Trend Analysis and Forecasting**: By analyzing current trends and client preferences, ChatGPT, in conjunction with DALL.E 3, can predict and visualize future trends in real estate and interior design, aiding professionals in staying ahead in their field.

In summary, the integration of DALL.E 3 with ChatGPT presents a transformative solution for the real estate and interior design industries. By combining the power of visual AI with advanced natural language processing, it offers a more efficient, engaging, and client-focused approach to property showcasing, design visualization, and client consultations. This technological synergy is set to redefine the standards of presentation and customer interaction in these sectors.

IX. Event Planning and Management:

In event planning, DALL.E 3 can be used to create conceptual visuals for event layouts, themes, and decorations, helping clients to visualize and tailor their events according to their preferences.

The integration of DALL.E 3 with ChatGPT presents a groundbreaking development in the field of event planning and management, providing innovative solutions that enhance creativity, efficiency, and client engagement. This combination of advanced AI technologies has the potential to revolutionize how events are conceptualized, planned, and executed. Here's an exploration of its impact on event planning and management:

1. **Visualizing Event Concepts**: DALL.E 3's ability to generate detailed and realistic images, when coupled with ChatGPT's descriptive prowess, allows event planners to visualize and present event concepts and themes to clients in a more vivid and tangible way. This visual representation helps clients better understand and engage with the proposed ideas.

2. **Customized Theme Creation**: For themed events, DALL.E 3 can create images that capture specific themes or atmospheres, guided by the textual inputs and detailed descriptions from ChatGPT. This aids in creating a unique and tailored event experience for each client.

3. **Venue Layout and Design**: Utilizing DALL.E 3 for generating layouts and designs of event spaces, combined with ChatGPT's ability to articulate spatial arrangements, helps in efficient planning of the venue setup. It allows for a clear visualization of space utilization, guest movement, and overall aesthetics.

4. **Marketing and Promotional Materials**: The integration is a boon for creating marketing and promotional materials for events. DALL.E 3 can generate eye-catching visuals for invitations, banners, and social media posts, while ChatGPT provides compelling and relevant textual content, enhancing the overall appeal and reach of the event.

5. **Interactive Client Consultations**: This AI integration enables a more interactive and responsive consultation process with clients. As clients express their ideas or preferences, the AI can instantly generate corresponding visuals, leading to a dynamic and engaging planning experience.

6. **Cost-Effective Prototyping**: Event planners can use DALL.E 3 to create prototypes or mock-ups of event setups, decorations, and themes. This visual prototyping is not only cost-effective but also helps in making quick adjustments based on client feedback.

7. **Enhanced Vendor Communication**: The clear visual and textual descriptions generated by DALL.E 3 and ChatGPT aid in better communication with vendors and service providers, ensuring that the client's vision is accurately conveyed and executed.

8. **Real-Time Adaptation to Changes**: The ability to quickly produce new visualizations in response to changes in client preferences or logistical adjustments makes the planning process more adaptable and flexible.

9. **Educational Tool for Clients**: For clients new to event planning, this integration can serve as an educational tool. ChatGPT can explain various aspects of event planning in simple terms, while DALL.E 3 visually represents these concepts, making the process more accessible and understandable.

10. **Trend Analysis and Inspiration**: By analyzing current trends in event planning and client preferences, ChatGPT, along with DALL.E 3, can suggest and visualize contemporary and innovative event themes and designs, aiding planners in staying ahead in their field.

In summary, integrating DALL.E 3 with ChatGPT in the context of event planning and management offers a transformative approach, combining visual AI's power with sophisticated natural language processing. This technological synergy enables more efficient, creative, and client-focused planning and execution of events, redefining the standards of client interaction and presentation in the event planning industry.

X. **Customer Support and Service**:

Integrating DALL.E 3 with customer support systems allows businesses to provide more illustrative and informative responses to customer queries, improving the overall customer service experience.

The integration of DALL.E 3 with ChatGPT marks a significant advancement in the realm of customer support and service, heralding a new era of enhanced client interaction and problem-solving capabilities. This innovative combination of AI technologies offers businesses a novel approach to addressing customer needs, improving response quality, and enriching the overall service experience. Below is a comprehensive introduction to its applications in customer support and service:

1. **Visual Problem Solving**: DALL.E 3's ability to generate precise, context-specific images combined with ChatGPT's language understanding facilitates visual problem solving. For example, in technical support, customers can describe an issue, and the AI can generate visual aids or diagrams to guide them through the solution, making complex instructions more accessible and understandable.

2. **Enhanced Interactive Guides**: Traditional text-based user manuals or FAQs can be transformed into interactive, visual guides. DALL.E 3 can create relevant images or step-by-step visuals based on ChatGPT's textual descriptions, providing customers with an easier, more engaging way to understand product use, troubleshooting, and maintenance.

3. **Personalized Customer Responses**: By integrating these AI technologies, businesses can offer more personalized responses to customer inquiries. ChatGPT can understand the context and nuances of customer queries, and DALL.E 3 can create tailored images or illustrations to accompany responses, enhancing clarity and customer satisfaction.

4. **Training Customer Support Teams**: This integration is also beneficial for training customer service teams. By simulating various customer scenarios and generating corresponding visuals, it provides a comprehensive training tool that helps support agents understand and respond to customer needs more effectively.

5. **Visual Aids for Multilingual Support**: In multilingual support environments, DALL.E 3 can generate universal visual aids that transcend language barriers, complementing ChatGPT's ability to converse in multiple languages. This makes customer service more inclusive and accessible to a global customer base.

6. **Automated Response Enhancement**: In automated customer support systems like chatbots, integrating these technologies can significantly enhance the quality of automated responses. Visual aids can add value to text-based answers, making automated interactions more informative and helpful.

7. **Product and Service Customization**: For businesses offering customizable products or services, this integration allows customers to visually convey their preferences or customizations, which the AI can interpret and visualize in real-

time. This leads to a better understanding of customer requirements and higher satisfaction with the final product or service.

8. **Real-Time Feedback Visualization**: Customers providing feedback can be instantly shown visual changes or improvements based on their suggestions, fostering a more interactive and responsive feedback process.

9. **Marketing and Promotion**: Customer support channels often double as opportunities for marketing and promotion. By creating visually appealing product suggestions or promotional materials in response to customer interactions, businesses can enhance cross-selling and upselling strategies.

10. **Handling Complex Queries with Visual Data**: For complex queries involving data interpretation, DALL.E 3 can generate charts, graphs, or infographics based on data provided by customers, making it easier for support agents to provide informed, accurate responses.

Conclusion,

The integration of DALL.E 3 with ChatGPT in the business sector offers a multitude of advantages, from enhancing marketing and branding efforts to improving product development, customer experience, and content creation. It empowers businesses to be more creative, efficient, and customer-centric, thereby driving growth and innovation in an increasingly competitive market. This technology is not just a tool for visual creation; it is a transformative force that redefines the way businesses interact with their customers and manage their operations, heralding a new era of AI-assisted business excellence.

Prompts:

1. Marketing and Branding: "Create a realistic photograph of a team of marketing professionals, consisting of a Caucasian woman and a Hispanic man, brainstorming in a modern office with digital screens displaying dynamic brand designs."

2. Product Visualization and Prototyping: "Generate a realistic photograph showing a diverse group of engineers (a Black woman, an Asian man, and a Middle-Eastern woman) using advanced computer software to design and prototype a new tech gadget."

3. Customized Customer Experiences: "Illustrate with a realistic photograph a retail scene in a boutique with a South Asian female customer experiencing a virtual reality headset, guided by a Caucasian male sales assistant, in a personalized shopping environment."

4. E-commerce Enhancements: "Create a realistic photograph of a young, Black female entrepreneur managing an online store from her laptop, surrounded by various products and a digital analytics dashboard in the background."

5. Content Creation and Management: "Generate a realistic photograph showing a Middle-Eastern man and a Hispanic woman collaboratively working on digital content creation using multiple monitors in a creative studio setting."

6. Training and Educational Resources: "Illustrate with a realistic photograph a corporate training session, where a diverse group of employees, including a South Asian man and a Caucasian woman, are engaged in an interactive digital workshop."

7. Enhancing Presentations and Reports: "Create a realistic photograph of a business team, including an Asian woman and a Black man, actively discussing over a high-tech table displaying interactive data visualization for a business report."

8. Real Estate and Interior Design Visualization: "Generate a realistic photograph of a real estate agent, a Caucasian man, showing a 3D virtual home tour on a tablet to a prospective Hispanic female buyer in a real estate office."

9. Event Planning and Management: "Illustrate with a realistic photograph an event planning team, consisting of a Middle-Eastern woman and an Asian man, strategizing over a digital interactive event layout on a large screen in an office."

10. Customer Support and Service: "Create a realistic photograph of a customer service center, where a Black woman is assisting a client over a video call, surrounded by monitors displaying customer service software."

The concept of Business Applications is illustrated in the generated image, depicting a modern marketing

The image illustrating the concept of Business Applications in a modern marketing environment has been generated. It captures a diverse team of professionals in a brainstorming session, with elements like digital marketing analytics, innovative strategies, and a contemporary office setup. Feel free to observe the details in the image.